THERAPEUTIC RECREATION:
CASES AND EXERCISES

Barbara C. Wilhite Ed.D., C.T.R.S.
M. Jean Keller Ed.D., C.T.R.S.

THERAPEUTIC RECREATION: CASES AND EXERCISES

Barbara C. Wilhite Ed.D., C.T.R.S.
M. Jean Keller Ed.D., C.T.R.S.

Venture Publishing, Inc.
State College, Pennsylvania

Cover Design: Margaret Ream
Production: Bonnie Godbey
Printing and Binding: Thomson-Shore, Inc.

Library of Congress Catalogue Card Number 91-68519
ISBN 0-910251-50-9

CONTENTS

Chapter Two
Individual Therapeutic Recreation Program Planning   41

Chapter Three
Implementing Individual Therapeutic Recreation
    Program Plans   85

Chapter Four
Leadership in Therapeutic Recreation   121

Chapter Five
Evaluation in Therapeutic Recreation   157

Chapter Six
Selected Issues in Therapeutic Recreation 191

Preface

The idea for *Therapeutic Recreation: Cases and Exercises* was born one day in conversation between the two authors. We were lamenting the fact that most therapeutic recreation students had limited working experience. Without such experience, principles and theories abstracted from the literature had little reality for them. We needed a way of socializing students into the complex therapeutic recreation process prior to an internship. We also realized that successful therapeutic recreation specialists were challenged daily with situations that demanded the ability to go beyond "this is how it is done," and search for creative new alternatives.

This text grew out of notions that, in addition to knowledge, therapeutic recreation specialists emerge as effective by developing a particular way of thinking about people with disabilities and a belief in the role of therapeutic recreation in the rehabilitation and habilitation of people with mental, physical, social, and emotional disabilities. As students and teachers, we found that a process of discovery was critical to effective learning and consequently an important teaching device. Since case method is a vehicle for discovery and offers an opportunity to think about people with disabilities and therapeutic recreation processes and techniques, this book is a logical consequence.

The Cases in The Text

The cases and issues presented in this text are real and restless. Therapeutic recreation is a profession fraught with stress, change, reward, and above all, challenge. Some of these elements emerge from our interactions with clients, professionals, administrators, institutions, and communities. Some come from within therapeutic recreation specialists as they struggle to define their role and to be the best they can be. In addition, history tells us that each era has multiple forms of restlessness and change. We have witnessed an increase in the use of harmful substances, a growing number of people with AIDS, a rapid expansion of people with depression, a society with an increasing divorce and suicide rate, a growing population of older adults and fewer children, and indeed, an ever increasing need for therapeutic recreation professionals.

The cases of *Therapeutic Recreation: Cases and Exercises* are based on actual situations. Some are virtually complete reports of therapeutic recreation situations, while others are partial reports to show open-endedness and to stimulate alternative lines of discussion. The cases are short enough to avoid having discussions bog down in a confusion of detail and yet long enough to enable precise understanding of problems.

The Case Study Method

The case method is accepted as a way of developing inexperienced students and as a way of broadening mature, experienced therapeutic recreation specialists. Case study requires the use and application of substantive content, technical and general knowledge, relevant information, and common sense; therefore, the cases in this text are to be used with other textbooks, articles, and resources that provide information about therapeutic recreation and its practice.

The specific questions at the end of each case are intended to stimulate initial inquiry into issues or topics related to or prompted by the individual case. In almost every instance the listed questions should be followed by additional questions such as "Why?" "Why not?" and "What then?" In no case do the questions exhaust all possibilities for discussion.

Many of the cases, particularly those with personal exchanges, lend themselves to effective role-playing. While preparation for role-playing outside of the learning environment may produce beneficial knowledge, spontaneous role-playing may produce even more meaningful learning experiences. Other experiences such as simulations, panel discussions, interviews, field trips, invited presentations, and video tapes are suggested to challenge learners. In this way, *Therapeutic Recreation: Cases and Exercises,* can serve as a supplemental text to all therapeutic recreation courses.

The Challenges of Case Study Analysis

A common hazard for learners is the rejection of a case due to what is perceived as insufficient information. Seldom is all desirable or useful information available for analyzing and resolving therapeutic recreation issues. Therapeutic recreation specialists must use information available and do the best they can with what they have. Furthermore, the main issue of many situations is to determine what additional information can be obtained before adequate analysis can be made and appropriate action taken. Specialists must decide whether additional information is worth getting, whether it is meaningful and relevant, and whether it can be secured in time to be useful.

Learners may also conclude that two cases are identical, not just similar. Since many factors affect the behavior of people and the circumstances within which they react and interact, no two cases *are* identical, although they may be similar.

Beginners in case analysis should be cautioned to recognize their feelings and prejudices. Sifting case facts through our feelings and prejudices (knowingly, or unknowingly) tends to slant and bias the facts. Learners occasionally search for the "right" answer or solution to cases. Although some answers or solutions are better than others, there are no "right" ones.

Readers will recall the children's puzzles with little animals hidden in the branches and foliage of a tree, contrived in such a way that you had to study the drawing, turning it at all angles to find the hidden, camouflaged creatures. They clung to the branches, disappeared in the foliage, or, in extremes, were etched in the sky and clouds. The artist may have placed as many as fifteen camouflaged creatures in a sketch. If you were able to find them all, you were indeed perceptive. These puzzles encouraged intellectual freedom and individual creativity. So too, *Therapeutic Recreation: Cases and Exercises* encourages readers to apply what they already know, discover the unknown, seek new solutions, and enjoy the delightful challenge of analyzing and synthesizing the known and unknown into the practice of therapeutic recreation. It is suggested that the text be used as a companion text with others throughout the entire therapeutic recreation curriculum to enhance the growth and development of therapeutic recreation specialists. Additionally, *Therapeutic Recreation: Cases and Exercises* may be used in training and in-servicing with therapeutic recreation specialists in various settings.

Sincere Thanks

This text would not have been possible without the contributors of the various cases. These individuals, both practitioners and educators, shared their experiences so that others may learn to be successful therapeutic recreation specialists. Their names are listed on the page following this preface. Each chapter, along with its cases, was reviewed by leading professionals in therapeutic recreation: **Dan R. Ancone**, William S. Hall Psychiatric Institute, Columbia, SC; **Teresa Boeger**, Meridian Point Rehabilitation Hospital, Scottsdale, AZ; **joan burlingame**, Idyll Arbor, Inc., Ravensdale, WA; **Cynthia Carruthers**, University of Nevada, Las Vegas, NV; **Cathy O'Keefe**, University of South Alabama, Mobile, AL;

Bob Raynor, Medical University of South Carolina, Charleston, SC; **Thomas K. Skalko**, Florida International University, Miami, FL; and **Virginia Wood**, Sea Pines Rehabilitation Hospital, Melbourne, FL. Their expertise in the subject area provided insight to the authors. **Marcia Jean Carter**, University of Northern Iowa, Cedar Falls, IA, reviewed the entire text and provided assistance to the authors. Her comments and suggestions are reflected in *Therapeutic Recreation: Cases and Exercises*.

The authors wish to extend their appreciation to those agencies and individuals who provided pictures for the text. These include American Diabetes Association, Georgia Affiliate, Inc., Atlanta, GA; Camp John Marc Myers, Dallas, TX; Georgia Golden Olympics, Winder, GA; Georgia Recreation and Park Association Senior Citizens Camp, Conyers, GA; Muscular Dystrophy Association of Georgia, Inc., Tucker, GA; Sea Pines Rehabilitation Hospital, Melbourne, FL; Shepherd Spinal Center, Atlanta, GA; and Marcia Jean Carter, Cedar Falls, IA.

The authors also wish to thank their respective employing educational institutions, the University of Georgia and the University of North Texas, for their support and assistance. Appreciation is extended to Warren Leamon for his editorial assistance, to Donna Berend, Lovis Miller, and Leslie Weltner for assistance with case preparation, and to Brenda Arnold for her word processing assistance.

Barbara C. Wilhite

M. Jean Keller

Case Contributors

Linda Aldrich
McLean Hospital
Boston, MA

Mary L. Anderson
Mankato State University
Mankato, MN

Marcia Jean Carter
University of Northern Iowa
Cedar Falls, IA

Joanne Ardolf Decker
Mankato State University
Mankato, MN

Phyllis Grimes
Georgia Department of Corrections
Atlanta, GA

Bruce Hatalski
Seaborne Hospital
Dover, NH

Jeff Hoffman
The Arden Hill Life Care Center, Inc.
Goshen, NY

Christine Z. Howe
State University of New York
Brockport, NY

Susan Hudson
University of North Texas
Denton, TX

I. Roy Hunter
Kansas State University
Manhattan, KS

Alfred G. Kaye
Patricia Neal Rehabilitation Center
Knoxville, TN

Greg Little
Hattiesburg, MS

Arlene Marmer
Rancho Los Amigos Medical Center
Downey, CA

Marjorie J. Malkin
Southern Illinois University
Carbondale, IL

Lovis W. Miller
Texas Women's University
Denton, TX

Gerald S. O'Morrow
Radford University
Radford, VA

Lou Powell
University of New Hampshire
Durham, NH

Peggy Powers
Springfield College
Springfield, MA

J. Robert Rossman
University of North Texas
Denton, TX

Ruth V. Russell
Indiana University
Bloomington, IN

Case Contributors — continued

Janet Sable
University of New Hampshire
Durham, NH

Barbara Trader
Shepherd Spinal Center
Atlanta, GA

Carol Weber
Governor's Council on Developmental
  Disabilities for Georgia
Atlanta, GA

Jeff Witman
Kent State University
Kent, OH

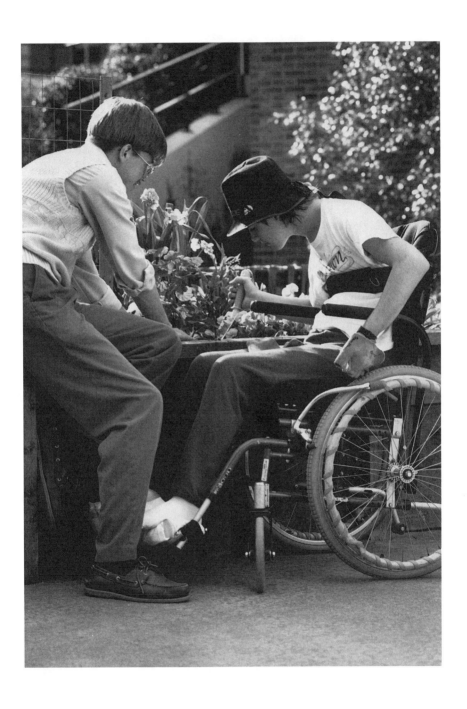

Introduction

An Overview

Therapeutic recreation, and the various settings in which it occurs, is growing and changing at a rapid pace. To meet present challenges, therapeutic recreation specialists must be able to apply theoretical, philosophical, and ethical principles to the design and implementation of therapeutic recreation programs and services. This case study text focuses on actual situations where therapeutic recreation specialists are challenged to translate principles and theories into practice and application. The study of these case histories, exercises, role-playing, and structured field experiences may improve the practice of therapeutic recreation on a day-to-day basis. Additionally, the laboratory experiences these exercises provide, prior to or in conjunction with actual field placement, should increase the effectiveness of classroom learning and the professional preparation of therapeutic recreation specialists.

The goal of this book is to promote sound practice and application of therapeutic recreation principles, theories, and research findings in situations comparable to those experiences therapeutic recreation professionals and paraprofessionals encounter. Practice exercises, simulating realistic events, provide a safe environment in which taking risks, testing ideas, evaluating decisions, and comparing outcomes are encouraged. In this way therapeutic recreation specialists can learn from their mistakes without harming anyone by them. The exercises, however, are not limited to preprofessional education. They also provide a means to assess the skills of graduate students without therapeutic recreation undergraduate degrees. In addition, practicing professionals and paraprofessionals are provided opportunities to refine problem-solving and decision-making skills and continue their professional development.

This book focuses on the following aspects of therapeutic recreation and its practice.

Chapter One   *Assessment in Therapeutic Recreation* presents a definition of individual assessment and examines its use in clinical and community service delivery settings. Assessment techniques and methods are highlighted and characteristics of comprehensive individual assessments are discussed.

Chapter Two   *Individual Therapeutic Recreation Program Planning* examines the establishment of individual goals and objectives based on comprehensive assessments and the development of individual program plans. This chapter also covers principles for analyzing, selecting, and adapting activities and interventions. Selected intervention techniques, including behavior management, sensory stimulation, reality orientation, remotivation, resocialization, relaxation, and assertiveness training are discussed.

Chapter Three *Implementing Individual Therapeutic Recreation Program Plans* presents a range of topics including the role of therapeutic recreation specialists, documentation and record keeping, risk management, the team approach, and utilization of community resources.

Chapter Four   *Leadership in Therapeutic Recreation* examines leadership styles, presents guidelines for effective leadership, and highlights techniques for improving communication and teaching skills. This chapter also presents selected teaching strategies, leader assistance techniques, and leadership concerns.

Chapter Five   *Evaluation in Therapeutic Recreation* discusses the purpose of conducting individual evaluations and defines evaluation criteria. Approaches to formative and summative evaluation are presented.

Chapter Six   *Selected Issues in Therapeutic Recreation* highlights a range of topics including philosophy, values, ethics, advocacy, normalization-integration, nontraditional settings, and diverse client populations.

Administrative and management concerns, as they pertain to individual clients, are interspersed throughout the chapters. The chapters' texts are not definitive and should only serve as a means of review for the content and knowledge areas. Because it is critical for users of this text to supplement their preprofessional and/or professional development with outside reading, each chapter includes a bibliography of reference citations and a listing of additional resources; cases are supplied with selected references. Learners will discover that references may not directly apply to a case, but will add insight into a situation or issue.

All six chapters focus on therapeutic recreation services and programming strategies with individual clients and present case histories and scenarios which incorporate a variety of disabling conditions in clinical and community settings. The case histories and scenarios vary in length and complexity. Each case, however, describes a particular situation and includes information about the individual(s) involved, the setting, and other key factors. A series of suggested discussion questions and exercises follows each case study. Consistent with the multidimensional nature of therapeutic recreation, some cases are carried from one chapter to another. Learners will need to refer to the chapter where the case originated to review the complete scenario. Page numbers are indicated within the text (and in the index) to make this cross referencing easier.

- Discussion questions require learners to organize pertinent information, identify and analyze problems, determine indicators of successful experiences, identify possible courses of action, and develop individual program plans.
- In-class exercises require learners to practice various skills highlighted in the scenarios.
- Role-playing requires learners to represent key individuals in the scenario, simulating possible outcomes of a variety of problem-solving solutions.
- Field experience exercises require learners to interact in particular settings with professionals and individuals with disabilities. Learners will be required to observe situations, gather and analyze information about particular problems, and then present their observations and recommendations.

Although the methodological process of sorting, classifying, and analyzing case information may vary according to the preferences of learners and teachers, diagnosing basic problems should be a common objective of all processes. Identifying and stating the basic problem of the case should generally be a starting point.

Some of the case histories and scenarios may necessitate a review of related literature which is pertinent to the case, but is not discussed explicitly in the text. For example, learners may want to review literature relating to such items as specific disabilities or illnesses, treatment interventions, and medications that are highlighted in the case.

This book is action-oriented in that it requires interaction and active participation through analyzing, synthesizing, problem solving, formulating individual plans, and evaluating outcomes. Learners are asked to undertake a number of assignments related to completing leisure assessments, developing goals and objectives, conducting activity analyses, writing progress notes, and developing evaluation plans.

The exercises presented in this book may be easily altered or expanded to accommodate learners' specific needs and interests. Practicing therapeutic recreation specialists and individuals with disabilities can provide invaluable insight into many of the situations and problems encountered in these exercises; hence it is recommended that they be invited to participate.

Bibliography

Bannon, J. (1981). *Problem solving in recreation and parks.* Englewood Cliffs, NJ: Prentice-Hall.

Brill, N. (1978). *Working with people.* New York, NY: Lippincott.

Glueck, W. F. (1978). *Cases and exercises in personnel.* Dallas, TX: Business Publications.

Duncombe, L. W., Howe, M. C., and Schwartzberg, S. L. (1988). *Case simulations in psychosocial occupational therapy* (2nd ed.). Philadelphia, PA: Davis.

Shank, P. A. (1988). *Case study guidelines.* Farmville, VA: Longwood College.

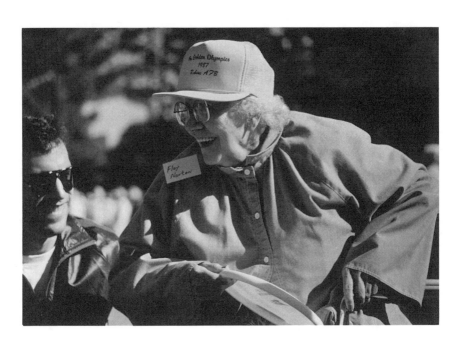

Chapter One

Assessment in Therapeutic Recreation

Therapeutic recreation specialists are responsible for helping clients develop, express, and maintain a personally chosen interdependent leisure lifestyle and, in the process, eliminate or minimize barriers that prevent or limit the attainment of this goal (Howe-Murphy and Charboneau, 1988; Peterson and Gunn, 1984). For a leisure lifestyle to be appropriate and meaningful, it must reflect clients' strengths, needs, and interests. Services must be provided based on clients' needs and preferences rather than on attempts to fit them into preexistent programs. The concept of interdependence values the interrelatedness of all aspects of clients—cognitive, physical, social, affective, spiritual—and the relationship between clients and their environments. An interdependent leisure lifestyle emphasizes that at various times, individuals need support and assistance from others to develop, express, and maintain appropriate and meaningful lives as they relate to leisure. Interdependent leisure functioning recognizes that seeking support and assistance is part of the give and take of life and is one way clients achieve autonomy and control.

Assessment is the process through which knowledge is obtained about clients, and their functional abilities related to school, work, leisure, and family. It establishes a baseline or starting point and provides a foundation for identifying needs, determining interests, formulating goals, selecting appropriate activities, developing intervention strategies, and evaluating progress. Assessment is a multidisciplinary effort involving clients, therapeutic recreation specialists, family members, significant others, and representatives of professions and agencies committed to meeting clients' needs.

Purposes of Assessment

For leisure experiences to satisfy clients' needs and interests, these experiences should be designed based on accurate and comprehensive assessment of how clients actually function in various environments, what they hope to gain through leisure involvement, and what skills will be needed to facilitate full participation. Through assessment, therapeutic recreation specialists are able to identify programs or services that address clients' needs by supporting and utilizing their strengths and interests. Determining existing skills and behaviors enables therapeutic recreation specialists to identify and target behaviors that need maintenance or remediation to promote interdependent leisure functioning. The assessment processes and outcomes also provide information to direct therapeutic recreation specialists in the selection of appropriate intervention and facilitation techniques for use with clients.

Approaches and Techniques

By assessing clients' current level of performance, therapeutic recreation specialists can identify strengths and needs relative to personal preferences and provide direction for determining individualized goals. Therapeutic recreation specialists must then consider with clients which activities they might enjoy and are appropriate. Leisure pursuits should be chosen in conjunction with clients when possible, since personal preference is central to developing one's leisure lifestyle. Therapeutic recreation specialists must also take into account an agency's mission, goals and resources as assessment instruments and procedures are selected.

Important questions to consider and discuss with a client during the assessment phase include:

(1) How does he currently spend his free time? What are his present leisure skills?

(2) What does he like? dislike?

(3) What does he see as the benefits of participation in recreation activity (e.g., making friends, being active, feeling useful, learning a new skill)?

(4) What recreation activities appear to interest him, even if he does not currently participate in them?

(5) Of all the explored activities which appear to interest him most, how much time does he spend participating in any single activity or in utilizing a specific piece of recreation equipment? When presented with multiple leisure opportunities, how quickly does he respond to a particular activity or item?

(6) What personal or activity adaptations are needed to promote full or partial participation in his chosen activity?

(7) What resources (e.g., discretionary money, equipment, materials) does he have available which can be used in leisure?

(8) What functional skills (e.g., cognitive, physical, social, affective, adaptive behaviors, independent living skills) can be maintained or developed during leisure?

A client's need to acquire specific skills, or the need to make personal or activity adaptations, should reflect both his activity preferences, and the demands and opportunities of his community. "Best practice assessment includes a comprehensive evaluation of the local environment, as well as the individual" (Wilcox and Bellamy, 1987, p. 31). Assessing the environment, as well as the client, facilitates the identification of needed personal and environmental adaptations. Limitations of the client, and the physical as well as attitudinal barriers within the community, can then be reduced or eliminated so that maximum leisure functioning can be obtained.

Assessment questions pertaining to a client's environment might include:

(1) What recreation activities does he presently pursue in the home?

(2) What resources, such as recreation facilities, services, and transportation, are available?

(3) What environmental adaptations are needed to enable him to participate, at least at some level, in his chosen activity?

(4) With whom does he spend most of his leisure time?

(5) What are the values and preferences of his nondisabled family members, peers, and other caregivers relative to specific recreation activities?

Identifying Needs, Interests, and Skills

A variety of resources can provide useful assessment information. That coming from clients is referred to as subjective information while that coming from others is referred to as objective information. In many instances, clients themselves are the most significant provider of assessment information. Various techniques are used to gather cognitive, social, physical, affective, or leisure assessment information from available resources.

Skillful observation, one technique for gathering assessment data about clients, involves knowing what to look for and how to observe significant factors in clients' general appearance and behavior (O'Morrow and Reynolds, 1989). Observation techniques must be practiced to be perfected.

Therapeutic recreation specialists can identify many clients' needs and interests simply by observing them in a variety of situations. For some clients, including those who are nonverbal, this may be the best assessment technique available. Formal observation methods, such as frequency measures, interval recording, and time sampling (Crawford and Mendell, 1987; Dattilo and Murphy, 1987; Fine and Fine, 1988; Navar, 1984) make possible very specific and accurate observations. Through narrative recording (Cooper, 1981), therapeutic recreation specialists observe clients during a specific time frame, noting items of significance. Some therapeutic recreation specialists will record the frequency of a behavior, others will document the duration of a specific behavior, and still others will define whether a behavior occurred during specified periods.

Strengths, areas of need, and interests can also be identified by interviewing and listening to clients, family members, and other significant individuals. Interviewing family and other caregivers is particularly important when clients are very young (Fine and Fine, 1988) or unable to express themselves. Additionally, interviews with other professionals such as teachers, counselors, and caseworkers can provide useful information about clients. Interviews can be conducted formally or informally and formats will vary. Therapeutic recreation specialists must structure interviews to obtain reliable and valid information.

Assessment may also include the use of assessment instruments designed to identify clients' skills and behaviors. Many agencies use activity checklists, leisure interest questionnaires, and skill inventories designed to be in keeping with the agency's operational framework and to present client profiles.

Standardized assessment procedures are valuable because they have been rigorously designed and include measures of validity and reliability. If therapeutic recreation specialists choose a standardized instrument, they should ascertain how well the instrument measures what it is intended to measure (validity) as well as the accuracy or consistency of the instrument's findings (reliability). In addition, standardized assessment instruments help to eliminate any biases therapeutic recreation specialists might have (O'Morrow and Reynolds, 1989). Several standardized assessment instruments currently being used in therapeutic recreation include the Comprehensive Evaluation in Recreation Therapy (CERT) scale (Parker, Ellison, Kirby, and Short, 1975), Leisure Activities Blank (LAB) (McKechnie, 1975), State Technical Institute Leisure Assessment Process (STILAP) (Navar, 1980), and Leisure Diagnostic Battery (LDB) (Witt and Ellis, 1987). While there are numerous other standardized instruments available to obtain cognitive, social, physical, affective, and leisure information, these four tools are highlighted because they are frequently used by therapeutic recreation specialists.

The CERT scale, designed for use in short-term, acute care psychiatric settings, identifies and defines behaviors relevant to therapeutic recreation. General lifestyle behaviors, as well as performance in individual and group therapeutic recreation activities are included in the CERT scale. The LAB explores patterns of leisure interests as well as the psychological significance of those patterns. It may be most appropriate for use with older children and adolescents (Fine and Fine, 1988). STILAP was designed to identify leisure participation patterns of adults in rehabilitation settings. The patterns are categorized into leisure competency areas and guidelines are provided for future leisure skill development. The LDB, one of the most comprehensive measures in therapeutic recreation, focuses on the leisure functioning of typical children and youth as well as those who have orthopedic or cognitive disabilities. This instrument consists of a series of scales which measure indicators of leisure ability. Collectively, these measurements enable therapeutic recreation specialists to determine clients' perceptions of freedom in leisure and to identify factors that might limit their perception of personal freedom.

Additional assessments are available to measure leisure satisfaction, interests, attitudes, and participation. Assessments may also provide measures of functional abilities and skills clients demonstrate within their environment. An example of a functional-environmental assessment would be the client's ability to use public transportation.

Though there is concern in the field of therapeutic recreation over the paucity of standardized instruments (Witt, Connolly, and Compton, 1980; Dunn, 1984; Loesch and Wheeler, 1982), the use of informal, nonstandardized assessments does not necessarily result in imprecise findings (Wilcox and Bellamy, 1987). In fact, when used in isolation, the results of formal assessments may provide a limited view of clients' capabilities. To be useful, the findings of formal assessments must be studied in concert with information obtained from additional instruments through a variety of techniques (Loesch and Wheeler, 1982; O'Morrow and Reynolds, 1989). Assessment information may also be obtained by reviewing health and social histories; medical and psychiatric records; academic, developmental and adaptive tests results; and basic demographic data including age, sex, education, and occupation. Participation in team meetings, consisting of various professionals, family members, and/or clients, can also provide useful assessment information.

Essential Characteristics of Assessment Procedures

Therapeutic recreation specialists must determine the purpose of the assessment prior to selecting the instrument and procedure. Specialists then identify which procedure(s)—interview, observation, inventory, test—can provide information that will enable them to make appropriate program planning decisions with clients. There is no one approach that can be used with all individuals. The decision on which approach to use is influenced both by characteristics of a client and by the ability of a specialist to utilize and interpret accurately the results of a given procedure.

Assessments may be *criterion referenced*; that is, they evaluate clients based on some expectation perceived to be necessary for functioning in a leisure environment. An example of a criterion is "adults with mental retardation will be able to manage all activities of daily living in order to participate in the residential camp." Assessments may also be *norm referenced*; that is, they compare clients' performance to a larger (reference) group. For instance, most adults with mild mental retardation are able to manage all activities of daily living. Norm referenced assessments are frequently used to determine a client's eligibility for services; however, these assessments have limited value for determining a client's actual skill level (burlingame and Blaschko, 1991).

McLoughlin and Lewis (1986) point out that assessment procedures must be compatible with clients' skills and should capitalize on their strengths rather than penalize their limitations. Considering clients' developmental and functional levels, along with specific characteristics such as health status and disabling conditions, enables therapeutic recreation specialists to determine the suitability of a potential assessment procedure.

Therapeutic recreation specialists must also establish the practicality of the assessment procedure (Carruthers, Sneegas, and Ashton-Shaeffer, 1986). Even the most comprehensive, sophisticated assessment procedure will not provide accurate information unless therapeutic recreation specialists are qualified to administer, score, and interpret the instrument, and have adequate time. The feasibility and practical usability of assessment procedures should be considered in relation to the client, agency, staff, and situation.

Fine and Fine (1988) state that the most important characteristic of assessment procedures may be therapeutic recreation specialists' judgement. Interpreting the findings of an assessment procedure is both a difficult and crucial aspect of the assessment process. Ultimately, it is the responsibility of therapeutic recreation specialists to determine if the assessment results obtained accurately depict clients' strengths, potentials, and limitations. All elements of the assessment process should be taken into account when interpreting assessment data.

Summary

Assessment is the first step to creating opportunities with clients to experience leisure in a personally meaningful and appropriate manner. Therapeutic recreation specialists must recognize the varying levels of clients' abilities, knowledge, skills, and interests as well as the range of factors which make up the environment in which these clients live. Specialists should gather this information through a well-planned, systematic examination involving a variety of assessment techniques.

Assessment leads to the development of general statements about what clients can and hope to gain through recreation participation. The following chapter, *Individual Therapeutic Recreation Program Planning,* describes how clients' expectations are translated into goals and objectives and how individual therapeutic recreation program plans are developed.

Bibliography

burlingame, j. and Blaschko, T. M. (1991). *Assessment tools for recreational therapy: Red book #1.* Ravensdale, WA: Idyll Arbor.

Carruthers, C., Sneegas, J. J., and Ashton-Shaeffer, C. A. (1986). *Therapeutic recreation: Guidelines for activity services in long term care.* Urbana-Champaign, IL: University of Illinois.

Cooper, J. O. (1981). *Measuring behavior* (2nd ed.). Columbus, OH: Charles E. Merrill.

Crawford, M. E. and Mendell, R. (1987). *Therapeutic recreation and adapted physical activities for mentally retarded individuals.* Englewood Cliffs, NJ: Prentice-Hall.

Dattilo, J. and Murphy, W. D. (1987). *Behavior modification in therapeutic recreation.* State College, PA: Venture Publishing, Inc.

Dunn, J. K. (1984). Assessment in therapeutic recreation. In C. A. Peterson and S. L. Gunn, *Therapeutic recreation program design: Principles and procedures* (2nd ed.) (pp. 267-320). Englewood Cliffs, NJ: Prentice-Hall.

Fine, A. H. and Fine, N. M. (1988). *Therapeutic recreation for exceptional children: Let me in, I want to play.* Springfield, IL: Charles C. Thomas.

Howe-Murphy, R. and Charboneau, B. G. (1987). *Therapeutic recreation intervention: An ecological perspective.* Englewood Cliffs, NJ: Prentice-Hall.

Loesch, L. C. and Wheeler, P. T. (1982). *Principles of leisure counseling.* Minneapolis, MN: Education Media Corporation.

McKechnie, G. E. (1975). *Manual for leisure activities blank.* Palo Alto, CA: Consulting Psychology Press.

McLoughlin, J. and Lewis, R. (1988). *Assessing special students.* Columbus, OH: Charles E. Merrill.

Navar, N. (1984). Documentation in therapeutic recreation. In C. A. Peterson and S. L. Gunn, *Therapeutic recreation program design: Principles and procedures* (2nd ed.) (pp. 212-266). Englewood Cliffs, NJ: Prentice-Hall.

Navar, N. (1980). A rationale for leisure skill assessment with handicapped adults. *Therapeutic Recreation Journal, 14*(4), 21-28.

O'Morrow, G. S. and Reynolds, R. P. (1989). *Therapeutic recreation: A helping profession* (3rd ed.). Englewood Cliffs, NJ: Prentice-Hall.

Parker, R. A., Ellison, C. H., Kirby, T. F., and Short, M. J. (1975). The comprehensive evaluation in recreational therapy scale: A tool for patient evaluation. *Therapeutic Recreation Journal, 9*(4), 43-52.

Peterson, C. A. and Gunn, S. L. (1984). *Therapeutic recreation program design: Principles and procedures* (2nd ed.). Englewood Cliffs, NJ: Prentice- Hall.

Project LIFE. (1988). *LIFE forms, the LIFE training guide.* Chapel Hill, NC: Project LIFE, Curriculum in Leisure Studies and Recreation Administration, University of North Carolina at Chapel Hill.

Wilcox, B. and Bellamy, G. T. (1987). *A comprehensive guide to the activities catalog.* Baltimore, MD: Paul H. Brookes.

Witt, P. A., Connolly, P., and Compton, D. M. (1980). Assessment: A plea for sophistication. *Therapeutic Recreation Journal, 14*(4), 5-8.

Witt, P. A. and Ellis, G. (1987). *The leisure diagnostic battery: User's manual.* State College, PA: Venture Publishing, Inc.

Suggested Readings

Certo, N. J., Schleien, S. J., and Hunter, D. (1983). An ecological inventory to facilitate community recreation participation by severely disabled individuals. *Therapeutic Recreation Journal, 17*(3), 29-38.

Dunn, J. K. (1989). Guidelines for using published assessment procedures. *Therapeutic Recreation Journal, 23*(2), 59-69.

Dunn, J. K. (1988). Establishing reliability and validity in evaluation instruments. *Journal of Park and Recreation Administration, 5*(4), 61-70.

Ellis, G. D. and Niles, S. (1985). Development, reliability and preliminary validation of a brief leisure rating scale. *Therapeutic Recreation Journal, 18*(1), 50-61.

Ferguson, D. D. (1983). Assessment interviewing techniques: A useful tool in developing individual program plans. *Therapeutic Recreation Journal, 17*(2), 16-22.

Howe, C. Z. (1989). Assessment instruments in therapeutic recreation: To what extent do they work? In D. M. Compton (Ed.), *Issues in therapeutic recreation: A profession in transition* (pp. 205-223). Champaign, IL: Sagamore.

Howe, C. Z. (1984). Leisure assessment instrumentation in therapeutic recreation. *Therapeutic Recreation Journal, 18*(2), 12-18.

Kennedy, D. W. (1985). Using the leisure activities blank with spinal cord injured persons: A field study. *Adapted Physical Activity Quarterly, 2*(3), 182-188.

Levy, J. (1982). Behavioral observation techniques in assessing change in therapeutic recreation/play settings. *Therapeutic Recreation Journal, 16*(1), 25-32.

McMahon, R. J. (1984). Behavioral checklists and rating scales. In T. H. Ollendick and M. Hersen (Eds.), *Child behavioral assessment* (pp. 80-105). New York, NY: Pergamon.

National Therapeutic Recreation Society. (1990). *The best of the therapeutic recreation journal: Assessment.* Alexandria, NY: National Recreation and Park Association.

Stumbo, N. J. (1982). Systematic observation as a research tool for assessing client behavior. *Therapeutic Recreation Journal, 17*(4), 53-63.

Stumbo, N. J. and Rickards, W. H. (1986). Selecting assessment instruments: Theory in practice. *Journal of Expanding Horizons in Therapeutic Recreation, 1* (Fall 1986), 1-6.

Watts, J. H., Brollier, C., and Schmidt, W. (1989). Why use standardized patient evaluations? Commentary and suggestions. *Occupational Therapy in Mental Health, 8*(4), 89-96.

CASES 1 and 2
CORA AND MARIA

The following case studies concern two women in treatment at a public psychiatric hospital in a southern state.

A series of assessment procedures was used in gathering the data. The chief physician evaluated each woman to assess her current level of depression, suicidal risk, and substance abuse pattern. For these purposes, the Beck Depression Index Fasttest (Beck and Beamesderfer, 1974) and Hopelessness Scale (Beck, Weissman, Lester, and Trexler, 1974) were administered. Substance abuse and suicidality were rated using scales from the Life Crisis Inventory (Kiev, 1977).

A demographic questionnaire completed by each woman, along with medical records data, were reviewed by the therapeutic recreation specialist. The following standardized instruments were administered by the therapeutic recreation specialist: (1) the Leisure Satisfaction Scale (Beard and Ragheb, 1980); (2) the Perceived Freedom in Leisure Scale-Short Form Version B (Witt and Ellis, 1985); and (3) the Life Satisfaction Scale (Lohmann, 1980).

The therapeutic recreation specialist conducted structured interviews, consisting of open-ended and closed-form questions, with both Cora and Maria. These interviews were largely based upon the Weissman and Paykel (1974) Social Adjustment Scale and concerned the roles women may play as mother, spouse, neighbor, worker, and family member. The therapeutic recreation specialist attempted to validate the data gathered regarding leisure and life satisfaction. Other questions were added to explore gender identity, interpersonal relationships, perceived freedom and control, and leisure interests, history and participation.

Selected References for Case Studies

American Psychiatric Association. (1987). Diagnostic and statistical manual of mental disorders (3rd ed. revised). Washington, DC: Author.

Beard, J. G. and Ragheb, M. G. (1980). Measuring leisure satisfaction. *Journal of Leisure Research, 12*(1), 20-32.

Beck, A. T. and Beamesderfer, A. (1974). Assessment of depression: The depression inventory. In P. Pichot (Ed.), *Modern problems in pharmacopsychiatry,* (Vol. 7), Basel, Switzerland: Karger.

Beck, A. T., Weissman, A., Lester, D., and Trexler, L. (1974). The measurement of pessimism: The hopelessness scale. *Journal of Consulting and Clinical Psychology, 42*(6), 861-865.

Joint Commission on Accreditation of Healthcare Organizations. (1991). Alcoholism and other drug dependence services. In *Accreditation Manual for Hospitals* (pp. 3-9). Chicago, IL: Author.

Kiev, A. (1977). *The suicidal patient: Recognition and management.* Chicago, IL: Nelson Hall.

Lohmann, N. (1980). A factor analysis of life satisfaction, adjustment and morale measures with older adults. *International Journal of Aging and Human Development, 11*(1), 35-43.

Malkin, M. J. (1986). *Leisure attitudes of suicidal female psychiatric clients.* Unpublished doctoral dissertation, University of Georgia, Athens, GA.

Malkin, M. J., Howe, C. Z., and Del Rey, P. (1989). Psychological disability and leisure dysfunction of female suicidal psychiatric clients. *Therapeutic Recreation Journal, 23*(1), 36-46.

Parker, R. A., Ellison, C. H., Kirby, T. F., and Short, M. J. (1975). The comprehensive evaluation in recreational therapy scale: A tool for patient evaluation. *Therapeutic Recreation Journal, 9*(4), 43-52.

Weissman, M. M. and Paykel, E. S. (1974). *The depressed woman: A study of social relationships.* Chicago, IL: University of Chicago Press.

Witt, P. A. and Ellis, G. D. (1985). Development of a short form to assess perceived freedom in leisure. *Journal of Leisure Research, 17*(3), 225-233.

Case 1

CORA

Cora, a 39 year old black woman, is an alcoholic. She is small, trim and fashionably dressed with a neatly arranged hair style. She is quietly reflective and responds appropriately to questions.

Cora has been sad and anxious the last four months and has been drinking heavily. For the ten days prior to admission she had been having auditory and visual hallucinations.

Cora lives with her parents and her son, in addition to several younger siblings, in an urban area apartment. She is not married, but she has a boyfriend, who also drinks heavily. She feels she will never marry since the father of her son refused to marry her. The following results of psychometric and leisure assessments were reported for Cora:

Beck Depression Scale—9 (moderately depressed)

Beck Hopelessness Scale—2 (minimal)

Life Satisfaction Scale—12 (32 possible, this score indicated low satisfaction with life)

Perceived Freedom in Leisure Scale—4.04 (compared to research group mean of 3.9, S.D. 0.7)

Leisure Satisfaction Scale—95 (compared to research group mean of 84.9, S.D. 19.6). Highest scores for subscales were 17 (out of 20 possible) for the educational aspects of leisure satisfaction, and 18 for the relaxational aspects. Lowest subscores were 15 for the social and physiological aspects of leisure and 14 for the aesthetic aspects.

Based upon Kiev Life Crises scales, Cora was currently diagnosed as alcohol dependent and was rated as depressed, but nonsuicidal.

Cora is somewhat dissatisfied with her leisure experiences as indicated by her response that she would enjoy activities more if she were more involved in planning them. She participated in recreational activities that were readily available to her. She does feel that she freely chooses her activities. She concluded, "I simply do what is available and easy."

Cora noted that drinking more than she should resulted in her hospitalization. She admitted that drinking during her after-work hours, weekends, holidays, and when unemployed, indicates a leisure or recreational problem. She stated that her major limitation is the problem she has been having with her "jealous" boyfriend. Lack of money, family responsibilities, as well as lack of motivation and confidence have also limited her participation in recreational activities.

Cora enjoys dancing, partying, playing softball and basketball, reading, watching TV, and listening to music. She is not interested in pursuing any new activities at present. She prefers to do things with friends, rather than alone or with family, but has recently spent much time alone. She sometimes participates in recreational activities to please her friends or boyfriend, to relieve boredom, for personal enjoyment, to forget or escape problems, or to improve both her health and her appearance. She sometimes has too much free time, especially when she is unemployed. The problems leading to her hospitalization have caused her to reduce her participation in previous activities. She feels she is not having much fun lately due to her jealous boyfriend. He will not let her go to parties and dance, so she spends a lot of time alone with him. She does occasionally participate in recreational activities with her son. Cora is satisfied that her life is meaningful and purposeful. However, she is not satisfied with the variety in her life, her energy level, her chance to enjoy nature, her activities with friends or family, her chances to be creative, or how her life is going in general.

A high school graduate, Cora had been working full time until she was laid off two months ago, due to lack of work for her company. She consistently appeared to value work over leisure, and stated that her personal ambitions could best be realized on the job. She would prefer to be famous for something she had done on her job, than in her free time. She disagreed that it is more important for her to be good at free time activities than work activities. However, she reported recreational activities were more satisfying to her than work, and recreational activities expressed her talents and abilities better than her job activities. If she were to describe herself to someone, she would talk about work and free time activities equally.

Cora reported having approximately six close friends with whom she maintains weekly contact. She does not discuss feelings and some private issues with her friends, because she wants to keep some things to herself. She has had diminished social contacts recently due to her jealous boyfriend. If they go out with other people, it creates arguments. Cora does continue to attend church and go to family dinners and get-togethers. She has felt lonely recently, even when around other people. She has felt bored during her free time but usually found something to do to relieve the boredom.

Cora reported a mixed evaluation of her internal/external control in leisure. She stated that her successes and failures were due partly to luck. She is not, for example, a very good basketball player, but occasionally makes some lucky shots. Other successes are sometimes due to her abilities. She loves dancing and has won several dance contests. She feels that most of the events and happenings in her life are under the control of other people.

Cora agreed that she can be as good as she wants to be in her recreational activities, that she can usually decide with whom she participates, and that she can participate in a way that makes the activity enjoyable for everyone. She disagreed that she can usually convince other people to go along with activities that she wants to pursue, and that she can keep bad things from happening during a recreational activity.

Cora feels she is a traditional, "feminine" woman, but that her career choices may be limited because she is a woman. She participates in some activities many may consider "masculine" such as basketball and fishing. She can do minor car repairs such as changing tires. She does not feel women should be in charge of men on the job, but feels they could be in charge of men during recreational activities.

DISCUSSION QUESTIONS

1. In what respects has alcohol dependence affected Cora's leisure lifestyle? *limited her choices*

2. How have difficulties with interpersonal relationships affected Cora's leisure lifestyle?   *isolation*

3. Discuss issues of identity (work, leisure, gender) for Cora. How could these issues affect independent leisure or social functioning?

4. The use of criterion referenced assessments is receiving increased emphasis. Discuss the differences between criterion and norm referenced assessments and the advantages and disadvantages of using each type in therapeutic recreation.

5. Consider the use of the Leisure Diagnostic Battery's (LDB) Perceived Freedom in Leisure scale. Would you have recommended this instrument for clinical assessment in Cora's case? Why? Did this scale provide any additional insight to assist the therapeutic recreation specialist? Is the LDB criterion or norm referenced?

6. Consider the use of the Comprehensive Evaluation in Recreational Therapy (CERT) scale. Would you recommend this scale for clinical assessment in Cora's case? Why? Is the CERT Scale criterion or norm referenced?
7. Results of standardized tests sometimes conflict with information received in interviews. Why might that occur? Discuss areas where this occurred in Cora's case. How does a therapeutic recreation specialist report discrepancies in assessment data gathered from a client?
8. Is race, marital status, or age of any importance in interpreting the assessment data gathered about Cora? If so, how or why?

Case 2

MARIA

Maria, a 27 year old Hispanic female, is currently hospitalized on her seventh admission. She was hospitalized under a physician's certificate as dangerous to herself or others. Her current level of suicidality is judged moderate, although she has been seriously suicidal in the past, when definite suicidal plans were evident, or actual attempts occurred. Maria was reported to be depressed and sad for two weeks prior to admission. She stated she needs help for depression. Her primary diagnosis is bipolar disorder, depressed type. She is currently prescribed lithium carbonate.

Maria has been divorced for one and one-half years, since her husband left her. She has had financial problems caring for her three children. She and the children have been living with her parents in a private suburban home. Other relatives live nearby.

Maria completed two years of technical school. A secretary/bookkeeper, she has repeatedly quit jobs, as she has difficulty concentrating. She was working full-time just prior to her hospitalization.

clinical
or motivational

Maria is tall, large-framed and quite overweight, appearing to have gained weight since her last admission. During the interview she was strongly opinioned, often paused briefly, and then responded to questions with a thoughtful response. Her intelligence and vocabulary seemed to be above average.

The following results of psychometric and leisure tests were reported for Maria:

Beck Depression Scale—5 (mild depression)

Beck Hopelessness Scale—2 (minimal)

Life Satisfaction Scale—26 (out of 32 possible, fairly high)

Perceived Freedom in Leisure Scale—5 (research group mean was 3.8, S.D. 1.1)

Leisure Satisfaction Scale—108 (group mean 75.7, S.D. 23.7). Highest subscale scores were 20/20 scored in subscales for the educational, psychological, social, and relaxational aspects of leisure.

Maria was rated on the basis of Kiev scales as having no substance abuse disorder, and as being moderately suicidal.

When questioned about the problems which brought her to the hospital this time, Maria stated she was losing track of time, becoming very "inwardized" and depressed. She reported no physical problems or disabilities. Maria stated that she was satisfied with her recreational activities and that she had no recreational or leisure problems, although her participation has been limited recently due to her depression. She indicated that she freely chooses her recreational activities.

Maria cited lack of money, family responsibilities, lack of motivation, confidence and energy, and fear of failure as factors limiting her participation in recreational activities. Activities she enjoys include bowling, cake decorating, volleyball, creative writing, reading, talking, and singing. Maria reported that when not depressed, she has lots of energy. She stated she used to read a lot but has had trouble concentrating in recent years. She also stated she would like to rejoin her church choir.

Maria claimed to prefer doing things alone rather than with friends or family. This is a recent change as she used to dislike being alone. In the past, she spent time alone reading or writing. Now she spends time alone thinking and has learned to like being by herself.

Maria indicated the following reasons for participating in recreational activities: to relieve boredom; to forget or escape problems; and for personal enjoyment. She indicated she has too much free time at present, due to being unemployed. The problems leading to her hospitalization have, as noted, limited her participation in recreational activities. She has maintained her church activities, even when depressed, but stated she has had virtually no participation in her hobbies during the past two years.

Maria's future plans span a couple of years and concern the relationship between her children and herself. She has "mixed" satisfaction with the variety in her life, her opportunities to be creative and how her life is going in general. She is satisfied with the things she does with her friends and family, and very satisfied with her opportunities to enjoy nature and the meaning and purpose of her life. Maria disagreed that she can best realize her ambitions on the job rather than during her free time. She also disagreed that she would rather be famous for something she had done on the job rather than in her free time. But she adds that it is false that it is more important to be "good at" free time activities than at a job. She disagreed, for two reasons, (1) that her recreational activities are more satisfying than her work, and (2) she is unemployed at the present time and recently has participated in little if any recreational activities, except church.

Maria has dropped most of her friends due to her depression. She does maintain contact with two church friends. She is usually able to discuss her feelings and private matters with her friends. She stated she only has girlfriends, no male friends. Maria reported she often feels uncomfortable, ill at ease, tense, and shy in social situations. She used to avoid most social interactions, but believes she is now more aware of and in control of herself.

Maria agreed that her successes in leisure and recreation were due to her own abilities or efforts, but she feels that work or leisure events are not always under her control. She feels that whether or not she is as good as she wants to be at recreational activities depends on many factors. She used to be able to convince others to participate in activities, but does not try anymore. Maria decides who she participates in activities with and can usually help other participants have more fun in an activity. She denied that she can enable everyone to have more fun, or that she can keep bad things from happening in recreational activities.

In terms of sex role orientation and social constraints, Maria stated that she is limited in her career choices more because of her lack of education than because she is a woman. She has enjoyed activities in her leisure most people consider to be "masculine" such as repairing cars and riding motorcycles with her ex-husband.

Maria does not feel women should be in charge of men at work or leisure. She feels people need to be as respectful of others as they are deserving of respect.

DISCUSSION QUESTIONS

1. Discuss the effects of bipolar disorder, depressed type upon Maria. You may want to review this diagnosis in the *Diagnostic and Statistical Manual of Mental Disorders* (3rd ed. revised).
2. Discuss issues of identity (work, leisure, gender). How could these issues affect Maria's independent leisure or social functioning?
3. Depression, suicide, and related behaviors are often dyadic, involving one or more significant other. How have difficulties with interpersonal relationships affected Maria?
4. Consider the use of the Leisure Diagnostic Battery's (LDB) Perceived Freedom in Leisure scale. Would you have recommended this instrument for clinical assessment in Maria's case? Why? Did this scale provide any additional insight to assist the therapeutic recreation specialist? Is the LDB criterion or norm referenced?
5. Consider the Comprehensive Evaluation in Recreation Therapy (CERT) scale. Would you recommend this scale for clinical assessment in Maria's case? Is the CERT Scale criterion or norm referenced?
6. Results of standardized tests sometimes conflict with information received in interviews. Why might this occur? Discuss areas where this occurred in Maria's case.
7. The therapeutic recreation specialist observed that Maria seemed to verbally maintain an optimistic front despite difficulties. In addition, her diagnosis of bipolar disorder indicates that a manic phase may occur as her depression decreases. A manic phase is characterized by elevated mood, grandiosity, or euphoria (American Psychiatric Association, 1987). How would these two factors affect results of testing? Could these two factors have influenced her perfect score on the Perceived Freedom in Leisure scale?
8. Consider Maria's diagnosis, admissions histories, and medication. Could she be at risk for early problems with reality orientation? Based on your answer, present a rationale for or against administering a reality orientation assessment to determine a baseline.

Case
3

MAGNOLIA HILLS

Magnolia Hills is a 25 year old congregate residence for older adults. A four-story building with a basement, parking lot, and landscaped grounds, Magnolia Hills gives the appearance of a contemporary residence hall. Constructed to meet the accessibility standards at the time it was built, Magnolia Hills has barrier-free apartment units, ramps, and elevators. The entire building is hooked up to an emergency intercom, and the residence is in compliance with all federal and state codes governing nondiscrimination, equal housing opportunity, and standards of health and safety.

The first floor, which is ground level, houses the administrative offices, a reception area, a spacious lobby, a multipurpose meeting room, and a dining room which opens to a brick patio with gas grill facilities. The dining room itself is set up cafeteria style, with a buffet serving line. The upper floors have one bedroom and studio apartments; the former for couples and roommates, the latter for single persons. Residents provide their own furnishings. Each floor also has a comfortable lounge with card tables, chairs, and sofas.

Magnolia Hills is a private facility. The rental rates are set at fair market value and are affordable for middle income individuals or couples. Almost all of the residents are on fixed incomes, with their financial resources composed of Social Security, private pensions, personal investments, savings, and assistance from adult children. The rental rate includes one meal a day, which is served at noon. Residents prepare their other two daily meals in their own kitchens. Special meals and festivities are planned for all major holidays.

Magnolia Hills' administrative staff includes a director, an activities coordinator, a part-time coordinator of volunteers, and an office manager, who also serves as bookkeeper, secretary, and receptionist. The director is responsible to a board of directors who must approve all major expenditures and policy revisions. The current director has a bachelor's degree in health administration and a master's degree in gerontology.

The activities coordinator has a bachelor's degree in social work and a master's degree in recreation administration, with a concentration in therapeutic recreation. Both she and the director had several years of professional experience prior to assuming their positions at Magnolia Hills. The part-time volunteer coordinator was a special education teacher for eight years. The office manager, a high school graduate, has been with Magnolia Hills for over ten years.

Since its opening, Magnolia Hills, with room for 200 residents, has been filled to capacity. Initially open to individuals 55 years and older who were no longer able to or desired to live independently, Magnolia Hills' only additional admission criterion was the applicant's ability to walk independently or with the use of a cane. Individuals using crutches, walkers, wheelchairs, or other assistive devices were not admitted because they would not be able to go through the cafeteria line unassisted.

Based on the nation's changing population demographics, increasing longevity and a growing waiting list, Magnolia Hills recently raised the minimum age for admission to 65. Of the 200 current residents, 100 percent are white; 98 percent are female; 92 percent are widowed, divorced, or never married; 80 percent are high school graduates, with 30 percent of that number being college educated. Ranging in age from 67 to 94, the current population has an average age of 79 years.

As the population of Magnolia Hills has aged, there has been an increase in the incidence of chronic conditions that tend to occur with greater longevity: diabetes, memory impairment, sensory impairment, heart and respiratory diseases, hypertension, and depression. In the latter condition, a physiological connection between sensory deprivation and drug-induced (e.g., heart medications, antibiotics, sleeping medications) neurological depression may be contributing to feelings of loneliness. It is harder for residents to initiate and maintain social interactions if physiologically depressed. Each of these conditions can affect autonomous functioning to some extent.

As the residents are getting older, their needs are changing. Recognizing that programing must be expanded to keep pace with the needs of their changing population, the activity coordinator's first priority was to provide opportunities for socialization beyond special holiday meals and weekly worship services. However, she and the director both recognized that this was only an intermediate step. To plan and implement an effective program, they needed to conduct a systematic and comprehensive assessment of the residents' ongoing needs.

With the approval of the board of directors, a therapeutic recreation consultant was hired. With support and direction from the activities coordinator, the consultant would be responsible for developing and implementing an assessment program. You are that consultant. You have agreed to develop, implement, and evaluate a comprehensive and systematic assessment at Magnolia Hills.

The director and activities coordinator have emphasized that they want to examine more than the residents' physical and cognitive functioning. They want your assessment to include social and affective functioning and the role of recreation and leisure in each individual's life. You have all the rights and responsibilities of an administrative staff member: office space; access to your colleagues, the residents, and all records; word processing; and any other items typically needed to work in a professional setting.

DISCUSSION QUESTIONS

1. What is the immediate assessment problem to be solved or the question(s) to be answered? How does the statement of a problem affect a therapeutic recreation specialist's approach to solving it?
2. What personal, educational and professional resources are you going to need to fulfill your role?
3. What existing tools or devices are available to measure physical, cognitive, affective, social, and leisure functioning of older adults? Where and how can these assessment tools be located? How can they be adapted for use in this situation?
4. If you construct your own assessment tools or devices, how can you ensure that they are reliable, valid, and practical for your purposes?
5. How are you going to analyze the assessment data you obtain? How are you going to report that data so that they can be used by the activity coordinator, director, and board of directors?
6. How do you anticipate the interpretation of the data will influence the decisions Magnolia Hills' staff and board will be making?
7. How are you going to evaluate the effectiveness of the assessment instruments, procedures, and processes you selected?

8. An important part of the assessment process is to help deter-
    mine when a resident has reached a level of need which
    qualifies him for additional services or funding from a govern-
    ment agency and/or third party payer. Examples of services
    include services for the blind, "meals on wheels," or hearing
    evaluations. What would be the role of the therapeutic recrea-
    tion consultant in this situation?

IN-CLASS EXERCISES

1. Play "The Game of Aging Concerns" available from the
    American Association of Homes for the Aged Publications,
    1129 20th Street, NW, Suite 400, Washington, DC 20036-
    3489, (202)296-5960.

FIELD EXPERIENCES

1. Visit a congregate living center for older adults in your area so
    that you get a sense of this type of facility, setting, clients, and
    recreation programming.
2. Invite an activity coordinator from a congregate living center
    to meet with the "consultants" in developing the assessment
    program for Magnolia Hills.
3. Interview several older adults who reside in a congregate living
    center to become better acquainted with this population and
    their potential leisure needs.
4. Conduct a leisure needs assessment with a local congregate
    senior facility as a class project.
5. Conduct a literature review of gerontological assessment tools
    that might be relevant to designing a leisure needs assessment
    with older persons.
6. Invite a state or federal surveyor of residential programs for
    older adults to discuss pertinent regulations and requirements
    relating to recreation programs.
7. Invite community officials, such as a representative from the
    health or fire department, to meet with the class and provide
    information on codes and regulations as they relate to recrea-
    tion programming.

Selected References for Case Study

Howe, C. Z. and Qui, Y. (1988). The programming process revisited: Assumptions underlying the needs based models. *Journal of Park and Recreation Administration, 6*(4), 14-27.

Howe, C. Z. (1987). Selected social gerontology theories and older adult leisure involvement: A review of the literature. *Journal of Applied Gerontology, 6*(4), 448-463.

Ragheb, M. G. and Griffith, C. A. (1982). The contribution of leisure participation and leisure satisfaction to the life satisfaction of older persons. *Journal of Leisure Research, 14*(4), 295-306.

Riddick, C. C. and Daniel, S. N. (1984). The relative contribution of leisure activity and other factors to the mental health of older women. *Journal of Leisure Research, 16* (2), 138-148.

Retsinas, J. (1989). Functioning and perceived distress. *Clinical Gerontologist, 8*(4),46-47.

Salamon, M. J. and Conte, V. A. (1988). *Life satisfaction in the elderly scale (LSES)*. Odessa, FL: Psychological Assessment Resources, Inc.

Wing, J. K. (1989). The measurement of "social disablement": The MRC social behavior and social role performance schedules. *Social Psychiatry and Psychiatric Epidemiology, 24*(4), 173-178.

Case 4

EDITH

Edith Miller, a 69 year old white female, lives in a 75-bed private for-profit licensed long-term health care facility in a rural midwest community. Residents range in age from 65 to 102 years. An individual care plan is completed for each resident. Quarterly meetings are conducted with primary care givers and team representatives from nursing, dietary, social services, and activities. Residents are invited to participate in these quarterly meetings. Team members establish goals for each resident based on assessed needs. Residents must consent, when able, to specific goals before they can be implemented. The nursing staff reviews each resident's status monthly.

The neighboring community, 10 miles away, is a college town of approximately 40,000 residents. The facility does not own transportation vehicles, but staff on occasion use their cars to take residents to this community. Weekly and special events, including church services, are sponsored by organizations from the college town.

Mrs. Miller was placed in the facility three years ago by her husband, who is employed in the nearby community. Their three children all live out-of-state. Mrs. Miller was admitted with a diagnosis of Alzheimer's disease. Symptoms of the disease, which began ten years ago, have progressively worsened over time.

Current assessment information reveals secondary impairments of depression, ulcerative colitis, and hypothyroidism. Medications include: Metamucil, Tbsp, b.i.d. at meal times; Haldol, 1 milligram, q.i.d. at bedtime; and p.r.n., Tylenol for pain or headache. Also noted, elevate legs to reduce edema; p.r.n., LOA.

Chart notes indicate unexpected mood swings, agitation, combative behavior, incontinence, dislike of loud noises including voices of others and high volume TV, decreased walking balance, limited attending skills, upset with religious activities, difficulty with feeding, definite likes and dislikes of specific staff, resistive behaviors when toileting and bathing, limited responses which are usually nonverbal, and flat affect. Staff report they are unable to determine when Mrs. Miller is listening to or hearing their conversations. Activities Mrs. Miller appears to enjoy include walking with staff assistants or her husband, listening to low volume TV or radio music, watching movies, and attending parties with food.

The primary team goals have included enabling Mrs. Miller to recognize her primary caregiver, limiting the striking of others, maintaining her weight, cooperating with staff during activities of daily living, and maintaining socially appropriate contact. Nursing goals have also included preventing decubitus ulcers and establishing the proper dosages of the appropriate medications. Dietary goals focus on self-feeding and attending to eating while at meals. Social service goals focus on developing and maintaining skills associated with interpersonal interactions.

As the newly hired full-time therapeutic recreation specialist, you realize that it is time to reevaluate and develop individual therapeutic recreation program goals for Mrs. Miller.

DISCUSSION QUESTIONS

1. What functional difficulties commonly experienced by persons with Alzheimer's disease will be of concern to you as you attempt to obtain an accurate assessment of Mrs. Miller's strengths, areas of need, and interests as they relate to therapeutic recreation? How will you conduct your assessment so that the effect of functional difficulties is minimized?

2. Why is it important to note compensatory methods Mrs. Miller might use to overcome functional deficits?

IN-CLASS EXERCISES

1. Current assessment information is listed in this case. Is there a need to obtain additional assessment information? If so, identify the desired information along with sources and methods you will utilize to obtain it.

2. Obtain and review a summary of the Omnibus Budget Reconciliation Act (OBRA) of 1987. How does this legislation impact assessment procedures and techniques?

3. Under OBRA legislation, every individual admitted to a nursing facility must be administered the same assessment. Obtain a copy of the *Minimum Data Set for Nursing Home Resident Assessment and Care Screening (MDS)*, a general admission tool, from a local nursing home. Are the questions which

address residents' recreation needs and patterns adequate to plan an individual program? If not, what additional assessment procedures or techniques would you recommend?

FIELD EXPERIENCES

1. Invite a spokesperson from an Alzheimer's and Related Diseases Chapter to speak to the class about the disease and the disabling conditions associated with it.

Selected References for Case Study

Burnside, I. M. (1984). Interviewing the aged. In I. M. Burnside, *Working with the elderly: Group process and techniques* (pp. 7-18). Monterey, CA: Wadsworth Health Sciences.

Burnside, I. M. (1984). Interviewing the confused aged person. In I. M. Burnside, *Working with the elderly: Group process and techniques* (pp. 19-33). Monterey, CA: Wadsworth Health Sciences.

Cunningham, W. R. and Brookbank, J. W. (1988). *Gerontology: The psychology, biology, and sociology of aging.* New York, NY: Harper and Row.

Farran, C. J. and Keane-Hagerty, E. (1989). Communicating effectively with dementia patients. *Journal of Psychosocial Nursing, 27*(5), 13-16.

Eisdorfer, C. and Friedel, R. O. (Eds.). (1979). *Cognitive and emotional disturbances in the elderly.* Chicago, IL: Yearbook Medical Publishers.

Greenblatt, F. S. (1988). *Therapeutic recreation for long-term care facilities.* New York, NY: Human Science Press.

Herring, G. H. (1985). *An Alzheimer's primer, 1984.* Denton, TX: Center for Studies in Aging, North Texas State University.

Lyman, K. A. (1990). Staff stress treatment of clients in Alzheimer's care: A comparison of medical and nonmedical day care programs. *Journal of Aging Studies, 4*(1), 61-79.

Omnibus Budget Reconciliation Act. (1987). Public Law 100-203. Section C. Nursing Home Reform, Part I. Medicare, Part II., Medicaid.

Mace, N. and Rabins, P. (1981). *The 36 hour day: A family guide to caring for persons with Alzheimer's disease, related dementing illnesses, and memory loss in later life.* Baltimore, MD: Johns Hopkins University Press.

Medicare and Medicaid. (Tuesday, February 2, 1989). Requirements for longterm care facilities: Final rules with requests for comments *Federal Registry, 54*(21), 5316-5373.

Sanders, P. (1990). *Activity care plans for long term care facilities.* Houston, TX: M & H Publishing.

Weiner, M. B., Brok, A. J., and Snadowsky, A. M. (1987). *Working with the aged, practical approaches in the institution and community* (2nd ed.). Norwalk, CT: Appleton-Century-Crofts.

West, H. L., Chafetz, P. K., and Rice, C. (1987). Issues in the development of Alzheimer's disease special care units. *The Southwestern Journal of Aging, 4*(1), 59-66.

Zgola, J. M. (1987). *Doing things: A guide to programming activities for persons with Alzheimer's disease and related disorders.* Baltimore, MD: Johns Hopkins University Press.

Film

History Taking With the Elderly. Southern Illinois University School of Medicine, P.O. Box 19230, Springfield, IL 62794-9230, (217) 782-2860.

Audio Cassette

Alzheimer's Disease and Other Cognitive Disorders. America's Society on Aging, 833 Market St., Suite 512, San Francisco, CA 94103, 1-800-537-9728.

Resources

Geriatric Resources, Inc. 5450 Barton Drive, Orlando, FL 32807, (404) 282-8711. (Sensory stimulation products for Alzheimer's type dementias and geriatric rehabilitation.)

```
┌─────────────────────┐
│                     │
│                     │
│        Case         │          TODD
│         5           │
│                     │
│                     │
└─────────────────────┘
```

Todd Smith, a 26 year old white male with a diagnosis of Down's syndrome, was referred for assessment by his family physician. His parents, who are his legal guardians, had expressed concern about the increased frequency of behavioral problems in his home and at the Lakeshore Service Center. Specifically, they noted an increased frequency of interpersonal aggression, sustained periods of yelling and self-injurious behavior.

The Smiths also reported increased frustration at their inability to effectively manage their son's self-injurious behavior. Their threats to "tie his hands" "sometimes work." He was recently admitted to the state institution to determine the possible medical and psychological bases for his behavior and for development of a treatment program.

When discussing the possibility that Todd's behavior may have some attention-getting elements, Mr. Smith reported that "he gets more attention than most kids—he has unlimited access to TV, toys, selected foods, etc." Still, Mr. and Mrs. Smith believe that Todd's increased frequency of behavior problems may be due to "boredom."

Todd's test scores indicated performance in the severe range of mental retardation. Mr. Jim Hill, Lakeshore Adult Service Center, reported that Todd was enrolled in their lowest functioning class. This class primarily addresses basic daily living skills.

Mr. Hill also reported that Todd has demonstrated an increased frequency of aggressive behavior toward other Center clients and staff. He reported that initially Todd would "attack primarily the meek and elderly on the bus," but that he had recently begun to strike out at familiar people, including people he liked.

With regard to behavioral strategies, Mr. Hill reported that in the past, time-out and raising his voice had been somewhat effective in managing Todd's hitting and noncompliance, but that these techniques were becoming increasingly less effective. Mr. Hill indicated that a verbal direction to put his hands in his lap is effective in decreasing Todd's self-abuse.

Todd was observed by the therapeutic recreation specialist during an evaluation session conducted by the psychologist. During the session, Todd demonstrated one period of sustained yelling while his parents were still in the room. He yelled until his father raised his voice, after which he ceased. He also demonstrated one episode of self-abuse, again with his parents in the room. He stopped after his mother threatened to tie his hands.

Following a period of compliance and cooperation after his parents left the room, Todd was observed to engage in a series of what appeared to be "testing" behaviors with the examiner. After appearing to become bored with table activities, he engaged in a series of progressively disruptive behaviors (e.g., pounding the table, leaving the chair, lifting the table, upsetting the wastebasket). After each behavior in the sequence, he looked at the examiner. When no attention was provided, he engaged in more disruptive behavior. This series of events occurred four times during the session. On two occasions it culminated with his voluntary return to his chair (the expectation), and on the remaining two occasions, with his father entering the room and verbally reprimanding him.

When completing simple activities, Todd's performance improved when given paired physical and verbal prompts. Pretzels and the combination of pretzels and social praise were very effective in facilitating Todd's compliance with simple directions. He appeared to understand the relationship between his compliance with a request and the reinforcer as he often looked at the pretzels or reached for them following his compliance. Social praise alone was not shown to be an effective reinforcer for Todd.

Boredom, desire for attention, and/or frustration with his inability to communicate may be reasons for Todd's disruptive behavior. Increasing Todd's repertoire of leisure skills, which he may eventually use independently or with minimal prompting and assistance, may reduce his boredom and thus serve to decrease his frustration and undesirable behavior.

DISCUSSION QUESTIONS

1. What type of assessment information will you need in order to recommend a therapeutic recreation program plan for Todd?
2. What are some potential objective and subjective sources for the assessment data identified in question one? For each source you identify, describe and justify the method you will use to collect the data. Be specific when identifying standardized leisure assessments, and justify why you would use these instruments. State the reliability, validity, and feasibility of the instruments selected.

3. Assuming you agree that increasing Todd's repertoire of leisure skills is a desirable outcome of his participation in a therapeutic recreation program, you will need to know more about his current level of functioning. Identify questions you would like to have answered in these areas:
   a. physical domain,
   b. cognitive domain,
   c. social domain,
   d. affective domain, and
   e. past leisure patterns and expressed areas of preference.
   How would you discover answers to the questions you have raised?
4. Is evaluation of Todd's home and Center environments important in this situation? If yes, what do you want to know about these environments?
5. What would you do during an on-site assessment visit to Todd's home and/or Center?
6. Do you think there are additional reasons for Todd's disruptive behavior? If so, identify these reasons and discuss other possible desired outcomes of his participation in a therapeutic recreation program.

IN-CLASS EXERCISES

1. Develop a list of Todd's strengths, areas of need, and interests. Identify behaviors that need remediation or improvement for effective leisure functioning to occur.

FIELD EXPERIENCES

1. Visit a therapeutic recreation specialist who works with individuals who have moderate to severe mental retardation. Discuss methods utilized to conduct assessments. Obtain copies of assessment protocols, instruments, and techniques, if possible, that might be appropriate for use with Todd. Ask the therapeutic recreation specialist you visit to review your responses to the questions above. Report your findings in class and share written information.

Selected References for Case Study

Crawford, M. E. and Mendell, R. (1987). *Therapeutic recreation and adapted physical activities for mentally retarded individuals.* Englewood Cliffs, NJ: Prentice-Hall, Inc.

Datillo, J. and Murphy, W. D. (1987). *Behavior modification in therapeutic recreation.* State College, PA: Venture Publishing, Inc.

Mittler, P. and McConachie, H. (Eds.). (1983). *Parents, professionals and mentally handicapped people: Approaches to partnership.* Cambridge, MA: Brookline Books.

Mulick, J. A. and Kedesdy, J. H. (1988). Self-injurious behavior, its treatment, and normalization. *Mental Retardation, 26*(4), 223-229.

Schleien, S., Cameron, J., Rynders, J., and Slick, C. (1988). Acquisition and generalization of leisure skills from school to the home community by learners with severe multihandicaps. *Therapeutic Recreation Journal, 22*(3), 53-71.

Schleien, S., Kiernan, J., and Wehman, P. (1981). Evaluation of an age-appropriate leisure skills program for moderately retarded adults. *Education and Training of the Mentally Retarded, 16*(1), 13-19.

Schoen, S. F. (1986). Decreasing noncompliance in a severely multihandicapped child. *Psychology in the Schools, 23,* 88-93.

Wehman, P. and Schleien, S. J. (1981). *Leisure programs for handicapped persons: Adaptations, techniques and curriculum.* Austin, TX: PRO-ED.

Wehman, P. and Schleien, S. J. (1980). Relevant assessment in leisure skill training programs. *Therapeutic Recreation Journal, 14*(4), 9-20.

Chapter Two

Individual Therapeutic Recreation Program Planning

Individual program planning in therapeutic recreation indicates there is a need for intervention and service delivery with the intention of altering clients' personal and/or leisure functioning. Early leaders in therapeutic recreation, such as Ball, Frye, and Peters, were among the first to describe a continuum concept of therapeutic recreation intervention leading to desired change.

Ball (1970) provided an interpretation of the continuum concept in her depiction of a sequence of steps through which a client progresses until he reaches a "true recreative experience." These steps are shown in Figure 2.1.

In Ball's model, a client first moves through a functionally deficient level in which he participates in recreation just for the sake of "reality participation." The client then acquires attitudes, skills, and knowledge regarding recreation participation, and gradually begins to exercise personal recreation participation choices.

	EXPERIENCE	TYPE OF TIME	MAJOR MOTIVATION
1.	Activity for sake of activity	Obligated time	Drive is outer-directed
2.	Recreation education	Obligated time	Drive is outer-directed
3.	Therapeutic recreation	Unobligated time	Motivation is inner-directed but choice of experience is limited
4.	Recreation	Unobligated time	Motivation is inner-directed

Figure 2.1
Steps to a recreative experience. From *Therapeutic Recreation Journal* 4(1) (p. 18) 1970. Reprinted with permission of the National Recreation and Park Association.

Frye and Peters (1972) furthered the continuum concept by describing the relationship between the control or authority imposed by therapeutic recreation specialists and the freedom experienced by clients. Their diagram was adapted from a leadership model for business managers developed by Tannenbaum and Schmidt (1958). Frye and Peters acknowledged that a client's disability might initially limit his participation in a truly recreative experience. It is important to provide a range of leisure opportunities offered in situations and settings which vary in their restrictiveness. Frye and Peters' model is illustrated in Figure 2.2.

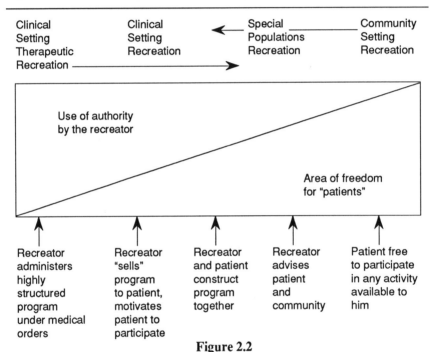

Figure 2.2

A continuum of therapeutic recreation. From *Therapeutic Recreation: Its Theory, Philosophy, and Practice* (p. 43) by V. Frye and M. Peters, 1972, Harrisburg, PA: Stackpole Books. Copyright 1972 by Stackpole Books. Reprinted by permission.

Gunn and Peterson (1978) expanded these early ideas concerning a continuum and developed the "Therapeutic Recreation Service Model." This model served as the backbone for the development of the therapeutic recreation philosophical position statement endorsed by the National Therapeutic Recreation Society (1982). A later version of the model (Peterson and Gunn, 1984) is presented in Figure 2.3.

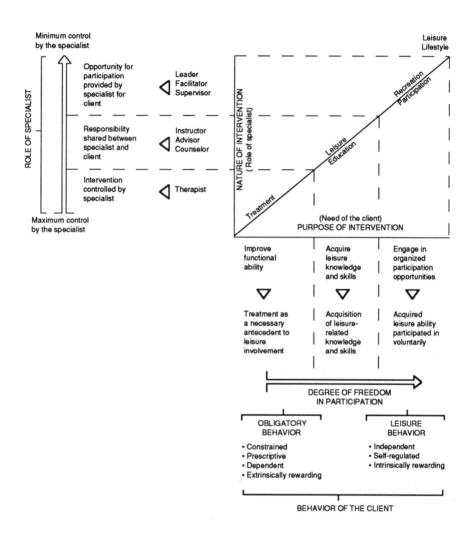

Figure 2.3

Therapeutic recreation service model. From *Therapeutic Recreation Program Design: Principles and Procedures* (2nd ed.) (p. 44) by C. A. Peterson and S. L. Gunn, 1984, Englewood Cliffs, NJ: Prentice-Hall. Copyright 1984 by Prentice-Hall. Reprinted by permission.

As depicted in this model, the interaction that occurs during the therapeutic recreation process is sometimes directed toward resolving an existing problem. At other times, the goal is to enhance nonproblematic functioning and encourage further personal development. This model helps therapeutic recreation specialists determine the scope of practice based on the resources and limitations of clients and agencies.

While other leaders in the field of therapeutic recreation have expressed variations on these early concepts regarding a continuum of services (Carter, Van Andel and Robb, 1990; Howe-Murphy and Charboneau, 1987; O'Morrow and Reynolds, 1989), a concept of personal freedom remains paramount. A primary goal of therapeutic recreation intervention is to maximize clients' personal freedom so that they might truly experience leisure. Witt (1982) indicated that therapeutic recreation attempts to create freedom *from* constraints in the individual or environment and freedom *to* make choices and act at will.

While various models of individual therapeutic recreation program planning have been developed, all stress the importance of helping clients achieve maximum interdependent leisure functioning. In this discussion of individual therapeutic recreation program planning, eight steps will be highlighted: (1) determining direction; (2) selecting content and process; (3) analyzing activities; (4) selecting activities; (5) modifying activities; (6) selecting appropriate interventions; (7) considering service delivery options; and (8) developing a written plan.

Determining Direction

When therapeutic recreation specialists attempt to discover what is preventing maximum interdependent leisure functioning, they must consider the question of where to begin. "Problems" related to clients' current functioning levels can be discovered through reviewing assessment data and formulating a list of strengths, areas of need, and interests. By analyzing this list, therapeutic recreation specialists can determine which areas need to be addressed first and how clients' strengths and interests might be used to ameliorate problems. Crawford and Mendell (1987) advise specialists to target first those deficiencies that are prerequisites to other desired skills. In addition, the resolution of some problems will require assistance from other members of a multidisciplinary team or from various community representatives (O'Morrow and Reynolds, 1989). This individual program planning process includes clients' perceptions of problems and their expectations of service participation.

Desired client outcomes and behaviors can then be stated as observable short- and long-term goals for which a client will strive and toward which a therapeutic recreation specialist will direct his programmatic efforts. According to Peterson and Gunn (1984), there are no universal definitions distinguishing short-term and long-term goals. The length of time implied by the term will vary from agency to agency. Frye and Peters (1972) state that the various dimensions of the therapeutic recreation continuum imply a discrimination between short- and long-term goals. Thus, the therapeutic recreation specialist might think of short-term goals as the acquisition of behaviors and skills needed in order to accomplish the intent of the long-term goals. Wilcox and Bellamy (1987) point out that activities directed toward accomplishing short-term goals should be combined with efforts directed toward accomplishing long-term goals. For example, if a client's long-term goal is to develop social interaction skills, she can participate in a nonverbal small group activity even before she has demonstrated the ability to respond verbally to leader or participant initiated questions.

In their most useful form, these goals are restated as measurable objectives—specific behaviors that are to be demonstrated within a specified period of time, under a certain set of conditions, and judged by a predetermined standard or criterion. They are often referred to as behavioral objectives, performance measures, or outcome statements. These objectives: (1) identify what the client will be doing to demonstrate the intent of the objective (the behavior); (2) explain the situation under which the behavior will occur, such as "on request..." "without assistance..." "when given a choice of..." (the conditions); and (3) describe the criteria by which the client's progress will be evaluated, such as accuracy, amount of time, and form. Objectives are often stated in one of three domains: cognitive, affective, and psychomotor (Kennedy, Smith, and Austin, 1991). They may also be written as outcomes to be achieved in one or more of the therapeutic recreation service functions: rehabilitation or treatment, leisure education, or recreation participation (Peterson and Gunn, 1984). Rehabilitation or treatment should address functional deficiencies that could limit leisure involvement. Leisure education should focus on the knowledge required for successful leisure participation and recreation participation should provide opportunities for utilizing leisure-related skills while participating in activities of choice.

Selecting Content and Process

Once therapeutic recreation specialists have determined clients' goals, activities and approaches must be selected. Activity *content* refers to the specific activity or combination of activities (e.g., table games, sports, crafts, leisure education program, music, drama, dance) that will be used to address individual objectives. In essence, content is "what" will be done. *Process* refers to the specific leadership interaction and intervention techniques that will be used, as well as the activity structure or format. In other words, process is "how" the content will be presented to clients.

Activities and approaches are selected that contribute to clients' objectives and reflect preferences and other personal and/or environmental characteristics. Peterson and Gunn (1984) state that content and process should also produce the desired result "with the least expenditure of time, energy, or resources" (p. 118).

Analyzing Activities

As the individual program planning process unfolds, therapeutic recreation specialists must analyze potential activities to determine what clients' abilities are necessary for successful participation. Activity analysis is conducted independent of clients; that is, without a specific individual in mind. Through activity analysis therapeutic recreation specialists learn what activity characteristics contribute to the accomplishment of clients' objectives.

To engage in activities requires action in at least three behavioral areas—cognitive, affective, and psychomotor—and may also involve social and spiritual areas. When analyzing the cognitive aspects of activities, therapeutic recreation specialists should consider necessary academic skills, such as reading, math, and spelling, as well as such things as the type and amount of memory required, and degree of concentration and/or strategy involved.

Analysis of affective aspects should take into account the various emotional responses likely to be stimulated by the activity (Peterson and Gunn, 1984). Does the activity relieve stress, allow the participant to communicate feelings, or promote creativity? Is the activity fun, stimulating, or exciting? Does frustration commonly arise from engaging in the activity?

When analyzing the psychomotor aspects of activities, therapeutic recreation specialists might determine the type of manipulative movement involved, the degree of mobility or the level of exertion and endurance required. Various types of sensory demands (e.g., sight, hearing, touch) inherent in the activity should be specified.

Examples of the social aspects of an activity that therapeutic recreation specialists might analyze include the degree of cooperation or competition and opportunities for interaction with individuals without disabilities and of the opposite sex. Determining the amount of communication required (vocal and nonvocal) and the general types of interactions which occur (e.g., contact with the environment, leaders, or others) will also help therapeutic recreation specialists understand social skills needed by clients to successfully participate in activities.

Spiritual aspects of activities do not pertain just to a specific religion but include the opportunity to care for others, to experience spiritual value in the aesthetic sense—beauty, awe, and grandeur—and to gain peace of mind. As activities are analyzed in the spiritual area, concepts of helplessness, control, perceived freedom, and reciprocity should be considered.

Selecting Activities

Once potential activities have been identified, the appropriateness of each selection must be determined. As previously discussed, this decision is based on the activity's potential contribution to clients' goals and objectives (desired changes), interests and abilities, and characteristics of their living environments.

Limitations of a client or his environment should not be the primary reason for rejection of an activity. To the contrary, recognizing limitations should include determining the need for, interest in, and ability to develop necessary participation skills. Personal skills and capabilities needed for participation in the activity of choice may be acquired through leisure education or skill development programs. Environments in which clients live, work, or recreate may be capable of supporting efforts to acquire and utilize recreation participation skills. If not, the feasibility of environmental adaptations can be explored and determined before making activity selections.

Some clients may not readily indicate their personal preferences and interests. In such situations, it may be necessary to encourage participation in a wide variety of activities that contribute to clients' goals and objectives so that, over time, therapeutic recreation specialists may rank individual preferences from most to least favorite activities.

Wuerch and Voeltz (1982) provide additional insight regarding the selection of activity content. According to these authors, it is helpful when activity selections are also valued and supported by people with whom clients come into contact. The activity's appeal and adaptability to peers without disabilities, family members, and other caregivers should be considered.

In addition, Wuerch and Voeltz (1982) suggest that therapeutic recreation specialists and clients should consider how participation skills can extend beyond a specific recreation activity and setting. "For an activity to be functional, a person must be able to perform under a range of conditions" (Wilcox and Bellamy, 1987, p. 64). Emphasis should be placed on developing a variety of transferable competencies and establishing opportunities for clients to practice newly acquired skills in a number of different settings. For example, participating in a painting class in a special recreation program could expand in a variety of ways, such as painting as a hobby, or painting a set for the community theater.

Modifying Activities

To facilitate clients' participation in therapeutic, educational, or recreational activities, specialists may have to make modifications that involve individual, programmatic, or environmental changes which will reduce or eliminate barriers. Therapeutic recreation specialists and clients should work together to develop activity adaptations and modifications. For example, specialists may simply ask: "How can you best do this?"; "What would allow you to perform this more easily?"; or "How does this feel?" These adaptations should be individualized and designed to highlight clients' abilities rather than disabilities.

Activities can be modified in several ways (Howe-Murphy and Charboneau, 1987; Project LIFE, 1988; Wehman and Schleien, 1981; Wuerch and Voeltz, 1982). The *materials or equipment* might be modified. In addition to homemade equipment and devices, commercially marketed items are available (Nesbitt, 1986).

The activity could also be modified by changing *procedures and/or rules*. Clients may sit or walk rather than stand or run. Additional trials (strikes, throws, misses, etc.) may be permitted and extra players may be added. Playing dimensions (size of court, height of net or basket, etc.) may be altered as well. Clients can also be challenged to design their own procedures and rules, thus creating new activities.

Therapeutic recreation specialists can change the *way activities are introduced and presented.* For example, they can use simple rather than complex words, suggest physical prompts, offer guidance, demonstrate the task, and emphasize more than one sense (touch, sight, hearing, etc.). *Lead-up activities* can be used to prepare clients for full participation in an original activity (Wehman and Schleien, 1981). For example, kickball, whiffle ball, and/or the use of a batting tee can be lead-up activities to prepare clients for participation in baseball.

The *environment* in which an activity takes place may also require modification. For example, accessible parking, ramps, drinking fountains, and toilets may be needed, as well as lifts, grab bars, nonslip and nonabrasive floor surfaces, level play areas, adequate lighting, and reduced background noise.

Selecting Appropriate Interventions

Intervention techniques are used to bring about desired client change or improvement. Peterson and Gunn (1984) point out that the intervention strategy should be chosen in light of clients' characteristics, objectives, program content, and therapeutic recreation specialists' ability to use the techniques. Since no one approach will be appropriate for all clients, therapeutic recreation specialists should strive to develop proficiency in a variety of techniques. Several intervention techniques are discussed.

Behavior management is based on learning theory and involves the systematic use of various strategies and techniques to alter observable and measurable client behaviors. Clients' behaviors may be considered a problem, and thus targeted for change, if they occur too often, not often enough, or inappropriately (e.g., in the wrong place or at the wrong time). Accordingly, therapeutic recreation specialists may wish to decrease, increase, or change certain behaviors. When clients' behaviors are considered appropriate, maintaining these behaviors should be emphasized.

A variety of behavioral techniques may increase desired behaviors. For example, a behavioral or contingency contract is a written agreement between a therapeutic recreation specialist wishing to change a behavior and the client whose behavior is to be changed. The contract specifies the required behavior and the consequence(s) contingent on the performance of the required behavior. Token economy, another example of a behavioral technique, is a reinforcement system in which tokens are earned when previously defined behaviors are performed. The tokens have no specific value, but may be exchanged for rewards such as objects, activities, and privileges (Kazdin, 1980). Additional techniques, such as task analysis and skill sequencing, verbal cuing, and physical prompting are discussed in other chapters of the text.

Sensory training, which utilizes various activities to improve one's perception and interpretation of stimuli, is directed toward all five senses, and includes kinesthetic awareness, tactile stimulation, smelling, listening, tasting, and visual activities (Barns, Sack, and Shore, 1973). Sensory training has been used extensively with clients who have severe or profound mental retardation and with older clients who are regressed and/or disoriented.

Remotivation, resocialization, and reality orientation are intervention techniques often used with a variety of clients such as older adults who are disoriented, individuals who have head injuries, and people who are in transition to community settings. Remotivation and resocialization approaches promote renewal of interests and establishment of relationships through group interaction. Remotivation group sessions follow a structured five-phase process centered around a chosen theme (Leitner and Leitner, 1985). Resocialization group sessions are less structured and encourage awareness of self and others. In reality orientation, clients are continually oriented to basic personal and current information including time, place, names, events of the day, and things in the environment. To be most successful, all caregivers must use reality orientation continually with clients (Barns et al., 1973).

Therapeutic recreation specialists are increasingly using *relaxation* activities to reduce stress. One of the most popular techniques is progressive relaxation (Jacobson, 1974), in which the individual alternately relaxes and tenses each major muscle group, thereby achieving a feeling of deep relaxation. Other relaxation techniques may include deep breathing, meditation, Hatha Yoga, T'ai Chi Ch'uan, biofeedback, and imagery. Often, these various techniques are used in combination.

Interactions with others can be a source of considerable stress. *Assertiveness training* is an attempt to reduce stress by teaching more effective coping techniques. It is believed that the assertive person is more relaxed in interpersonal situations. Assertiveness training has been found to be an effective approach for dealing with depression, anger, resentment, and interpersonal anxiety (Davis, Eshelman, and McKay, 1986).

Considering Service Delivery Options

As previously discussed, a continuum of leisure opportunities will enable clients to have more interdependent leisure lifestyles. This continuum of services could include *segregated* programs which are only for clients with disabilities. Segregated recreation programs may be used when clients lack prerequisite activity skills.

Special recreation programs may also be used. These programs still feature disability-specific groupings but are less specialized and focus on developing leisure attitudes and skills necessary for community leisure opportunity participation. Often these services are physically integrated; that is, they take place in community environments such as bowling alleys, shopping malls, theatres, restaurants, and parks.

Fully or *socially integrated* programs promote clients' participation with nondisabled participants in regular community recreation activities. Based on the abilities and limitations of clients, assistance, modification, and adaptation may still be used to achieve full integration. When developing the individual program plan, therapeutic recreation specialists must consider a range of leisure opportunities offered in situations and settings with as few restrictions as possible.

Developing a Written Plan

The written individual therapeutic recreation program plan, a "visible manifestation of the intervention process" (Howe-Murphy and Charboneau, 1987, p. 215), is a way of assuring and documenting that quality and appropriate services are being delivered (Carruthers, Sneegas, and Ashton-Shaeffer, 1986). Documentation, the record keeping process associated with individual program planning, is essential for noting client progress and maintaining appropriate intervention techniques.

In comprehensive individual program plans, the services of different disciplines, including therapeutic recreation, are integrated, and a designated staff member is responsible for monitoring the plan and serving as primary advocate for a client. These plans may be referred to as Individualized Treatment Plans (ITPs), Individualized Habilitation Plans (IHPs), or Individualized Service Plans (ISPs), depending on the setting. Generally, individualized program plans are developed by a multidisciplinary team involving staff who evaluate and deliver services to clients. Involvement of clients and their families is elicited whenever possible. These plans are reviewed regularly by team members to ensure appropriate integrated and coordinated services are continued.

In addition to the comprehensive individual program plan developed by a multidisciplinary team, personnel in each service area, such as therapeutic recreation, usually develop and maintain a separate, detailed individual program plan. The individual therapeutic recreation program plan includes the outcomes or goals established with a client (including those relating to discharge), measurable objectives that relate to the goals, activity content and leadership methods which will be utilized to achieve selected goals, anticipated time frame for accomplishment of goals, and time intervals at which outcomes will be reviewed.

The individual therapeutic recreation program plan can be written in a format known as *SOAP*. Utilizing the *SOAP* format, a written plan would include *s*ubjective assessment information, *o*bjective assessment information, therapeutic recreation specialists' conclusion or *a*ssessment concerning clients' problems, and a *p*lan for ameliorating the problems. Some therapeutic recreation specialists add *e*valuation as a fifth component to this format—*SOAPE*. In the evaluation component, therapeutic recreation specialists identify information sources necessary to determine goal attainment and reporting strategies

Summary

This chapter has focused on procedures relating to therapeutic recreation individual program planning phases. Once desired client changes are identified and goals and objectives relating to these changes are formulated, then a written plan for accomplishing expected outcomes is designed. This individual plan includes the selection of specific activities (content) and leadership approaches (process) that will be used to accomplish objectives. The delineation of expected outcomes constitutes the basis for documenting and evaluating individual progress toward and eventual accomplishment of goals and objectives.

The individual assessment and planning phases discussed in Chapters One and Two have provided the basis for implementing the individualized therapeutic recreation program. Program implementation is discussed in Chapter Three, *Implementing Individual Therapeutic Recreation Program Plans*.

Bibliography

Ball, E. L. (1970). The meaning of therapeutic recreation. *Therapeutic Recreation Journal, 4*(1), 17-18.

Barns, E. K., Sack, A., and Shore, H. (1973). Guidelines to treatment approaches: Modalities and methods for use with the aged. *The Gerontologist, 13,* 515-522.

Carter, M. J., Van Andel, G. E., and Robb, G. M. (1990). *Therapeutic recreation: A practical approach.* Prospect Heights, IL: Waveland Press.

Carruthers, C., Sneegas, J. J., and Ashton-Shaeffer, C. A. (1986). *Therapeutic recreation: Guidelines for activity services in long term care.* Urbana-Champaign, IL: University of Illinois.

Crawford, M. E. and Mendell, R. (1987). *Therapeutic recreation and adapted physical activities for mentally retarded individuals.* Englewood Cliffs, NJ: Prentice-Hall.

Davis, M., Eshelman, E. R., and McKay, M. (1986). *The relaxation and stress reduction workbook* (2nd ed.). Oakland, CA: New Harbinger.

Frye, V. and Peters, M. (1972). *Therapeutic recreation: Its theory, philosophy, and practice.* Harrisburg, PA: Stackpole Books.

Gunn, S. L. and Peterson, C. A. (1978). *Therapeutic recreation program design: Principles and procedures.* Englewood Cliffs, NJ: Prentice-Hall.

Howe-Murphy, R. and Charboneau, B. G. (1987). *Therapeutic recreation intervention: An ecological perspective.* Englewood Cliffs, NJ: Prentice-Hall.

Jacobson, E. (1944). *Progressive relaxation.* Chicago, IL: The University of Chicago Press, Midway Reprint.

Kazdin, A. (1980). *Behavior modification in applied settings.* Homewood, IL: Dorsey.

Kennedy, D. W., Smith, R. W., and Austin, D. R. (1991). *Special recreation: Opportunities for persons with disabilities* (2nd ed.). Dubuque, IA: William C. Brown.

Leitner, M. J. and Leitner, S. F. (1985). *Leisure in later life: A sourcebook for the provision of recreational services for elders.* New York, NY: Haworth Press.

Lewis, J. A. and Lewis, M. D. (1983). *Management of human service programs.* Monterey, CA: Brooks/Cole.

National Therapeutic Recreation Society. (1982). *Philosophical position statement of the National Therapeutic Recreation Society.* Alexandria, VA: National Recreation and Park Association.

Nesbitt, J. A. (Ed.). (1986). *The international directory of recreation-oriented assistive device sources.* Marina Del Rey, CA: Lifeboat Press.

O'Morrow, G. S. and Reynolds, R. P. (1989). *Therapeutic recreation: A helping profession* (3rd ed.). Englewood Cliffs, NJ: Prentice-Hall.

Peterson, C. A. and Gunn, S. L. (1984). *Therapeutic recreation program design: Principles and procedures* (2nd ed.). Englewood Cliffs, NJ: Prentice-Hall.

Project LIFE. (1988). *LIFE forms, the LIFE training guide.* Chapel Hill, NC: Project LIFE, Curriculum in Leisure Studies and Recreation Administration, University of North Carolina at Chapel Hill.

Tannenbaum, R. and Schmidt, W. H. (1958). How to choose a leadership pattern. *Harvard Business Review, 36*(2), 95-101.

Wehman, P. and Schleien, S. (1981). *Leisure programs for handicapped persons: Adaptations techniques, and curriculum.* Austin, TX: PRO-ED.

Witt, P. A. (1982). *The leisure diagnostic battery user's guide.* Denton, TX: Division of Recreation and Leisure Studies, North Texas State University.

Wilcox, B. and Bellamy, G. T. (1987). *The activities catalog: An alternative curriculum for youth and adults with severe disabilities.* Baltimore, MD: Paul H. Brookes.

Wuerch, B. B. and Voeltz, L. M. (1982). *Longitudinal leisure skills for severely handicapped learners: The Ho'onanea curriculum component.* Baltimore, MD: Paul H. Brookes.

Suggested Readings

Austin, D. R. (1991). *Therapeutic recreation: Processes and techniques* (2nd ed.). Champaign, IL: Sagamore.

Austin, D. R. and Crawford, M. E. (Eds.). (1991). *Therapeutic recreation: An introduction.* Englewood Cliffs, NJ: Prentice-Hall.

Bachner, J. and Cornelius, E. (1978). *Activities coordinator's guide.* Washington, DC: U. S. Government Printing Office.

Baumgart, D., Brown, L., Pumpian, I., Nisbet, J., Ford, A., Sweet, M., Messina, R., and Schroeder, J. (1982). Principle of partial participation and individualized adaptations in educational programs for severely handicapped students. *The Association for the Severely Handicapped Journal, 7* (Summer 1982), 17-27.

Dattilo, J. and Murphy, W. D. (1987). *Behavior modification in therapeutic recreation.* State College, PA: Venture Publishing, Inc.

Kohut, S., Kohut, J. J., and Fleishman, J. J. (1979). *Reality orientation for the elderly.* Oradell, NJ: Medical Economics.

Mager, R. F. (1972). *Goal analysis.* Belmont, CA: Fearon Publishers.

Mager, R. F. (1977). *Preparing instructional objectives* (2nd ed.). Belmont, CA: Fearon Publishers.

Mosey, A. C. (1973). *Activities therapy.* New York, NY: Raven Publishers.

Presbie, R. and Brown, P. (1977). *Physical education: The behavior modification approach.* Washington, DC: National Education Association.

Riddick, C. C. and Keller, M. J. (1990). Developing recreation services to assist elders who are developmentally disabled. *Activities, Adaptation and Aging, 15*(1/2), 19-34.

Teaff, J. D. (1990). *Leisure services with the elderly.* Prospect Heights, IL: Waveland Press.

Toepfer, C. T., Bicknell, A. T., and Shaw, D. O. (1974). Remotivation as behavior therapy. *The Gerontologist, 14*(5), 451-453.

Turnbull, H. R., Turnbull, A. P., Bronicki, G. J., Summers, J., and Roeder-Gordon. (1989). *Disability and the family: A guide to decisions for adulthood.* Baltimore, MD: Paul H. Brookes.

Wehman, P. (1977). Application of behavior modification techniques to play problems of the severely and profoundly retarded. *Therapeutic Recreation Journal, 11*(1), 16-21.

Wilhite, B., Keller, M. J., and Nicholson, L. (1990). Integrating older persons with developmental disabilities into community recreation: Theory to practice. *Activities, Adaptation and Aging, 15*(1/2), 111-129.

Case 1

RECREATION IN CORRECTIONS

The Jackson Correctional Institution (CI) houses most of the geriatric inmates within the Department of Corrections, as well as those with visual or hearing impairments and physical disabilities. Some of these inmates are also classified as either mentally retarded, mentally ill, or both.

Of the over six hundred inmates at Jackson CI, 55 use wheelchairs, 13 are legally blind (some with total blindness), 20 have hearing impairments (seven with total deafness), and 20 use canes and walkers. Over 70 percent of all inmates are over fifty years of age. A few inmates have no special problems and are at the institution primarily to maintain the day-to-day operations, such as yard maintenance, laundry operation, office and dormitory cleaning.

Treatment, leisure education, and recreation participation activities are provided, offering opportunities for relieving the stress and anxiety of incarceration, expanding knowledge of leisure interests, and learning to use free time wisely after incarceration. Within the last year, the recreation staff at Jackson CI have obtained the latest adaptive equipment and supplies, participated in training, implemented specialized programs, and added additional adapted facilities to better serve these inmates' recreational needs and interests.

Outside recreation facilities include completely accessible paved basketball and volleyball courts (with adjustable goals/nets for wheelchair activities), a softball field, a ten station putt-putt golf course, horseshoe pits, a garden area, a shuffleboard court, benches and picnic tables, and a walking path. Inside recreation facilities include a 60' x 84' multipurpose room (containing billiard tables, pinball, darts, a projection screen television, a stage area for concerts and other performances, and tables for table games), weight, music, and leathercraft rooms, a woodworking shop, and a recreation office. Also, there is a conference room for activities such as leisure education.

The Jackson CI recreation staff include two therapeutic recreation specialists, two general recreators, and the therapeutic recreation supervisor, who has administrative responsibility over all recreation staff. Written documentation including assessments, treatment plans, and progress notes is maintained for each inmate with a mental illness or mental retardation diagnosis.

Several therapeutic recreation programs initiated within the last year have significantly contributed to inmates' habilitation. The leisure education class has as its goal "to educate inmates about the meaning of leisure and its importance in their lives." The two-days-per-week course provides opportunities to explore areas such as self-awareness, leisure awareness, decision making, skills acquisition, and community resources. Inmates are expected to discover how they were experiencing leisure prior to incarceration and to use their uncommitted time in socially acceptable ways during incarceration and after release.

"Get Fit While You Sit" is an activity for inmates who are wheelchair users or who are older and in need of maintaining or building upper body strength. Inmates exercise their upper bodies three times weekly, with a therapeutic recreation specialist, using a video presentation. Many of the inmates have indicated that this exercise regimen has enabled them to be more independent in transferring to and from their wheelchairs as well as in other self-care areas.

Recreation activities for inmates with visual impairments include mobility training taught by a staff member from rehabilitation services. Braille recreation supplies, such as backgammon games and checkers, are available. Inmates have access to "talking books" (taped westerns, romance, science fiction, biblical stories, etc.), and the institution's library has braille newspapers, magazines, and books. Recreation activities for inmates with hearing impairments include a sign class which is also offered for hearing inmates and staff. The interest of inmates with hearing in this sign class has helped to decrease the isolation of the inmates with hearing impairments. Special programs include talent shows, dance contests, magic shows, band concerts, and weekly movies with popcorn.

IN-CLASS EXERCISES

1. Develop an individualized program plan for the following inmates, highlighting major problems, goals, and intervention strategies:

    a. William, incarcerated for committing first degree murder, is a "passion killer": he killed his wife after discovering that she was having an affair with another man. This was his first offense and he will be eligible for parole in seven years. He is 38 years old and has a degree in engineering. According to administrative records, his behavior while in prison has been that of a "model prisoner."

      William has a severe hearing impairment, but he reads lips well and signs adequately. His overall health is good and he says that he enjoys weight training, running, cards, basketball, and volleyball. In addition, he would like access to various reading materials and training on the facility's personal computers.

    b. Mark, who has been in and out of prison during the past ten years, was arrested last year for selling drugs to young children. He is 28 years old and dropped out of school in the 9th grade. He is considered to have borderline mental retardation and was served by special education classes in school. He is unmarried with one child. His mother and brothers live in a nearby city, but have "disowned" and have no contact with him. The administration has had to restrict his privileges several times over the last three months because of his violent outbursts against other inmates. The administration will use the next three months as a trial period to determine whether he will be granted parole. Mark is in good overall health and is interested in weight training, running, basketball, and volleyball.

Selected References for Case Study

Aguilar, T. E. (1986). Recreation: An untapped resource. *Corrections Today, 48*(2), 173-178.

Anderson, S. C. (1991). Corrections. In D. R. Austin and M. E. Crawford (Eds.), *Therapeutic Recreation: An Introduction* (pp. 352-372). Englewood Cliffs, NJ: Prentice-Hall.

Calloway, J. (Ed.). (1981, February). Correctional recreation: A long-time need. [Special issue]. *Parks and Recreation.*

Hambrock, M. C. (1988). Correctional recreation: Get your program off and running. *Corrections Today, 50*(7), 143-136.

Harris, G. A. and Watkins, D. (1987). *Counseling the involuntary and resistant client.* College Park, MD: American Correctional Association.

McCall, G. (Ed.). (1981, April). Issues in correctional recreation. [Special issue]. *Journal of Physical Education and Recreation.*

Case 2

BENJAMIN

Mr. and Mrs. Johnson, recently divorced, share custody of their three children. They came to the Center for Comprehensive Psycho-Educational Services seeking an evaluation of their son's behavioral difficulties. Benjamin lives with his mother and two younger sisters, ages 7 and 2-1/2 years, and spends one weekend a month with his father. Reportedly, he usually gets along well with his sisters but is sometimes "mean" to them. His parents were specifically concerned about his difficulty controlling his temper as evidenced by verbal aggression and temper tantrums, refusal to complete homework assignments, and inability to accept parental disciplinary actions, usually evidenced by rebellious behaviors such as refusing to eat at mealtimes.

Benjamin's extra curricular activities include Boy Scouts, baseball, swimming, and board games. His parents reported that he gets along well with both peers and adults, although he sometimes complains about having no friends. Mr. Johnson perceived Benjamin as "unhappy," and Mrs. Johnson perceived him as "happy, but angry." Both reported that he has difficulty occupying himself independently. They also described him as very demanding—"always wanting something different." Mr. Johnson felt that Benjamin may "resent authority figures." Both reported that he has always had a high activity level and that his strengths include participation in physical activities. Also, he has periodically demonstrated high levels of motivation; he read 80 books during National Book Week.

Benjamin, a nine year old white male, is currently in a regular third grade classroom. His teacher stated that he fails to bring in his homework or complete assignments even though he is very capable of doing the work. Although he always gives the appearance of working and his grades are adequate, he often does not finish on time and his performance is inconsistent. His teacher also reported that Benjamin tries hard to please and has a strong need for approval, but responds to discipline by smirking or "acting" contrite. Socially, Benjamin is popular and is often sought out by other children.

Evaluators at the Center concluded that Benjamin is a verbal child who openly and enthusiastically discussed his interest in swimming and other sports activities. He spoke favorably about his peer relationships and stated that there were "a lot of kids" who liked him.

He explained that the reason for his evaluation was that "I lose my temper," and he stated that he does so because he often feels unjustifiably punished. He acknowledged that he loses his temper primarily at home, rather than in school or with friends. His explanation for not completing his homework was that "it's boring," and he preferred to play with peers. He could not appreciate the value of completing his work "because we just get more of the same work." He believed that within the past several weeks he had improved his school work because the class was now getting prizes for correct and timely completion of paperwork. His father also rewarded him, during his monthly visits, for completing his homework. His intellectual test data suggest that he is functioning in the average to high range of intelligence for his age. His academic test data are consistent and suggest above grade level performance in math and reading and approximate grade level performance in spelling.

Benjamin's actions during the interview suggest that he is capable of optimal learning. He appeared to be motivated to perform tasks to the best of his ability, was reflective and purposeful in his approach to tasks, enjoyed challenging activities, and was persistent on difficult items. He was compliant, cooperative, and seemed to enjoy working for and receiving social reinforcement. He refused, however, to discuss the issue of his parents' divorce. His responses to certain interview questions suggest that he is aware of his difficulty in controlling his temper and recognizes that it creates problems for himself and his family. "I love my Mom and Dad and sisters and I want all of us to be a happy family."

According to evaluators at the Center, Benjamin apparently needs a variety of challenging activities. Given his ability level and his developmental need to be in control, he may resent limitations placed on him at school and at home. He also may not understand the positive consequences for completion of homework since from his standpoint, he "just gets more work." Because he tends to view himself as someone who is unable to meet anyone's expectations and who is "in trouble" a great deal of the time, he may often appear angry or unhappy. Yet, rather than expressing these feelings, he may give the impression that he does not care. Benjamin also seems to have repressed his sadness about his parents' recent divorce.

You are a therapeutic recreation specialist at the Center for Comprehensive Psycho-Educational Services who has been asked to participate in the development of an individualized program plan for Benjamin. Your challenge is to suggest ways that social and leisure activities may contribute to ameliorating present problems. In addition, you are to make recommendations about Benjamin's possible participation in the Center's after school and weekend recreational activities.

DISCUSSION QUESTIONS

1. Identify Benjamin's strengths, areas of need, and interests. How will you use Benjamin's strengths and interests to work on his specified problems?
2. What would be the desired outcomes of therapeutic recreation intervention for Benjamin?

3. Describe any behavior management strategies you will recommend in Benjamin's individual program plan.
4. The Center's after school and weekend recreation programs take place in a "special recreation" format but are often physically integrated. Do you think Benjamin could benefit from a specialized program such as this? If so, what criteria would determine when these services were no longer appropriate for him?
5. Benjamin is already involved in community recreation such as Boy Scouts and organized sports. How would you address continued community recreation involvement in Benjamin's individualized program plan?
6. What activities could you suggest to Benjamin's parents to assist him in engaging in meaningful and purposeful leisure experiences at home alone and with his sisters?

Selected References for Case Study

De Salvatore, H. G. (1989). Therapeutic recreators as family therapists: Working with families on a children's psychiatric unit. *Therapeutic Recreation Journal, 23*(2), 23-29.

Fine, A. H. (1988). An overview of behavioral management strategies. In A. H. Fine and N. M. Fine, *Therapeutic recreation for exceptional children: Let me in, I want to play* (pp. 301-312). Springfield, IL: Charles C. Thomas.

Goldfarb, L. A., Brotherson, M. J., Summers, J. A., and Turnbull, A. P. (1986). *Meeting the challenge of disability or chronic illness: A family guide.* Baltimore, MD: Paul H. Brookes.

Kleiber, D. A., Ashton-Shaeffer, C., Malik, P. B., Lee, L. L., and Hood, C. H. (1990). Involvement with special recreation associations: Perceived impacts in early adulthood. *Therapeutic Recreation Journal, 24*(3), 32-44.

Sheridan, S. M., Kratochwill, T. R., and Elliot, S. N. (1990). Behavioral consultation with parents and teachers: Delivering treatment for socially withdrawn children at home and school. *School Psychology Review, 19*(1), 33-52.

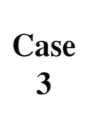

Case 3

CHARLES

Charles Brown, a 66 year old black male diagnosed with Guilian-Barre' syndrome, is two months post onset. Upper extremity and trunk strength have improved since onset so that he has regained nearly his full strength, but his lower extremity strength remains poor. He is a retired mechanic who likes to fish, hunt, work on old cars, and go boating.

Goal: To increase strength of his hip abductors.

Treatment Strategy: Adaptive aquatics program.

CINDY

Cindy Jones, an 18 year old white female who experienced a spinal cord injury as a result of a motor vehicle accident, is a T-5 complete paraplegic. She is seven weeks post accident, before which she was working as a secretary and pursuing a modeling career. Cindy demonstrates poor self-esteem and is fearful of community reentry. Her leisure interests included sewing, water skiing, snow skiing, playing tennis, listening to rock music, interacting with her pet dog, Bugs, and shopping.

Goal: To increase community functional social skills level to supervision. (At the supervision skill level, Cindy would require standby assistance, cuing, or coaxing without physical contact.)

Treatment Strategy: Social skills program.

JAMES

James Smith, a 12 year old white male with a head injury resulting from a motor vehicle accident, has a brain stem injury with characteristics of C-3 quadriplegia. He has a tracheostomy and a gastric tube and communicates with spitting sounds and by mouthing words. He is cognitively intact. He likes oldies music, Batman, animals, movies, football, and video games. He

is considered a gifted child. He presently feels very helpless and insecure.
Goal: To improve head control to neutral for 10 minutes.
Treatment Strategy: Animal assisted therapy program.

DISCUSSION QUESTIONS

You are a therapeutic recreation specialist in an acute physical rehabilitation center. You are working with each of the individuals described above.

1. Describe in detail how the specified treatment strategy could be used to achieve each goal. Analyze the treatment strategy and highlight the inherent components of the strategy as they relate to achieving the goal. Also discuss aspects of the strategy that can be manipulated by the therapeutic recreation specialist to achieve the goal.
2. Discuss at least one other treatment strategy that could be used effectively with each case.

IN-CLASS EXERCISES

1. Ask several therapeutic recreation specialists from physical rehabilitation facilities to attend a class presentation of students' responses to question one above and provide constructive critiques.
2. Invite an individual(s) with spinal cord injury to discuss his personal community adjustment, transition, and recreation activities.

FIELD EXPERIENCES

1. Assign small groups of students to each case and ask them to research the disability through library work, and personal contacts with rehabilitation specialists and persons with disabilities. Students will report their findings in class.

Selected References for Case Study

Basmajian, J. (Ed.). (1978). *Therapeutic exercise* (3rd ed.) Baltimore, MD: Williams and Wilkins.

Bloch, F. and Basbaum, M. (Eds.). (1986). *Management of spinal cord injuries*. Baltimore, MD: Williams and Wilkins.

Dunkin, M. A. and Ballew, T. (1990). The positive power of pets. *Arthritis Today*, May/June, 44-48.

Lasko, P. M. and Knopf, K. G. (1988). *Adapted exercises for the disabled adult*. Dubuque, IA: Eddie Bowers.

Lee, T. (1984). *Aquacise: Terri Lee's water workout book*. Reston, VA: Reston Publishing.

Rosenthal, M., Griffith, E., Bond, M., and Miller, J. (1990). *Rehabilitation of the adult and child with traumatic brain injury* (2nd ed.). Philadelphia, PA: F. A. Davis Company.

Trieschmann, R. (1988). *Spinal cord injuries: Psychological, social, and vocational rehabilitation* (2nd Ed.). New York, NY: Demos.

Wille, R. (1984). Therapeutic use of companion pets for neurologically impaired patients. *Journal of Neuroscience Nursing, 16*(6), 323-325.

Case 4

CHRIS

Chris is a seven year old white male with profound mental retardation. He has no measurable receptive or expressive language, possesses no self-help skills or body awareness, is ambulatory but with an unsteady gait, and his kinesthetic awareness is uncertain. He has full functioning of all five senses.

Chris has resided in a single parent household with his mother, who has limited education and earns a very low salary, two sisters, and one brother. Chris's family cares about him, but they have not known how to provide adequate stimulation and have therefore been able to do very little to address his needs. Chris's daily activities have consisted primarily of sitting idly and sleeping up to twelve hours a day. Thus, following a comprehensive assessment, during which it was determined that Chris's mother could no longer provide him with adequate care, he was admitted to an intermediate care facility for individuals with mental retardation.

Aaron, the therapeutic recreation specialist assigned to work with Chris, has completed an initial leisure assessment and is in the process of developing an individual habilitation plan. Reviewing Chris's leisure assessment, as well as assessments completed by other disciplines, Aaron noticed some strengths that could be used to address Chris's deficiencies. For example, Chris has adequate use of his five senses and good upper body movement. To assist in the development of an individualized therapeutic recreation program plan, Aaron needed to gain Chris's trust and establish communication with him. He also wanted to determine if Chris would respond when adequately stimulated. Since Chris could not demonstrate body awareness, Aaron selected body awareness as a leisure goal and also used it as a first step in getting to know Chris.

Aaron decided to work with Chris in a small room free of distractions. For the first session, Aaron sat on the floor in front of Chris with his legs over Chris's legs. In this position, Chris could not get up and was in close contact with Aaron. Next to Aaron was a bowl of Cheerios©, which the dietary assessment stated he liked, a softball size sponge, a bowl of warm water, and a towel. Aaron picked up a Cheerio©, held it to his eye and said, "Chris, look at me." The instant Chris made eye contact with him, Aaron put a Cheerio© in Chris's mouth. This action was accompanied by the verbal praise, "good!"

DISCUSSION QUESTIONS

1. Do you agree that the development of Chris's individual therapeutic recreation program plan will be enhanced through further exploration of his abilities and analysis of his interaction with the therapeutic recreation specialist? If yes, provide a rationale for this approach. What specific behaviors should the therapeutic recreation specialist be observing?
2. What are potential purposes of the sponge and warm water the therapeutic recreation specialist included in this session?
3. What behavior management techniques are being used in this scenario? Are there other techniques that could be included in Chris's plan? How long should external reinforcers and physical assistance be used?

4. Do you think the therapeutic recreation specialist needs to know more about Chris's interactions with his family? Why? How could the specialist involve Chris's family in the development of his individualized therapeutic recreation program plan?

IN-CLASS EXERCISES

1. Develop a list of activities Aaron could utilize to establish a positive rapport with Chris.
2. Develop one goal and accompanying objective for Chris in each of the three behavioral domains: cognitive, affective, and psychomotor. Provide examples of activities that could be utilized to achieve the objective in each behavioral domain.

Selected References for Case Study

Browder, D. M. (1987). *Assessment of individuals with severe handicaps: An applied behavior approach to life skills assessment.* Baltimore, MD: Paul H. Brookes.

Burch, M. R. Reiss, M., and Baily, J. S. (1985). A facility-wide approach to recreation programming for adults who are severely and profoundly retarded. *Therapeutic Recreation Journal, 19*(3), 71-78.

Dattilo, J. (1984). Therapeutic recreation assessment for individuals with severe handicaps. In G. Hitzhusen (Ed.), *Expanding horizons in therapeutic recreation XI* (pp. 147-157). Columbia, MO: University of Missouri.

Kim, Y. T., Lombardino, L. J., Rothman, H., and Vinson, B. (1988). Effects of symbolic play intervention with children who have mental retardation. *Mental Retardation, 27*(3), 159-165.

Wehman, P. (1977). *Helping the mentally retarded acquire play skills.* Springfield, IL: Charles C. Thomas.

Wilcox, B. and Bellamy, G. T. (1987). *The activities catalog: An alternative curriculum for youth and adults with severe disabilities.* Baltimore, MD: Paul H. Brookes.

Wuerch, B. B. and Voeltz, L. M. (1982). *Longitudinal leisure skills for severely handicapped learners: The Ho'onanea curriculum component.* Baltimore, MD: Paul H. Brookes.

Case 5

CORA

You were introduced to Cora in Chapter One, *Assessment in Therapeutic Recreation*, (p. 19) in which Cora was diagnosed as alcohol dependent with depression but nonsuicidal. Her drinking resulted in problems at home, at work, and in leisure. She is not married but has a boyfriend whom she describes as "jealous." Currently unemployed, Cora is somewhat dissatisfied with her leisure experiences but presently is not interested in pursuing new activities.

IN-CLASS EXERCISES

1. Write a problem list for Cora, indicating all problems revealed in the scenario. Identify which problems might be addressed by the therapeutic recreation specialist.
2. Develop an individualized therapeutic recreation program plan for Cora. Assume she will complete a 28-day substance abuse treatment program and then return home for outpatient treatment. Indicate appropriate intervention techniques such as assertiveness training, stress management, and leisure education, and explain why these are appropriate. Specify discharge criteria which include participation in Alcoholics Anonymous, or a similar group, for personal and social support. Include activities she can pursue with her son and/or her boyfriend.

DISCUSSION QUESTIONS

1. In completing the above questions, what information was most useful to you in writing the problem list or developing the individualized therapeutic recreation program plan? Is there additional information you might have collected during the assessment phase which could have assisted you in developing Cora's program plan?

FIELD EXPERIENCES

1. Ask a therapeutic recreation specialist who works in a substance abuse facility to critique your problem list and individualized therapeutic recreation program plan for Cora.
2. Take a field trip to a facility or unit serving persons with substance abuse problems and discuss with a therapeutic recreation specialist various factors to consider when designing individual plans with this population.

Selected References for Case Study

Bradley, A. M. (1988). Keep coming back: The case for a valuation of Alcoholics Anonymous. *Alcohol Health and Research World, 12*(3), 192-199.

Dilorenzo, T. M., Prue, D. M., and Scott, R. R. (1987). A conceptual critique of leisure assessment and therapy: An added dimension to behavioral medicine and substance abuse treatment. *Clinical Psychology Review, 7*(6), 597-609.

Diwan, S. (1990). Alcoholism and ideology: Approaches to treatment. *Journal of Applied Social Sciences, 14*(2), 221-248.

Faulkner, R. W. (1991). *Therapeutic recreation protocol for treatment of substance addictions.* State College, PA: Venture Publishing, Inc.

Lewis, M. J. (1990). Alcohol: Mechanisms of addiction and reinforcement. *Advances in Alcohol and Substance Abuse, 9*(1-2), 47-66.

McLaughlin, L. T. (1980). Leisure counseling with drug dependent individuals and alcoholics. *Leisurability, 7*(1), 9-16.

Ransom, G., Waishwell, L., and Griffin, J. A. (1987). Leisure: The enigma for alcoholism recovery. *Alcoholism Treatment Quarterly, 4*(3), 103-116.

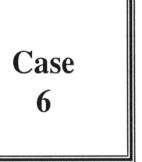

Case 6

LAURIE

Laurie, a five year old Japanese American, is admitted to Springfield Children's Hospital for a heart valve repair. This is her first hospitalization, and she and her parents are extremely anxious. During the preadmission tour, Laurie screamed and cried when role-playing a blood test. As the therapeutic recreation specialist at Springfield Children's Hospital, you work with patients on a twenty-five bed surgical unit prior to and following surgery. Laurie is a new patient on your unit.

DISCUSSION QUESTIONS

1. What are the developmental issues for a child in the preschool stage of life? Take into consideration the developmental characteristics of a five year old child.
2. Describe how "imaginary thinking" might affect Laurie's reaction to the things she sees and hears in the hospital.
3. Describe activities and approaches you would use during Laurie's hospitalization. Include preoperation education and pre- and postprocedural play. Discuss techniques for introducing activities to Laurie and her parents.
4. Suggest ways to alleviate the anxiety of Laurie's parents. How will you include Laurie's parents in the development of her individualized therapeutic recreation program plan? What would be their role during implementation of the plan?

IN-CLASS EXERCISES

1. View a videotape of preoperation education and pre- and post-procedural play conducted by a therapeutic recreation or child life specialist. Discuss the possible advantages and disadvantages of using these programs with children.

FIELD EXPERIENCES

1. Visit a child life and/or therapeutic recreation program in a children's hospital, talk with the specialists working in these programs and, if possible, observe an activity session. Report your findings in class.

ROLE-PLAYING

1. Role-play a preoperative play session including a therapeutic recreation specialist, Laurie, and Laurie's parents.

Selected References for Case Study

Brophy, J. and Erickson, M. T. (1990). Children's self-statements and adjustment to elective outpatient surgery. *Journal of Development and Behavior Pediatrics, 11*(1), 13-16.

DiCowden, M. (1990). Pediatric rehabilitation: Special patients, special needs. *Journal of Rehabilitation, 3*, 13-17.

Shrimali, S. and Broota, K. D. (1988). Effect of surgical stress on ego strength and perceived control. *Journal of Personality and Clinical Studies, 4*(1), 17-21.

Wolfer, J., Gaynard, L., Goldberger, J., Laidley, L. N., and Thompson, R. (1988). An experimental evaluation of a model child life program. *Children's Health Care, 16*(4), 244-254.

Yap, N. (1988). A critical review of pediatric preoperative preparation procedures: Processes, outcomes, and future directions. *Journal of Applied Developmental Psychology, 9*(4), 359-389.

Yap, N. (1988). The effects of hospitalization and surgery on children: A critical review. *Journal of Applied Developmental Psychology, 9*(3), 349-358.

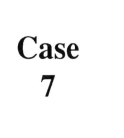

Case 7

EDITH

Mrs. Miller's situation was described in Chapter One, *Assessment in Therapeutic Recreation* (p. 31). Her primary diagnosis was Alzheimer's disease with secondary impairments of depression, ulcerative colitis, and hypothyroidism. She has resided in a long-term health care facility for three years. As the therapeutic recreation specialist, you were asked to develop individualized therapeutic recreation program goals for Mrs. Miller.

IN-CLASS EXERCISES

1. Develop individualized therapeutic recreation program goals and quarterly objectives for Mrs. Miller including activity content and processes. Also, specify evaluation criteria for Mrs. Miller's therapeutic recreation program plan. What role should Mrs. Miller and her husband play in developing her program plan?

DISCUSSION QUESTIONS

1. What activities might the assistants and Mr. Miller participate in to interact with Mrs. Miller?
2. Mrs. Miller must remain in her geriatric chair unless someone is available to assist her. She is losing weight as she becomes

less mobile and less capable of feeding herself. Suggest activities that will continue to stimulate her and maintain her energy level when lengthy time periods in the chair are required.

3. Is reality orientation an appropriate intervention technique for Mrs. Miller? Why or why not?

Selected References for Case Study

Buettner, L. L. (1988). Utilizing developmental theory and adaptive equipment with regressed geriatric patients in therapeutic recreation. *Therapeutic Recreation Journal, 22*(3), 72-79.

Coons, D. H. (1989). *Specialized domestic care units.* Baltimore, MD: The Johns Hopkins University Press.

Lasko, P. M. and Knopf, K. G. (1988). *Adapted exercises for the disabled adult.* Dubuque, IA: Eddie Bowers.

West, H. L., Chafetz, P. K., and Rice, C. (1987). Issues in the development of Alzheimer's disease special care units. *The Southwestern Journal of Aging, 4*(1), 59-66.

Zgola, J. M. (1987). *Doing things: A guide to programming activities for persons with Alzheimer's disease and related disorders.* Baltimore, MD: Johns Hopkins University Press.

Videos

My Mother, My Father; Because Somebody Cares; A Family Decision; Softfire; Where Do We Go From Here; Not Alone Anymore: Caring for Someone with Alzheimer's Disease; Wesley Hall: A special Life; Seven Days a Week: A Look at Quality Care in Nursing Homes; Helping People with Dementia in Activities of Daily Living. Terra Nova Films, Inc., 9848 S. Winchester Avenue, Chicago, IL 60643, (312) 881-8491.

```
┌─────────────────────┐
│ ┌─────────────────┐ │
│ │                 │ │
│ │     Case        │ │          ROBERT
│ │      8          │ │
│ │                 │ │
│ │                 │ │    The setting for this case is a transitional
│ └─────────────────┘ │    living center with five to eight residents,
└─────────────────────┘
```

Case 8

ROBERT

The setting for this case is a transitional living center with five to eight residents, young adult men and women with a variety of social, affective, physical, and cognitive disabilities. The center accepts residents following a six month trial period, and community placement in supervised apartments within four years is the ultimate goal. The center is staffed by social workers, daily living attendants, and program managers. Transportation is available via center and public vehicles. Residents are employed in the community in either full- or part-time positions. Staff members develop individual program plans with each resident which include responsibilities in the home as well as skill development in those areas that support their integration. With assistance of staff as needed, center residents arrange their own banking, health care, shopping, and social and family activities. A team meeting is held regarding each resident after each six month period and includes family or primary caregivers and community resource personnel such as speech therapists, special educators, and vocational counselors.

Robert, a thirty-year-old white male with Down's syndrome, was graduated from a public school special education workshop program and has been employed in a maintenance position four hours per day, five to six days per week, for five years at a fast food restaurant. He was referred to the center by the social worker through the special education system and the job training program. His parents support the placement and live in this community.

Robert has participated in therapeutic recreation programs offered by the city and a nonprofit agency since elementary school. He participated in Special Olympics while in school and continues to compete in bowling, skiing, and basketball. He resided in his family home until the recent move to the center. Robert's family is active in local swim and tennis clubs and often vacations together. Robert also attends a social club, participates in special events, and takes guitar lessons sponsored by the city therapeutic recreation program. Other recreation interests include listening to records, playing cards, and attending movies and major league sporting events.

To be able to live independently in supervised apartments, Robert must improve:

(1) Money management and budgeting skills. Robert is able to add, multiply, and divide, and deposit his paycheck in the bank. He tends, however, to carry too much discretionary money and does not attend when a vendor is returning change.

(2) Food preparation and weight watching skills. Robert is able to prepare microwave foods and select appropriate foods, yet eats too much unless someone sets limits. Unless someone else initiates the activity, Robert will not exercise voluntarily. Therefore, he has a tendency to be overweight.

(3) Decision-making skills. Robert tends to let others make decisions for him. He will express his likes and dislikes, if asked.

(4) Verbal expression. When he is excited or tired, Robert talks very rapidly and does not properly enunciate. This problem becomes most evident when he is excited by recreation activities or when new persons are present. He is currently receiving speech therapy.

(5) Ability to initiate and complete tasks. Robert completes tasks very willingly, and his work evaluations suggest that he is a motivated worker, but he is unable to initiate tasks independently. He can complete a task independently if he is given a list or if he follows a routine. If, however, the routine is altered or if he must initiate a task without prompting, the task most often remains undone.

If the above concerns are not resolved successfully, Robert's future could be limited to supervised group living arrangements such as the center or a return to his family home.

DISCUSSION QUESTIONS

1. The center's residents do not initiate physical activity on their own. Unless supervised, they tend to sit in front of the TV or video, or select passive activities like going to movies or watching professional sports. Many, like Robert, have weight problems. Discuss various activity content and processes that a therapeutic recreation specialist might include in Robert's

individualized therapeutic recreation program plan and also incorporate into the routine of the center to foster improved wellness and physical health of all residents.

2. Robert appears capable of living and working in the community. But he does not, at times, appear to be a "self-starter." Discuss activity content and process that a therapeutic recreation specialist might utilize to increase initiation.

3. Discuss how a community therapeutic recreation specialist might work with the residents and staff of the group home to develop appropriate recreation programs and services.

4. Discuss the pros and cons of Robert's continued participation in Special Olympics.

IN-CLASS EXERCISES

1. Develop an individualized therapeutic recreation program plan incorporating the areas in which Robert needs to improve his skills before moving into an apartment living setting. Consider Robert's needs in decision-making, expression of likes and dislikes, clarity of verbal expression, and money management/ budgeting skills.

2. Develop activity content and process for facilitating Robert's daily management of large blocks of free time (three to four hours per day after work, and on the weekends).

Selected References for Case Study

Carter, M. J. (forthcoming). *Designing therapeutic recreation programs in the community.* Reston, VA: American Alliance for Health, Physical Education, Recreation, and Dance.

Dattilo, J. and Murphy, W. D. (1991). *Leisure education program planning: A systematic approach.* State College, PA: Venture Publishing, Inc.

Dixon, J. T. (1980). Mainstreaming and leisure education for the mentally retarded. *Therapeutic Recreation Journal, 14*(1), 30-35.

Hawkins, B. (1987). Aging and developmental disability: New horizons for therapeutic recreation. *Journal of Expanding Horizons in Therapeutic Recreation, 2*(21), 42-46.

Hourcade, J. J. (1989). Special Olympics: A review and critical analysis. *Therapeutic Recreation Journal, 23*(1), 58-65.

Reiter, S. and Levi, A. M. (1981). Leisure activities of mentally retarded adults. *American Journal of Mental Deficiency, 86*(2), 201-203.

G. Allan Roeher Institute. (1989). *The pursuit of leisure: Enriching the lives of people who have a disability* (rev. ed.). Downsview, Ontario, Canada: Author.

Case 9

STEVEN

Steven, a 28 year old white male, was admitted to a 14-bed neurobehavioral unit for individuals with head injuries who exhibit severe behavioral deficiencies. Seven years ago, he was involved in a car accident resulting in a severe traumatic head injury. For Steven and other patients on the unit, management in a less restrictive setting has been unsuccessful. The two major treatment components used on this unit are behavioral and rehabilitation programs.

The behavioral program includes implementation of a specific behavioral plan for target behaviors. Client contracting with a token economy is often utilized as a behavioral management technique. Behavioral plan objectives are incorporated into each client's rehabilitation program. This program provides individual and group treatment in cognitive remediation, therapeutic recreation, occupational and physical therapy, and rehabilitation counseling. Therapeutic recreation services include the provision of leisure education, leisure and social skills development, community access, pet therapy, creative arts, and exercise.

Steven had a right frontal bone compound depressed fracture with epidural hematoma and complex facial and skull fractures with brain stem contusion. Immediately following the accident, he was comatose for three and one-half months. Currently he demonstrates right hemiparesis, right central facial weakness, and right ptosis. The neuropsychological evaluation reveals average intellectual functioning, significant memory impairment and impairment of visual organizational ability. He exhibited self-injurious behavior in the form of striking severe blows to the left side of his face and skull with his left fist. He would engage in this behavior up to thirty times a day. This self-injurious behavior and his violent outbursts toward others have led to the discontinuation of several specialized head injury treatment programs over the past seven years.

Prior to Steven's admission to the neurobehavioral unit, he was cared for at home. He typically got up at 4:00 a.m., spent most of the day watching TV and playing with a variety of children's games and toys, and usually went to bed around 9:00 p.m.

Over a period of four weeks, Steven was assessed by the therapeutic recreation specialist. The results of that evaluation are: Steven's present leisure interests include playing children's board games such as Candyland© and Chutes and Ladders©, watching TV, listening to music, making plastic car models, playing with Lego™ and Rubik's Cube™, and relaxing by taking naps. He prefers to spend time by himself or engaged in one-to-one activity with a staff or family member. He has difficulty entertaining himself, lacks initiative, and is dependent on others to structure his environment. He does not interact with other clients unless requested or structured by staff during scheduled groups. He is responsive only when staff make suggestions on ways to spend his free time. Steven uses a quad cane to ambulate short distances. He demonstrates significantly impaired judgement, and requires close supervision and frequent cues for safety.

Because Steven has a low threshold for frustration, he is easily frustrated when he does not win a game. This frustration results in self-injurious behaviors and to stop this behavior at home, family members offered him food. Consequently, he is 30 pounds over his desired weight.

To overcome severe dysarthria, Steven uses a letter board to communicate, a difficult and slow process because his hemianopsia interferes with his ability to scan for each letter. Steven is able, however, to use the communication board in conversations, appears to enjoy interacting one-to-one with staff, and responds appropriately when he engages in these interactions.

Steven often takes short naps or "breaks" during which he puts his head down and is nonresponsive for ten to thirty minute intervals before continuing his interaction or activity involvement. Recently, a seizure disorder was ruled out; thus, the cause of this behavior is unknown. During recreation activities requiring participants to take turns, Steven frequently puts his head down during others' turns but will respond to cues for his turn.

IN-CLASS EXERCISES

1. Identify Steven's strengths and areas of need. Develop three or four specific problems related to leisure functioning and write goal statements based upon your findings.
2. Develop an individualized therapeutic recreation program plan for Steven. Be sure to take into consideration his present behavioral status and low frustration tolerance, frequent napping and "breaks" throughout the day, and limited leisure interests. How might you use token economy, contracting, or other behavioral strategies to accomplish program plan objectives?
3. Look at the objectives you have developed for Steven and identify the behavior, conditions, and criterion for each.

FIELD EXPERIENCES

1. Visit a facility or unit that primarily serves persons with head injuries. Ask the therapeutic recreation specialist and/or other professionals to discuss characteristic behaviors of persons with head injuries and various treatment approaches and intervention strategies used with this population to facilitate rehabilitation.

Selected References for Case Study

Bennett, T. L. (1989). Individual psychotherapy and minor head injury. *Cognitive Rehabilitation, 8*(2), 14-18.

DiCesare, A., Parente, R., and Anderson, J. (1990). Personality change after traumatic brain injury: Problems and solutions. *Cognitive Rehabilitation, 8*(2), 14-18.

Leland, M., Lewis, F. D., Hinman, S., and Carrillo, R. (1988). Functional retraining of traumatically brain injured adults in a transdisciplinary environment. *Rehabilitation Counseling Bulletin, 31*(4), 289-297.

McLean, A., Temkin, N. R., and Dikmen, S. (1983). The behavioral sequelae of head injury. *Journal of Clinical Neuropsychology, 5*, 361-376.

Mulick, J. A. and Kedesdy, J. H. (1988). Self-injurious behavior, its treatment, and normalization. *Mental Retardation, 26*(4), 223-229.

Stumbo, N. J. and Bloom, C. W. (1990). The implications of traumatic brain injury for therapeutic recreation services in rehabilitation settings. *Therapeutic Recreation Journal, 24*(3), 64-79.

Case 10

TODD

The scenario involving Todd Smith was introduced in Chapter One, *Assessment in Therapeutic Recreation* (p. 35). Todd, a young adult with Down's syndrome that has resulted in severe mental retardation, was having problems with aggressive interpersonal behavior and self-abusive behavior. His parents and his supervisors at work believe the increased frequency of behavior problems may be caused by boredom, desire for attention, and/or frustration over his inability to communicate. Increasing Todd's repertoire of activities was suggested as one way to decrease his undesirable behavior.

DISCUSSION QUESTIONS

1. Identify and discuss the different characteristics of people with mild, moderate, severe, and profound levels of mental retardation.
2. What cognitive, affective, social, and physical characteristics associated with mental retardation in general, and with Todd in particular, will influence the development of his program plan?

3. Discuss behavior management techniques which can be used to teach leisure skills to Todd and, at the same time, decrease his aggressive, self-abusive behaviors.
4. Discuss how responses to questions two and three would change if Todd was also blind.

IN-CLASS EXERCISES

1. Develop a problem list for Todd that ranks his problems and prepare a justification for your ranking. As a class, agree on two specific problems a therapeutic recreation specialist could address.
2. Develop two leisure goals and accompanying measurable objectives to address the two problems identified above. Identify activities and approaches which can accomplish these goals and objectives. Critique your activity choices for their feasibility and appropriateness in this situation.
3. Select one of the activities you suggested in question two and prepare a narrative activity analysis. The activity analysis should include cognitive, affective, psychomotor, social, and spiritual areas. Identify modifications or adaptations, if any, that are appropriate for Todd.
4. Discuss how suggested activity modifications or adaptations would change if Todd was also blind.

FIELD EXPERIENCES

1. Using reference citations, present a justification for the belief that developing a leisure skill repertoire will facilitate positive behavior change in Todd. You will be required to investigate this issue through library research, personal observations, and interviews with professionals in the fields of mental retardation and therapeutic recreation before presenting your justification.

Suggested References for Case Study

Brimer, R. W. (1990). Persons with severe and profound mental retardation. In R. W. Brimer, *Students with severe disabilities: Current perspectives and practices* (pp. 21-51). Mountain View, CA: Mayfield.

Caplan, B. (Ed.) (1987). *Rehabilitation psychology desk reference.* Rockville, MD: Aspen.

Crawford, M. E. (1986). Development and generalization of lifetime leisure skills for multi-handicapped participants. *Therapeutic Recreation Journal, 20*(4), 48-60.

Funabiki, D., Edney, C. S., and Myers, J. (1982). Management of disruptive behaviors in therapeutic recreation settings. *Therapeutic Recreation Journal, 16*(4), 21-25.

Meyer, L. H. and Evans, I. M. (1986). Modification of excess behavior: An adaptive and functional approach for educational and community contexts. In R. H. Horner, L. H. Meyer, and H. D. Fredericks (Eds.), *Education of learners with severe handicaps: Exemplary service strategies* (pp. 315-350). Baltimore, MD: Paul H. Brookes.

Schleien, S. J., Light, C. L., McAvoy, L. H., and Baldwin, C. K. (1989). Best professional practices: Serving persons with severe multiple disabilities. *Therapeutic Recreation Journal, 23*(3), 27-40.

Chapter Three

Implementing Individual Therapeutic Recreation Program Plans

Carter, Van Andel, and Robb (1990) state that "the tasks undertaken during the assessment and planning phase result in a 'paper program' " (p. 145). This paper program, however, is useless unless therapeutic recreation specialists, along with clients, implement it in such a way that it will achieve the established goals and objectives. As therapeutic recreation specialists continually collect information about clients' recreation problems, reactions, and feelings, they may discover that clients are not achieving their desired behavioral changes. Thus, therapeutic recreation specialists must adjust the individual therapeutic recreation program plan as needed to accomodate clients' needs and to facilitate desired (planned) changes.

The success or failure of individual therapeutic recreation program plans depends heavily upon the personal and professional philosophy and skills of therapeutic recreation specialists (Carter, Van Andel and Robb, 1990; Howe-Murphy and Charboneau, 1987; O'Morrow and Reynolds, 1989). Just as specialists' personal and professional characteristics affect the design of an individual program plan, so will they affect implementation of the plan (O'Morrow and Reynolds, 1989). Therapeutic recreation specialists must be flexible and think of themselves as agents or initiators of change in clients and the environments in which they live, work, and play. Analytical, decision making, and communication skills are crucial to successful intervention.

Documentation and Record Keeping

The implementation of individual therapeutic recreation program plans requires systematic, ongoing collection of information. As Navar (1984) points out, therapeutic recreation specialists must "do what you say" (implement the program as planned) as well as "say what you do" (maintain accurate records when monitoring, evaluating, and revising the program). Documentation is important because it provides a record of both the process of intervention and the results. Such documentation is vital because therapeutic recreation specialists must be accountable for providing quality and appropriate services with clients. This information enables therapeutic recreation specialists to validate the need for these services and the resources necessary to deliver them (Schalenghe, 1987).

Documentation also facilitates communication with clients, their family members, fellow therapeutic recreation specialists, and planning team members. Good communication ultimately improves the quality of services and aids in the achievement of planned outcomes because it makes it possible for therapeutic recreation specialists to be consistent in their intervention content and approaches. Good communication also helps to keep clients' individual program plans relevant to their goals in that it provides ongoing information to individuals and staff which can be used to identify and facilitate necessary program revisions.

Therapeutic recreation specialists must also document program implementation to comply with various regulatory standards. The National Therapeutic Recreation Society has designed: (1) *Standards of Practice for Therapeutic Recreation Service*; and (2) *Guidelines for the Administration of Therapeutic Recreation Services* to help therapeutic recreation specialists carry out effective programs and services. The American Therapeutic Recreation Association has also developed recommended *Standards of Practice in Therapeutic Recreation*. Additional standards have been developed by various health care regulatory/accreditation agencies, including the Joint Commission on Accreditation of Healthcare Organizations (JCAHO), the Commission on Accreditation of Rehabilitation Facilities (CARF), the Health Care Financing Administration (HCFA), and the Accreditation Council for Services for Mentally Retarded and other Developmentally Disabled Persons (AC-MR/DD), to protect clients and give some assurance that quality services are being rendered.

Standards may also be developed by individual therapeutic recreation agencies. Though they must be in compliance with all standards of relevant regulatory authorities (Waterman, 1986), these agency standards are valuable because they are uniquely suited for the specific setting. For example, the Veterans Administration (VA) has developed the Systematic External Review Process (SERP), which provides specific guidelines in developing therapeutic recreation policies and procedures and yet allows individual agency flexibility (Donovan, 1987) as well as a more uniform approach to external program auditing (Donovan, 1987).

Following the development of individualized therapeutic recreation program plans, clients begin participating in either already existing or newly developed therapeutic recreation services. A major concern of therapeutic recreation specialists during program implementation is to gather and record data which indicate how clients are progressing toward their goals. Generally, specialists gather subjective and objective information which corresponds to stated expectations or outcomes. The nature and extent of record keeping often varies from agency to agency.

Navar (1984) points out that individual record keeping is primarily a concern of therapeutic recreation specialists working in clinical settings. Nevertheless, specialists working in community settings generally maintain attendance records, activity summaries, evaluations, incident reports, and minutes from staff meetings. In addition, specialists maintain individual progress records for skill-based activities such as an American Red Cross swimming course or a SCUBA course.

Progress notes are the result of the clinical method of recording information about a client into his chart or file (Navar, 1984), and there are internally and externally developed standards for therapeutic recreation practice that provide guidelines regarding what and when to chart. In clinical settings, documentation is usually organized chronologically and maintained in an individual record or "chart." This written information provides evidence that intervention with a client has occurred, the results of these interventions, and adjustments made in the program content or format.

Significant changes in individual behavior are usually reported in the progress notes when they occur (Carruthers, Sneegas, and Ashton-Shaeffer, 1986). Most agencies have schedules for when and how often client progress, regression, or lack of change is noted. Periodically, information from a number of individual progress notes should be summarized and reported in conjunction with an individual therapeutic recreation plan. O'Morrow and Reynolds (1989), however, caution against rigid limits on what, how much, and when to record. In their view, useful, relevant and timely documentation "is a professional and not a clerical activity" (O'Morrow and Reynolds, 1989, p. 150).

Progress notes should contain information pertinent to specific documentation standards for the agency. Various guidelines for determining the content of progress notes can be found in the professional literature (Carruthers, Sneegas, and Ashton-Shaeffer, 1986; Miller, 1989; Navar, 1984). Examples of possible content include:

(1) Progress toward desired goals,
(2) Level and frequency of participation in activities,
(3) Interaction patterns with staff and peers,
(4) New patterns of behavior,

(5) Physical observations such as appearance and personal hygiene, posture, facial expressions, and movement,

(6) Information provided by a client or caregiver, and

(7) Plans for present and future actions related to a client's progress toward desired goals.

If the individual therapeutic recreation program plan was written using the *SOAP* method described in Chapter Two, progress notes are written in a specific format and referred to as *SOAP* notes. *SOAP* notes include *s*ubjective data (what a client says about the problem), *o*bjective data (what others say, observe or inspect about the problem), *a*ssessment of the problem (based on subjective and objective data), and a *p*lan for addressing the problem, now and in the future.

Since progress notes should prove that individual program plans are being followed and record clients' progress, they should provide accurate and complete records of clients' responses to interventions. Progress notes should be written clearly, objectively, and precisely in a behavioral language that describes exactly clients' words, actions, and conditions. The progress notes should not interpret clients' behavior. For example, a therapeutic recreation specialist describes behavior when he writes, "The individual was observed crying during the evening meal." When interpreting the behavior he writes, "The client is depressed." Precisely stated, objective documentation provides a better understanding of a client's actions than do generalizations. For example, a specialist should state that a client participated in an activity "three times a week" rather than "often." Therapeutic recreation specialists may need to include their professional interpretation regarding clients' behavior, but when stating their conclusions, they must identify the interpretation as their own and include the behavioral observations that led to this interpretation.

Carruthers, Sneegas, and Ashton-Shaeffer (1986) provide the following example of how to correctly document clinical judgement: "The resident has remained in her room for the last three days except for meal times. She will speak and respond with a smile when others initiate interaction, however, the verbalization is brief. It is felt by the therapeutic recreation specialist that the resident would like to interact more with her peers but feels somewhat uncomfortable and shy" (p. 59).

The Team Approach

Optimal care and treatment cannot be provided by just one profession, discipline, or service area, and in fact, care and treatment are enhanced by the efforts of more than one. Thus, it is common for many professional specialists to offer a variety of services to clients simultaneously. The multidisciplinary team combines these individual professional efforts to produce a single coordinated result. Team members work together to identify clients' needs, develop plans to meet these needs, periodically evaluate clients' responses to the plans, and revise the plans accordingly. In addition to this interdependence among disciplines, several other descriptions of how teams function have been suggested by various authors (Brill, 1976; Lynch, 1981; O'Morrow and Reynolds, 1989): (1) sharing a common goal or purpose; (2) consolidating knowledge and coordinating activities; (3) specifying tasks based on expertise of team members; (4) developing and monitoring intervention plans; and (5) communicating.

The composition of a team, as well as the roles its members play, may vary. Team membership may be determined by factors such as the specific setting in which therapeutic recreation services are delivered, the goal the team hopes to accomplish, and the length of time the team expects to work together. Likewise, team members' roles will be determined in large measure by clients' problems.

While the team concept seems appropriate and logical, certain aspects of group dynamics can stalemate the team and render it less effective. For instance, the pooling of knowledge and expertise characteristic of the team approach should enhance the quality and efficiency of individual program planning. A team member, however, may perceive a need to defend his or her role, profession, or area of expertise and this may hinder the maximizing efforts of other team members. Another problem that may arise from the team concept is a blurring of roles that results in a failure to distinguish among team tasks, producing ineffective and inefficient situations where no one team member accepts responsibility or feels accountable for the end result. Team conflict may also occur because of the very nature of interdependency. Even in the best team relationships, there are inevitable differences of opinions, approaches, and perceptions.

Effective team relationships depend heavily on good communication. In short, team members must want to communicate—to give, receive, and respond to information. This effort can be enhanced if team members explain specific professional terminologies and methodologies so that each member understands. When team members openly communicate, share responsibility for planning, and are accountable for carrying out team activities, achievement of clients' goals is maximized.

Risk Management and Legal Liability Concerns

When individual program plans are implemented, therapeutic recreation specialists must consider all possible risks and ensure a reasonable level of client safety. Van der Smissen (1980) identifies three major areas of risk management: (1) supervision of participants; (2) conditions of the environment; and (3) manner of conducting activities. Russell (1982) points out that personal injury or property loss usually arises from poor professional judgement, lack of adherence to current safety standards, infrequent inspections and repair of areas and facilities, and poor design of program formats and conduct. Specialists must respond to these concerns when implementing individual therapeutic recreation program plans. Can adequate supervision be provided? Are the facility and equipment in safe operating condition? Will the planned approaches allow reasonably safe participation? Though part of the recent attention to managing risks has been caused by an increasing emphasis on minimizing legal liability, Joseph, Fox, and Stearns (1980) suggest that risk management is essential to quality services and treatment. That is, when participation risks are kept at a minimum, a higher quality of care is possible.

Voelkl (1988) suggests a three-step process for managing risk. First, therapeutic recreation specialists, aided by all staff involved in the implemention of programs, must identify all possible risks to clients, staff, and facility. Once risks have been identified, specialists should determine the best approach to eliminating or minimizing the risks. Last, therapeutic recreation specialists must develop a plan describing how the risks will be handled. As in the case of individual program plans, risk management plans should help specialists decide whether to continue, modify, or terminate the program.

Identifying and Utilizing Community Resources

Implementing individual therapeutic recreation program plans often involves the use of community resources, and therapeutic recreation specialists must be knowledgeable about available community leisure opportunities and resources. Local libraries, many of which have developed community leisure directories or research files, are excellent sources for the names and locations of potential leisure service providers. Directories often contain names of associations, clubs, and organizations devoted to specific recreation interests or activities, as well as community centers and recreation facilities in the area. The library, itself, is a good resource, providing an abundance of information about potential recreation activities. The telephone book, both the white and yellow pages, also provides valuable information since it contains the telephone numbers and addresses of leisure service agencies and facilities. Finally, retailers selling equipment for recreation activities, or private and commercial facilities, such as bowling alleys, golf courses, and tennis clubs, can usually provide information about classes and other leisure opportunities.

Therapeutic recreation specialists will find it helpful to develop a leisure resource system that organizes the individuals and agencies according to the services they provide. The information contained in this system should include the contact person's name, agency or category affiliation (such as community recreation professionals, parents, school personnel, and civic group representatives), address, telephone number, and services provided. It should also include other useful program information such as costs, transportation requirements, registration deadlines, times of the week or month when a leader is available, education and background a resource person has to offer, and meeting time and location.

Discharge/Referral Networks

While clients are receiving treatment, one or more team conferences are usually conducted regarding discharge. Discharge planning requires a final client assessment based on identified problems and goals. The information obtained during discharge planning helps therapeutic recreation specialists make decisions about clients' status, readiness for discharge, and referrals.

O'Morrow and Reynolds (1989) state "a major obstacle to participation in leisure experiences following discharge is the poor link between the rehabilitation facility and community recreation agencies" (p. 188). This "poor link" could result in lack of future client progress or even regression (Navar, 1984). Referral systems are currently being created to help facilitate clients' return to the community. For example, Georgia and Illinois are instituting statewide discharge and referral processes to help clients pursue leisure opportunities as they move from institutions into communities. These networks are being developed through joint efforts by therapeutic recreation specialists working in hospitals, state facilities for people with mental retardation, nursing homes, psychiatric facilities, rehabilitation centers, and correctional institutions, and their community recreation counterparts. To aid in this process, some communities are developing directories of agencies offering leisure services and resources. The development of effective discharge and referral systems will demand a greater emphasis in the future.

Summary

Individual therapeutic recreation program plans remain just that—plans—until they are put into practice. Thus, the implementation phase of the individual therapeutic recreation program planning process could be considered the "make-it-or-break-it" phase. The success of planned interventions relies heavily on the personal and professional expertise of therapeutic recreation specialists. Excellent analytical, decision-making, and communications skills are necessary if specialists are to implement, monitor, and revise a plan, and document client progress. The risks of participation must be mimimized and the quality of intervention maximized. Therapeutic recreation specialists should identify and use community resources that contribute to successful leisure experiences.

During implementation, therapeutic recreation specialists work directly with clients. In the next chapter, *Leadership in Therapeutic Recreation*, guidelines for effective leadership will be highlighted.

Bibliography

Brill, N. I. (1976). *Teamwork: Working together in the human services.* Philadelphia, PA: J. B. Lippincott.

Carruthers, C., Sneegas, J. J., and Ashton-Shaeffer, C. A. (1986). *Therapeutic recreation: Guidelines for activity services in long term care.* Urbana-Champaign, IL: University of Illinois.

Carter, M. J., Van Andel, G. E., and Robb, G. M. (1990). *Therapeutic recreation: A practical approach.* Prospect Heights, IL: Waveland Press.

Donovan, G. (1987). You want me to do what? Regulatory standards in therapeutic recreation. In B. Riley (Ed.), *Evaluation of therapeutic recreation through quality assurance* (pp. 25-35). State College, PA: Venture Publishing, Inc.

Howe-Murphy, R. and Charboneau, B. G. (1987). *Therapeutic recreation intervention: An ecological perspective.* Englewood Cliffs, NJ: Prentice-Hall.

Joseph, E. D., Fox, L. A., and Stearns, G. (1980). *Management solutions for mental health.* Chicago, IL: Care Communications.

Lynch, B. (1981). Team building: Will it work in health care? *Journal of Allied Health, 10,* 240-246.

Miller, M. (1989). *Documentation in long term care facilities.* Alexandria, VA: National Recreation and Park Association.

Navar, N. (1984). Documentation in therapeutic recreation. In C. A. Peterson and S. L. Gunn, Therapeutic Recreation Program Design: Principles and Procedures (2nd ed.) (pp. 212-266). Englewood Cliffs, NJ: Prentice-Hall.

O'Morrow, G. S. and Reynolds, R. P. (1989). *Therapeutic recreation: A helping profession* (3rd ed). Englewood Cliffs, NJ: Prentice-Hall.

Russell, R. V. (1982). *Planning programs in recreation.* St. Louis, MO: C. V. Mosby.

Schalenghe, R. W. (1987). Foreward. In B. Riley (Ed.), *Evaluation of therapeutic recreation through quality assurance* (pp. ix-x). State College, PA: Venture Publishing, Inc.

van der Smissen, B. (1980, October). *Overview of liability in parks and recreation.* Paper presented at the National Recreation and Park Association Congress, Phoenix, AZ.

Voelkl, J. E. (1988). *Risk management in therapeutic recreation: A component of quality assurance.* State College, PA: Venture Publishing, Inc.

Waterman, F. (1986). *One-minute TR manager.* Unpublished manuscript.

Suggested Readings

American Therapeutic Recreation Association. (1991). *Standards of practice in therapeutic recreation.* Hattiesburg, MS: Author.

Commission on Accreditation of Rehabilitation Facilities. (1990). *Standards manual for organizations serving people with disabilities*. Tucson, AZ: Author.

Edginton, C. R. and Ford, P. M. (1985). *Leadership in recreation and leisure service organizations*. New York, NY: Macmillian.

Jewell, D. L. (1980). Documentation: Shibboleth for professionalism. *Therapeutic Recreation Journal, 14*(1), 23-29.

Joint Commission of Accreditation for Healthcare Organizations (1990). *The 1991 Joint Commission accreditation manual for hospitals*. Chicago, IL: JCAHO Publications.

Kaiser, R. A. (1986). *Liability and law in recreation, parks, and sports*. Englewood Cliffs, NJ: Prentice-Hall.

National Therapeutic Recreation Society. (1990). *Guidelines for the administration of therapeutic recreation services* (revised). Alexandria, VA: National Recreation and Park Association.

National Therapeutic Recreation Society. (1990). *Standards of practice for therapeutic recreation service* (revised). Alexandria, VA: National Recreation and Park Association.

Pluckhan, M. (1972). Professional territoriality: A problem affecting the delivery of healthcare. *Nursing Forum, 11*, 300-310.

Rankin, J. (1977). Legal risks and bold programming. *Parks and Recreation, 12*(7), 47-48, 67-69.

Riley, R. (Ed.). (1987). *Evaluation of therapeutic recreation through quality assurance*. State College, PA: Venture Publishing, Inc.

Teague, M. and Mobily, K. (1986). Litigation: A growing threat to community centers. *Therapeutic Recreation Journal, 20*(1), 18-31.

Case 1

AMANDA

Camp Adventure, a residential summer camp for children ages six through thirteen with various physical, psychological, and behavioral deficiencies, features a variety of indoor and outdoor activities, including Ping-Pong™, basketball, table games, movies, horseback riding, swimming, and hiking. The children attend camp for one month. One weekend during the month, families of the campers are invited to participate. The camp maintains a one-to-three staff/camper ratio. Each member of the senior staff is a certified therapeutic recreation specialist. All staff members receive in-service training to prepare them to work with the range of disabilities represented in camp. This year most campers have physical and sensory disabilities such as muscular dystrophy, cerebral palsy, and spina bifida, and visual and hearing impairments, while others have less recognizable disabilities including emotional or behavioral deficiencies and epilepsy.

Amanda, a ten year old white female with epilepsy and a visual impairment attending camp for the first time, is on a dual medication regimen of Tegretol and Clonopin and has been seizure free for six months. She will be entering the sixth grade in the fall and makes good grades. She has several close friends and is a Girl Scout.

Amanda is excited about camp but is anxious about the possibility of recurring seizures and negotiating skills in a new environment. She remembers the embarassment of experiencing seizures and running into the door when she entered a new school. Amanda has tunnel vision, yet can generally negotiate herself easily and safely. She is very self-conscious about her disabilities and prefers no one to know. Before coming to camp, Amanda and her parents met with a counselor regarding her anxiety.

At one of the biweekly group sessions, where the campers discuss their anxieties and concerns about camp and disabilities, Amanda's roommate expressed concern about Amanda's disabilities. The group spent time discussing these concerns.

DISCUSSION QUESTIONS

1. What responsibility does the staff have in handling Amanda's condition with regard to the other children's safety and comfort level while maintaining confidentiality?
2. What responsibility does the staff have in handling Amanda's condition with regard to Amanda's safety and comfort?
3. What specific activities will involve risks for Amanda and what safety precautions should be taken?
4. Epilepsy is considered to be a "hidden disability." Discuss other conditions that are "hidden."
5. What activities at camp would be adaptable for Amanda's visual impairment and why?

IN-CLASS EXERCISES

1. Invite a representative from a local epilepsy association to discuss this disability and intervention techniques that are appropriate if one is to work effectively with persons who have epilepsy.
2. Watch a videotape of an individual having a seizure that displays appropriate interventions. The Standard First Aid Course offered by the American Red Cross is an excellent resource.
3. Contact the local or state chapter of the American Council of the Blind and ask a representative to discuss various types of visual impairments and their implications for engaging in recreation experiences.
4. Invite a representative from the State Rehabilitation Services unit to discuss various services and adaptive devices that can help persons with visual impairments engage in meaningful recreation experiences.
5. Simulate a visual impairment while playing Ping-Pong™, basketball, or table games. Discuss your feelings about the activity, yourself, and the overall experience.

Selected References for Case Study

American Foundation for the Blind. (1991-92). *Publications Catalog.* 15 West 16th Street, New York, NY 10011.

Cornelius, D. (1980). *Inside out.* Washington, DC: Regional Rehabilitation Research Institute on Attitudinal, Legal and Leisure Barriers, George Washington University.

Hourcade, J. J. and Parette, H. P. (1986). Students with epilepsy: Counseling implications for the hidden handicap. *School Counselor, 33*(4), 279-285.

Kelley, J. D. (Ed.). (1981). Recreation programming for visually impaired children and youth. New York, NY: American Foundation for the Blind.

Mandell, C. J. and Fiscus, E. (1981). Understanding exceptional people. St. Paul, MN: West Publishing.

National Rehabilitation Information Center, 8455 Colesville Road, Suite 935, Silver Spring, MD 20910-3319 (Provides information, data-based computer searches, and copies of available articles on a wide range of disability-related topics).

Rehab briefs: Bringing research into effective focus. (Periodic summaries of research or disability topics; available through National Institute on Disability and Rehabilitation Research, Office of Special Education and Rehabilitation Services, U.S. Department of Education, Washington, DC 20202).

Weiss, C. and Jamieson, N. (1988). Hidden disabilities: A new enterprise for therapeutic recreation. *Therapeutic Recreation Journal, 22*(4), 9-17.

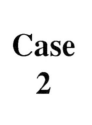

Case 2

RECREATION IN CORRECTIONS

You learned about the recreation program at Jackson Correctional Institute in Chapter Two, Individual Therapeutic Recreation Program Planning (p. 56). In the past, animals have been prohibited in this correctional institution. However, recreation staff at Jackson Correctional Institute have created interest in and support of a pet-facilitated therapy pilot project with the institution's Mental Health Supportive Living Unit inmates. The Department of Corrections' Commissioner has given approval for this project.

IN-CLASS EXERCISES

You are the therapeutic recreation supervisor at Jackson Correctional Institute:
1. Formulate possible program goals for inmates involved in the pet-facilitated therapy program.
2. Suggest content, formats, and processes for achieving each of the suggested program goals.
3. Based on program content, formats, and processes you suggested, what implementation questions should be answered before incorporating the pet-facilitated therapy program into an inmate's individualized program plan? Consider areas such as schedules, staff, resources, security, health regulations, documentation procedures, information dissemination, and evaluation criteria.
4. Finish each scenario by creating a possible positive outcome for each of the following inmates participating in this pet-facilitated program:
   a. A very regressed inmate with mental illness refuses to interact with the animals unless a staff member places a puppy in his lap.

     b. An inmate with mental retardation was afraid during the first session and said that he did not know how to pet the puppies.

     c. A large, quiet, male inmate with mental illness rarely exhibits enthusiasm or energy, except when participating in the pet program.

5. Brainstorm community agencies and resources that could help you implement the pet-facilitated therapy program at Jackson Correctional Institute.

6. Ask a therapeutic recreation specialist who implements a pet-facilitated therapy program to come to class and discuss risk management issues.

Selected References for Case Study

Anderson, S. C. (1991). Corrections. In D. R. Austin and M. E. Crawford (Eds.), *Therapeutic Recreation: An Introduction* (pp. 352-372). Englewood Cliffs, NJ: Prentice-Hall.

Dunkin, M. A. and Ballew, T. (1990). The positive power of pets. *Arthritis Today*, May/June, 44-48.

Grimes, P. (1990). Therapeutic recreation programs for special needs inmates. *Correctional Recreation Today*, 5(1), 7-8.

Haggard, A. (1985). A patient's best friend. *American Journal of Nursing*, 85(12), 1375-1376.

McCandless, P., McCready, K. F., and Knight, L. (1985). A model animal therapy program for mental health settings. *Therapeutic Recreation Journal*, 19(2), 55-63.

Thomas, R. G. and Thomas, R. M. (1988). The evolution of a prison adaptive-health program. *Journal of Correctional Education*, 39(1), 30-35.

Wilkes, C. N., Skalko, T. K., and Trahan, M. (1989). Pet Rx: Implications for good health. *Health Education*, 20(2), 6-9.

Case 3

CARPET CAPERS

You work as a therapeutic recreation specialist on a chemical dependency unit of a 120 bed for-profit hospital with a number of sister hospitals throughout the United States. The geographic region in which the hospital is based is currently experiencing a sharp recession and the hospital finds itself with major financial limitations. A decline in patients has created a financial deficit that has resulted in a twenty-five percent lay off of the hospital staff.

Despite these unsettling conditions, the administrator remains committed to therapeutic recreation services. She has recently invested a considerable amount of money in renovations to the therapeutic recreation area and has installed wall-to-wall carpet throughout the facility. Over the past few months, you have begun to notice an increase in the number of patients' injuries involving twisting of the ankles, knees, and hips that appear directly related to the new carpeted surface. You have also observed and documented one particular injury that resulted from a patient's sneaker catching in the carpet.

You report your suspicions to the therapeutic recreation director and suggest he report them to the administrator. He indicates that there is insufficient evidence to report this situation. In his discussion with you, the therapeutic recreation director also reiterates the financial crisis the hospital is facing and instructs you to evaluate the area and its potential for injuries and report back in two weeks.

DISCUSSION QUESTIONS

1. How will you go about evaluating the facility and potential risk areas so that you can prepare an adequate report for the therapeutic recreation director?
2. What evaluation questions do you need to answer to resolve this safety concern? How would you collect information about this problem in a two-week period?

3.   While you are evaluating the situation and preparing the report, you feel you cannot continue to have accidents in the therapeutic recreation area. Prepare a risk management plan for this area and determine how you can evaluate the effectiveness of this plan.

FIELD EXPERIENCES

1.   Invite an administrator and therapeutic specialist to class from a local chemical dependency facility to discuss risk management and possibly this particular case.

Selected References for Case Study

Dzingleski, L. (1987). The basic principles of managing risk. *Journal of Quality Assurance, 11*(Fall), 20-22.

Kibbee, P. (1988). Implementing a risk management program in a psychiatric facility. *Journal of Quality Assurance, 10*(1), 11-14.

Touchstone, W. A. (1984). Fiscal accountability through effective risk management. *Therapeutic Recreation Journal, 18*(4), 20-26.

Case 4

DAVID

David Jones, a 25 year old Hispanic male with spastic cerebral palsy, currently resides semi-independently in a four bedroom house with six other men who also have physical limitations. He moved to the semi-independent living service (SILS) home three months ago. Previously, he lived with his parents, who suggested a supervised living situation for David because he would be more independent and involved in the community. His parents had noted David tended to stay at home when he was not working. He is an only child and, according to his parents, has few friends. His cat, Sylvester, lives with him in his new home. David works at the Community Work Center Monday through Friday from 8:00 a.m. to 3:00 p.m. He operates a product packaging machine, a job he has held for two years. The Work Center is four miles from his new residence and David, who used to ride his bicycle to and from work, will now have to take the bus. His parents expressed concern about this arrangement because bicycling was his main source of independent physical activity.

Initial Therapeutic Recreation Program Plan

After living at the SILS home for two weeks, the therapeutic recreation specialist prepared the following individual therapeutic recreation program plan to present to the team for discussion:

Assessment

Diagnosis: Spastic cerebral palsy with speech impairment and slight learning disability.

Overall Observations: David is polite and reserved. He is a hard worker. In his leisure, David spends much time alone watching TV or playing with his cat, Sylvester. He enjoys riding his three-wheel bicycle, listening to music, and playing checkers with his father. He also enjoys his computer, but his knowledge and skills are quite limited at present.

Both of David's arms flex toward the front of his body with hands in a curled position. He maintains his mobility by walking on his toes with legs crossing in a scissors pattern. He is generally well-groomed, though he has difficulty maintaining good grooming over the course of the day.

Leisure-Related Problems

David is self-conscious about his physical appearance and mobility prob-lems. He tires easily and feels tense when he comes home from work. He is hesitant about socializing with others and about trying new activities.

Leisure Program Goals

Goal #1: To improve physical fitness.

Selected Activity: Bicycle riding with a peer.

Behavioral Objective: David will ride his three-wheel bicycle in the neighborhood with a peer bicycle rider for at least 30 minutes three days per week.

Goal #2: To utilize an appropriate relaxation activity after work.

Selected Activity: Listening to music, writing letters, playing with his cat, etc.

Behavioral Objective: Upon returning home from work, David will use one hour to relax and do what he prefers: writing letters on the computer, listening to music, watching TV, or playing with Sylvester.

Goal #3: To meet new people with whom he can socialize.

Selected Activity: Community Computer Club.

Behavioral Objective: David will join the Community Computer Club and attend meetings two times per week, from 6:00 p.m. to 8:00 p.m. (independently managing the bus) and meet at least one new friend within his first month of residence at SILS.

DISCUSSION QUESTIONS

1. After two weeks of living at the SILS home, David, his parents, and the SILS staff gathered for a team meeting. The meeting's purpose was to establish ongoing rehabilitation and maintenance goals for David. The therapeutic recreation specialist presented the program plan listed above. Place yourself in the role of various people at the team meeting and react to the therapeutic recreation program plan:
    a. David,
    b. David's parents,
    c. the vocational rehabilitation counselor,
    d. the house parent/program manager, and
    e. other team members (such as speech therapist, occupational therapist, physical therapist).
2. Is David's individual therapeutic recreation plan appropriate and realistic? How might the plan be improved?
3. How would the therapeutic recreation goals be integrated with the goals of other disciplines to create a comprehensive approach to David's overall program?

Selected References for Case Studies

Coyle, C. P. and Kinney, W. B. (1990). Leisure characteristics of adults with physical disabilities. *Therapeutic Recreation Journal, 24*(4), 64-73.

Condeluci, A. (1989). Empowering people with cerebral palsy. *Journal of Rehabilitation, 55*(2), 15-16.

Project LIFE. (1988). *LIFE forms, the LIFE training guide.* Chapel Hill, NC: Curriculum in Leisure Studies and Recreation Administration, University of North Carolina at Chapel Hill.

Schleifer, M. J. (1989). This has been a miserable fall: Problems of moving to a new community. *Exceptional Parent, 19*(3), 56-62.

Zoerink, D. A. (1989). Activity choices: Exploring perceptions of persons with physical disabilities. *Therapeutic Recreation Journal, 23*(1), 17-23.

Case 5

HEART-TO-HEART

During the initial assessment, Mr. Simpson, a black cardiac rehabilitation patient, reported two previous heart attacks and current attacks of angina and emphysema. He is currently taking nitroglycerin to stabilize angina symptoms. Mr. Simpson was told by a therapeutic recreation specialist that he had medical clearance to participate in nonvigorous activities. Mr. Simpson indicated that he understood his medical clearance explanation and agreed to take part in nonvigorous therapeutic recreation activities such as a low-level walking program.

The following morning, Mr. Simpson took part in morning aerobics, lead by a therapeutic recreation paraprofessional who had not met him and did not know his medical history. Near the completion of the aerobics class, the therapeutic recreation specialist who had assessed Mr. Simpson walked by and saw him participating. The therapeutic recreation specialist immediately met with Mr. Simpson and reinformed him of his medical clearance restrictions. Mr. Simpson stated that he fully understood and would comply.

Later this same morning, during a therapeutic recreation session, Mr. Simpson asked if he could participate in a slow pitch softball game. He was given the position of pitcher by the therapeutic recreation specialist in charge of his case and told to pitch the ball and not to make any attempt to catch or retrieve it. On the first play of the game, Mr. Simpson tried to field the ball, fell on his shoulder, and did not move for several seconds. Upon recovery, however, he insisted on continuing his role as pitcher.

DISCUSSION QUESTIONS

1. Do you believe Mr. Simpson's participation in the slow pitch softball game complies with his medical restrictions?
2. If Mr. Simpson insists he is fine, should he be allowed to continue to play? Why? Balance dignity of risk against prudent leadership.
3. How responsible is Mr. Simpson for administering his own program plan in therapeutic recreation?
4. What safeguards would you include in Mr. Simpson's plan? Why?
5. Should the therapeutic recreation paraprofessional conducting the morning aerobics activity have information on new patients participating in her programs? Why? How should information about new patients be disseminated to all therapeutic recreation staff members? Discuss possible intake procedures of new patients into therapeutic recreation programs.
6. Discuss the implications to Mr. Simpson and therapeutic recreation services if he had had a cardiac arrest during the morning aerobics activity.
7. Select a form of documentation, such as a progress note, incident report, or accident report, and record what happened concerning Mr. Simpson during the morning therapeutic recreation activities.

FIELD EXPERIENCES

1. Interview a therapeutic recreation professional with regard to this case and discuss each question. Compare the professional's responses with your own and determine the best solutions.

Selected References for Case Study

Herbert, W. and Herbert, D. L. (1988). Legal aspects of cardiac rehabilitation programs. *Physician and Sportsmedicine, 16*(10), 105-108, 111-112.

Hoeft, T. M. (1982). Leisure counseling: A component of cardiac rehabilitation and heart disease intervention programs. In L. L. Neal and C. R. Edginton (Eds.), *Exetra perspectives*: *Concepts in therapeutic recreation* (pp. 193-204). Eugene, OR: Center of Leisure Studies, University of Oregon.

Kozlowski, J. C. (1988). A common sense view of liability. *Parks and Recreation, 23*(9), 56-59.

McGuire, F. A. and Goodwin, L. (1991). Cardiac rehabilitation. In D. R. Austin and M. E. Crawford (Eds.), *Therapeutic recreation: An introduction* (pp. 320-332). Englewood Cliffs, NJ: Prentice-Hall.

Case 6

JOHN

John Watson, a 26 year old white male with bipolar disorder, is a resident at Clarion Mental Health Center, a 110 bed facility for persons with acute emotional disorders. Two years ago, he was hospitalized for compulsive exercising and symptoms of anorexia. Prior to this, he had been hospitalized four times in two years for depression or mania. Currently, John has difficulty expressing his emotions appropriately, a tendency to isolate himself from others, and difficulty with the use of free time.

During admission, John claimed that he did not need medication. In his words, he has been "playing games" with the doctors' minds: "I'm great, terrific, and physically healthy . . . I have the best self-esteem of anybody on the earth today! . . . I am better than anyone else on this earth because I have terrific talent musically and physically." Although John denies any specific psychotic symptoms, admissions staff noted erratic behaviors caused by excess energy, agitation, and aggression. He presents himself as casually dressed and moderately groomed. He is in an euphoric state, has fair eye contact, and denies any delusions or hallucinations at this time.

John's father is a construction worker with a history of several illnesses, and his mother, who graduated from college with honors, is a homemaker. His parents had high expectations that John would enter law or medical school. John, who was designated by the family as "the smart one," has one older brother, Robert, 31, and two sisters, 21 and 19.

During previous hospitalizations, John resisted participation in unit activities, group therapy, or individual recreation. He has few friends, keeps to himself most of the time, likes to listen to rock music, and plays the piano. Occasionally, he works out in the gym, takes walks, and attends picnics and outings if only one other individual or a small group is involved.

John is currently taking the following medications: Lithium, Tegretol, and Haldol.

Individual Therapeutic Recreation Program Plan

Following initial observations by admissions staff, John was referred to an adult treatment unit and assigned to therapeutic recreation for activity participation and observation. After an initial meeting with John and observing him in unit activities for three days, the therapeutic recreation specialist presented the following individualized therapeutic recreation program plan to the team for discussion.

Assessment

Diagnosis from Chart: Bipolar disorder—manic-depressive.
Overall Observations of Therapeutic Recreation Specialist: John appears
    to be experiencing grandiose delusions. His mood is euphoric. He has
    difficulty sitting still, his movements are hyperactive, and his attention

span is limited to approximately three minutes. He speaks to peers only when necessary, seeks attention of staff, and occasionally talks to himself. He tends to observe on the unit without getting involved in any specific recreation activities.

Leisure-Related Problems

John has difficulty expressing his emotions appropriately, a tendency to isolate himself from others, and difficulty with the utilization of free time.

Leisure Program Goals

Goal #1: To maintain physical fitness.
   Selected Activity: Participating in the YMCA Eagle Room physical fitness circuit.
Behavioral Objective: Upon visiting the YMCA Eagle Room with the therapeutic recreation specialist and becoming familiar with the proper use of equipment, John will complete the Eagle physical fitness circuit three times a week within six weeks.
Goal #2: To increase awareness of feelings.
Selected Activity: Keeping a personal journal.
Behavioral Objective: After receiving a journal, John will write daily about his feelings for the next thirty days, noting the situations that trigger his least desirable feelings.
Goal #3: To increase socialization skills.
Selected Activity: Attending a rock concert with at least one peer.
Behavioral Objective: After acquiring tickets to a rock concert, John will invite a peer and attend the concert within two weeks after admission.
Other Recommendations: While John is adjusting to his new environment, he should be assigned to one therapeutic recreation specialist with whom he begins building trust and rapport.

DISCUSSION QUESTIONS

1. After one week on the treatment unit, John's case was discussed by the treatment team for initial case review, and each member of the team presented an individual program plan for his or her discipline. The therapeutic recreation specialist presented the individual program plan outlined above. Place yourself in the role of various team members and react to the

individual therapeutic recreation program plan. What would be the reactions or concerns of:

   a. the social worker,
   b. the psychologist,
   c. the psychiatric nurse,
   d. the vocational rehabilitation counselor,
   e. the music therapist, and
   f. other team members?

2. How could the individual therapeutic recreation program plan be improved?
3. Identify several items in John's therapeutic recreation plan that may be difficult to implement and discuss why.
4. Would John be an appropriate participant in the stress management class offered at Clarion Mental Health Center? Why?
5. Do you think John would benefit from a structured reality orientation class? Why?
6. Discuss the relationship between the stages of pharmacological treatment for John with therapeutic recreation intervention. What problems relevant to these stages can be best addressed by therapeutic recreation?
7. If John's symptoms were similar, but his diagnosis was schizophrenia, would the therapeutic recreation specialist intervene differently? Why?

FIELD EXPERIENCES

1. Invite a treatment team from a mental health center to class to role play the treatment team meeting.
2. Ask a therapeutic recreation specialist with experience in a mental health setting to review your responses to each discussion question.

Selected References for Case Study

Kinney, W. B. and Sottile, J. (1990). Psychiatry and mental health. In D. R. Austin and M. E. Crawford (Eds.), *Therapeutic recreation: An introduction* (pp. 71-99). Englewood Cliffs, NJ: Prentice-Hall.

O'Morrow, G. S. and Reynolds, R. P. (1989). *Therapeutic recreation: A helping profession* (3rd ed.). Englewood Cliffs, NJ: Prentice-Hall.

Pakes, D. L. and Pakes, G. E. (1982). Antipsychotic drug effects and thera-
    peutic recreation program considerations. *Therapeutic Recreation
    Journal, 16*(1), 12-19.

Ost, L. G. (1987). Applied relaxation: Description of a coping technique
    and review of controlled studies. *Behaviour Research and Therapy,
    25*(5), 397-409.

Ruiz, D. S. (1982). Epidemiology of schizophrenia: Some diagnostic and
    sociocultural considerations. *Phylon, 43*(4), 315-326.

Case 7

EDITH

Edith Miller, 69 years old, was diagnosed with Alzheimer's disease and placed in a long-term healthcare facility three years ago by her husband, Mr. Miller, who is employed in a nearby college community.

You were introduced to Mrs. Miller's case in Chapter One, *Assessment in Therapeutic Recreation* (p. 31). In Chapter Two, *Individual Therapeutic Recreation Program Planning*, you were asked to develop goals and objectives for Mrs. Miller (p. 72). The following concerns evolved during the implementation of Mrs. Miller's therapeutic recreation program plan.

DISCUSSION QUESTIONS

1. During a team meeting, the nursing staff reported a change in medication in order to further arrest Mrs. Miller's aggressive behaviors. What information is needed by the therapeutic recreation specialist regarding this change and its implications for Mrs. Miller's activity participation? In general, how much should a therapeutic recreation specialist know about any client's medication?

2.   During a team meeting, the dietary staff reported their goal for Mrs. Miller was that she would eat snacks and finger foods without assistance. How might the therapeutic recreation specialist incorporate this information into her service goals?

3. Mr. Miller spends nearly two hours per workday and all day Sunday with his wife. Social service personnel have suggested he take more time for himself. His hobbies are traveling and gardening. How might the therapeutic recreation specialist assist? If the therapeutic recreation specialist supported Mr. Miller's present visiting behavior, how should she deal with this difference of opinion?

ROLE-PLAYING

1. Mrs. Miller becomes upset when groups present religious programs that differ from her own beliefs. Her family is concerned about this situation, and Mr. Miller decides to meet with the social service supervisor and therapeutic recreation specialist. How should these personnel respond to Mr. Miller's concerns? What appropriate activity substitutes could they identify for Mrs. Miller? What additional suggestions might they offer? In general, how should the therapeutic recreation specialist approach the inclusion of religious content in programs?

2. Mr. Miller and one of his daughters agree to accompany his wife, the therapeutic recreation specialist, a volunteer, and two other residents on an evening outing to the nearby college community. How should the therapeutic recreation specialist prepare Mr. Miller and his daughter for their participation with Mrs. Miller? What should be considered and included in the evening's activities? What additional suggestions might the therapeutic recreation specialist offer to maximize the probability for a successful and meaningful experience?

Selected References for Case Study

Austin, J. K. and Price, M. J. (1991). Health and safety considerations. In D. R. Austin, *Therapeutic recreation processes and techniques* (2nd ed.) (pp. 389-422). Champaign, IL: Sagamore.

Bonnardeaux, J. L. (1984). The effects of psychotropic drugs. *Impact of Science on Society, 34*(1), 35-47.

Hansen, S. S., Patterson, M. A., and Wilson, R. W. (1988). Family involvement on a dementia unit: The resident enrichment and activity program. *The Gerontologist, 28*(4), 508-510.

Keller, M. J. and Hughes, S. (1991). The role of leisure education with family caregivers of persons with Alzheimer's disease and related disorders. *Annual in Therapeutic Recreation, 2*, 1-7.

Quayhagen, M. P. and Quayhagen, M. (1988). Alzheimer's stress: Coping with the caregiving role. *The Gerontologist, 28*(3), 391-96.

Case 8

I'M OFF DUTY

Camp Summit is designed to provide outdoor living experiences to a variety of populations with disabilities. Funded by a private foundation and voluntary contributions, the camp is located near a major urban center in the northeast. For the last ten years leisure studies students from a local university have supplemented regular staff counselors during the weekend fall camping program. The university's involvement has served the three-fold purpose of enabling a smaller permanent staff to be hired during the year, providing students with experience in working with various populations, and offering a weekend camp experience to people with disabilities. Both camp personnel and the university faculty have maintained a good working relationship through the years and no problems have occurred, until today.

It is Monday morning and the assistant camp director, who was in charge over the weekend, has come to you, the camp director, with some disturbing information about the weekend's overnight activity. A group of university students spent the weekend at camp along with a group of nonambulatory teens with mental retardation. The day program was carried out effectively with both groups interacting and participating in a full program of activities. Saturday night, however, after the participants had been helped to bed, it seems that one of the university students drove to the local convenience store and purchased a six-pack of beer and returned to share it with two other students. According to your assistant director, the students sat outside one of the cabins talking and drinking for about an hour and a half before returning to their designated cabins for the night. The assistant director had no knowledge of the incident until the next day when one of the staff counselors who had been inside the cabin where the impromptu gathering took place told her about the event.

Your permanent staff members know that alcoholic beverages are strictly forbidden on camp premises. In addition, you suspect at least one, if not two of the university students may have been underage for the legal consumption of alcohol. At the same time, you are receiving the information third-hand and, while you have no reason to doubt your staff member, you feel less sure of the course you should take than if you had witnessed the event yourself.

DISCUSSION QUESTIONS

1. What would you, as the camp director, do in this situation?
2. If your assistant camp director had discovered the students instead of "hearing" about it, how would you have expected her to proceed?
3. How should this incident affect the relationship between the university and the camp?
4. Discuss possible liability issues related to this situation.

ROLE-PLAYING

1. One student assumes the role of the camp director and another the university faculty member involved. The camp director calls the university faculty member to discuss this issue. Carry out the dialogue.
2. Simulate the described situation and your interactions, as camp director, with the students upon discovering them with alcoholic beverages.
3. Play *The Game of Volunteer Management* which is designed to teach the concepts of volunteer management. The game is available from Volunteer Management, Avalon Hill Game Company, Department HL, 4517 Hartford Road, Baltimore, MD 21214.

FIELD EXPERIENCES

1. Invite a camp director into class to discuss this situation. Ask the camp director to consider issues such as risk management, liability, and standards of care during the discussion.

IN-CLASS EXERCISES

1. Design an orientation for university students participating in a weekend camp program. Describe and discuss the issues to be covered. If possible, conduct the orientation prior to an actual camp experience, then critique and modify it. Professionals could assist with this exercise.

Selected References for Case Study

Halloran, J. (1981). *Supervision: The act of management.* Englewood Cliffs, NJ: Prentice-Hall.

Johnson, R. L. (1984). What is your liability IQ? *Parks and Recreation, 19*(4), 48-52.

Kaiser, R. A. (1986). *Liability and law in recreation, parks, and sports.* Englewood Cliffs, NJ: Prentice-Hall.

Kirseh, S. and Culkin, D. (1986). *Managing human resources in recreation, parks and leisure services.* New York, NY: Macmillan.

Tedrick, T. and Henderson, K. A. (1989). *Volunteers in leisure: A management perspective.* Reston, VA: American Alliance for Health, Physical Education, Recreation, and Dance.

Case 9   A SUMMER OUTING

A group of patients from Green Hills Psychiatric Center went on an outing at a nearby park. The group consisted of twelve women, ages 19 to 43, with varying psychiatric diagnoses. Eight suffer from major depression—recurrent, without suicidal precaution. Two have been diagnosed with schizophrenia—undifferentiated. One has an obsessive-compulsive personality disorder and another a post traumatic stress disorder. Two of the women are recovering from anorexia and another woman has epilepsy and her seizures are not totally controlled by medication. All patients were granted a physician approval/release before going on the outing. Six staff accompanied the group: three therapeutic recreation specialists, two nurses, and one mental health technician.

According to documented hospital policy, the department planning the event is responsible for all related decisions. In this instance, the senior therapeutic recreation specialist was in charge of the outing.

It was July and the average temperature for the week was 95 degrees Fahrenheit. The group arrived at the outing site at 10:00 a.m. and everyone helped unload the food and supplies. The group then gathered at a shelter area near the lake. Various recreational activities such as paddleboats, horseshoe pits, and walking trails were located nearby. A group of four patients chose to go paddleboating and were accompanied by two therapeutic recreation specialists who were certified in lifesaving. Three patients played horseshoes nearby with another therapeutic recreation specialist. Three other patients went for a walk on the trails with a nurse. This last group left without indicating how long they would be gone.

Several participants and staff had finished their activities and were ready for lunch by 11:15 a.m. Two psychiatrists working with this group of patients arrived as planned at 11:45 a.m. to join in the picnic, but the group of walkers had not returned.

The entire group became concerned about the patients and nurse who had not returned from walking. Some of the remaining staff, including the two psychiatrists, decided to follow the road next to the walking trail in a van so that they could pick up the group of walkers and return them to the group. The psychiatrists' major concern was that the two patients with anorexia might overtax themselves and suffer serious medical consequences.

The group of walkers was found approximately four and one-half miles down the trail and all were glad for the ride back. One of the patients with anorexia reported dizziness and nausea when she returned to the shelter. The nursing staff checked vital signs and applied a cool compress. A short time later, the entire group of walkers, along with the rest of the group, ate lunch and drank plenty of beverages. After lunch, all patients played either cards or word games and chatted with each other. The group arrived back at the hospital at 2:30 p.m.

No serious problems arose with any of the walkers. All staff, however, understood the seriousness of the incident, and both staff psychiatrists severely reprimanded the nurse accompanying the patients on the walk for using poor judgement.

DISCUSSION QUESTIONS

1. Whose responsibility was it to clarify rules and guidelines for the outing? How should the division of labor between staff have been accomplished?

2. Were there adequate numbers of staff with patients at all times? If not, what would have been the most desirable ratio of staff to patients? What if only one therapeutic recreation specialist and two nursing staff were available for the activity?

3. What considerations should be made when planning such an outing? What was a desirable number of activity options in this instance and how should these have been decided? What would have been an effective method of communicating program planning decisions to the other staff members, including the psychiatrists?

4. What liability issues were involved in the incident of the four patients and one staff member who chose to walk? What is your reaction to the staff psychiatrists reprimanding the nurse?
5. How can a balance between clients' safety and the provision of meaningful community outings be maintained?

IN-CLASS EXERCISES

1. Prepare a risk management plan for this activity. A risk management plan is a set of policies, procedures, and regulations for conducting activities that are based on an analysis of participants, equipment, leaders, sites, conditions, and the activities themselves. Use the following outline to prepare the risk management plan:
    Event:
      Specific Activities:
      Dates and Times:
      Location:
      Conditions:
      Participants (specific characteristics):
      Leaders (age, number, qualifications, experiences):
      Equipment (type, number, condition):
      Supplies (type, number, condition):
      Policies and Procedures:
      Emergency Procedures and Numbers:

Selected References for Case Study

Dzingleski, L. (1987). The basic principles of managing risk. *Journal of Quality Assurance, 11*(Fall), 20-22.

Kibbee, P. (1988). Implementing a risk management program in a psychiatric facility. *Journal of Quality Assurance, 10*(1), 11-14.

Voelkl, J. E. (1988). *Risk management in therapeutic recreation: A component of quality assurance.* State College, PA: Venture Publishing, Inc.

Case 10

ROBERT

In Chapter Two, *Individual Therapeutic Recreation Program Planning*, you considered the case of Robert Wilson, a young adult male with Down's syndrome (p. 74). He currently resides in a transitional living center with five to eight other residents. He hopes to live independently in a community supervised apartment. Robert's strengths and areas of need were discussed in considerable detail in Chapter Two and you will need to review these before beginning the following exercises.

IN-CLASS EXERCISES

1. Develop a transitional plan for Robert to follow as he progresses from living within the center to community-supervised apartment living. Consider the most effective and efficient means to help him achieve his long-term objectives.

DISCUSSION QUESTIONS

1. Robert has progressed so that he is ready for placement in a supervised apartment in the community. A recreation center is within walking distance of the apartments where he will live. The recreation center's staff, though they have recreation degrees, have no experience with people with disabilities similar to Robert's. A planning meeting is set to discuss his transition during which someone from the recreation center will meet with the therapeutic recreation specialist, Robert, and Robert's family. How could the therapeutic recreation specialist help facilitate Robert's integration into community recreation?

ROLE-PLAYING

1. Role-play the situation described in the above discussion question. Students will assume the roles of recreation center director, therapeutic recreation specialist, Robert's mother and father, and Robert.

FIELD EXPERIENCE EXERCISES

1. Invite a community recreation professional(s) to visit class and discuss the issue of including persons with disabilities in generic community recreation programs. Try to ascertain concerns, apprehensions, misconceptions, and barriers, that might hinder successful integration attempts. In addition, try to determine the nature and extent of education/training that might help the community recreation professional to facilitate this process.
2. Visit a community recreation program in which people with disabilities are integrated into programs and services offered to the general public and discuss integration principles and practices.

Selected References for Case Study

Bullock, C. C. and Howe, C. Z. (1991). A model therapeutic recreation program for the reintegration of persons with disabilities into the community. *Therapeutic Recreation Journal, 25*(1), 7-17.

Carter, M. J. (forthcoming). *Designing therapeutic recreation programs in the community.* Reston, VA: American Alliance for Health, Physical Education, Recreation, and Dance.

Rynders, J. and Schleien, S. (1988). Recreation: A promising vehicle for promoting the community integration of young adults with Down's syndrome. In C. Tingey (Ed.), *Down's syndrome: A resource handbook* (pp. 182-198). Boston, MA: Little, Brown, and Company.

Schleien, S., Cameron, J., Rynders, J., and Slick, C.(1988). Acquisition and generalization of leisure skills from school to the home community by learners with severe multihandicaps. *Therapeutic Recreation Journal, 22*(3), 53-71.

Schleien, S. J. and Ray, M. T. (1988). *Community recreation and persons with disabilities: Strategies for integration.* Baltimore, MD: Paul H. Brookes.

Chapter Four

Leadership in Therapeutic Recreation

The implementation phase of individual therapeutic recreation program planning is described as the "make-it-or-break-it" phase that depends heavily on personal and professional skills of therapeutic recreation specialists. As O'Morrow (1980) stated, "There is no substitute for good leadership" (p. 139). These skills deserve additional attention because the quality of leadership is considered by many to be the key to the success of planned recreation interventions.

Understanding Leadership

In keeping with the predominant philosophical orientation of therapeutic recreation presented in Chapter Two, leadership will be defined based on the contributions of Robert Tannenbaum and his collaborators. Tannenbaum and Massarik (1957) define leadership as "interpersonal influence, exercised in situations and directed, through the communication process, toward the attainment of a specified goal or goals " (p. 3). Thus, in a broad sense, leadership in therapeutic recreation means influencing clients toward goal accomplishment.

In their leadership continuum, Tannenbaum and Schmidt (1958) describe a variety of situations and circumstances that could affect the way leaders choose to influence people toward the accomplishment of goals. As depicted in Figure 4.1, the continuum makes it possible for leaders to choose between the autocratic/democratic dichotomy and the task-versus-person orientation relating to McGregor's (1960) Theory X versus Theory Y leadership style.

At one end of the continuum, leaders are authoritarian and task-oriented and exert maximum control while focusing on the task of improving clients' functional abilities. Clients experience a minimum degree of freedom or choice. This style of leadership corresponds to rehabilitation or treatment goals of therapeutic recreation services. At the other end of the continuum, the leadership style is participatory and human relations-oriented, and therapeutic recreation specialists exert minimum control, allowing clients to experience maximum independence and autonomy. Tannenbaum and Schmidt (1958) did not intend to imply that the leadership style at one end of the continuum is better than the leadership style at the other. As clients

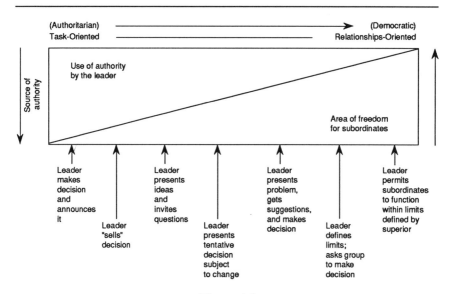

Figure 4.1
Continuum in leadership behavior. From "How to Choose a Leadership
Pattern" by R. Tannenbaum and W. H. Schmidt, 1958, *Harvard Business
Review*, (36)2, p. 95. Copyright 1958 by the President and fellows of Har-
vard College. Reprinted by permission.

progress along the continuum to interdependent leisure functioning, various
combinations of control and freedom will be determined by the: (1) characteristics of clients; (2) situation, i.e., goals clients are trying to accomplish
and the content, processes, and environment being used to achieve them;
and (3) skills, personality, and experiences of therapeutic recreation specialists. In short, changes in leadership style are dictated by clients as they
acquire the knowledge, skills, motivation, and behaviors to choose leisure
lifestyles.

Influencing Change

Planned change requires deliberate action. If therapeutic recreation specialists are to intervene effectively and enable clients to grow and develop, they
first need to recognize their potential as agents of change (Anthony, 1985;
Collingwood, 1972; Howe-Murphy and Charboneau, 1987). As change
agents, therapeutic recreation specialists engage themselves, clients, families, and the community in a process of assessing, planning, implementing,

and evaluating desired invidivual and environmental change. What characteristics must therapeutic recreation specialists possess to function effectively as change agents?

First and foremost, therapeutic recreation specialists must seek both personal and professional self-awareness and clarify their basic values and philosophical underpinnings. They must seek answers to personal questions such as, "Who am I?; How do I deal with my human needs?; What is important to me?; How do I choose to live my life?" If they know themselves, their abilities, and limitations, they will better understand the characteristics relevant to their role as helping professionals. Therapeutic recreation involves cooperative efforts directed at bringing about desired changes in clients and/or their environments. The question is not whether specialists *will* influence change, but rather *how*. To facilitate behavior change, therapeutic recreation specialists must understand clients, whose lives are to be changed, and the medium serving as both the means to and the goal of that change. To maximize self-determination and personal control, therapeutic recreation specialists must possess unwavering belief in the value and dignity of all human life, regardless of individual variation, and an awareness of the interdependence of human beings. In addition, specialists must cherish the meaning, purpose, and value of recreative and leisure experiences in their own and others' lives. The irreplaceable, satisfying human experiences referred to as recreation are vital for achieving and maintaining personal well-being. These experiences also serve as the medium for personal and environmental change.

Improving Helping Techniques

The achievement of a meaningful leisure lifestyle depends heavily on the development of behaviors, skills, and knowledge that enable clients to make choices and to gain full enjoyment and satisfaction from these choices. To help clients develop, therapeutic recreation specialists must be effective communicators and facilitators.

Effectively Communicating

Collective efforts directed toward achieving a desired goal imply communication, which occurs when those involved in the process of change exchange information and ideas, and achieve a common or shared understanding (Austin, 1991). Therefore, ability to communicate effectively is essential if therapeutic recreation specialists are to be successful leaders.

What are some of the skills required for effective communication? Attending, perhaps the most important communication skill and a necessary precondition of the helping relationship (Carkhuff, 1986) involves: (1) personal attentiveness; (2) observing; and (3) listening.

Personal attentiveness can be communicated through various nonverbal behaviors. For example, the therapeutic recreation specialist communicates his interest in the client when he faces her in a relaxed, forward-leaning body position and uses natural eye contact (not an unwavering stare), meaningful gestures such as head nodding and smiling, and animated facial expressions to convey his concentration and interest. These behaviors should be appropriate within the context of the situation and should not be exaggerated (Cormier, Cormier, and Weisser, 1984).

Carkhuff (1986) states that "we learn most of what we need to know about people by *observing* them" (p. 38) and suggests that effective communicators observe individuals' physical, emotional, and intellectual characteristics. For instance, observing body build, posture, and grooming helps ascertain whether a client has a high or low physical energy level, while observing certain postures and behavioral and facial expressions helps determine a client's feelings. As Carkhuff (1986) explains, drooped shoulders and head might indicate "down" feelings while a rigid posture might indicate tension. Slow or overly swift body movements or gestures may also indicate low affect or tension, respectively. Certain facial expressions can convey a variety of emotions such as happiness, anger, interest, or confusion. These same areas—posture, behavior and facial expressions—often provide clues about clients' intellectual readiness. The slouched posture could indicate a lack of readiness for intellectual tasks, while certain facial expressions often convey the level of interest in a task or experience or the ability to concentrate.

One way therapeutic recreation specialists can increase their ability to understand clients' communication is by *listening* carefully to what they say. While it may seem an easy, passive activity, listening is actually hard work and requires intense concentration. Listening improves when leaders know why they are listening, and in the therapeutic recreation process, the main reason for listening is to gather information needed to ameliorate problems and achieve goals. To gather this information, specialists must focus both on the words used by the client and on his tone, volume, and manner of presentation.

Thus, effective listening demands a strong focus on clients, during which therapeutic recreation specialists must try to rid themselves of external and internal distractions. To the extent possible, this means finding a place to interact that is private, and free from excessive noises or visual distractions. Perhaps more important, listening implies "being with" clients psychologically, which means temporarily suspending personal judgements about the information being conveyed, eliminating stereotypes or preconceived beliefs about the client, refusing to be preoccupied with personal concerns, or simply avoiding the tendency to daydream about future plans or tasks.

Certain verbal behaviors, such as "mm-hmm," "I see," "go on," encourage clients' communication and demonstrate continued interest (Cromier, Cromier, and Weisser, 1984). Therapeutic recreation specialists must avoid verbal interruptions or changes in topics that cut off or interfere with a client's expression. And since there may be a propensity for therapeutic recreation specialists to talk too much during personal interactions, silence is often an important aspect of verbal attentiveness. When used with good judgement, silence indicates a willingness to listen, allows communicators to collect their thoughts, and provides time for important observation and reflection.

Learning

Therapeutic recreation specialists work with clients to help them acquire and develop the attitudes, skills, and knowledge necessary to achieve and maintain their own leisure lifestyles. Russell (1986) distinguishes among the following types of learning. *Knowledge* is cognitive learning and includes an understanding of the concepts, information, or abstractions necessary to participate in an activity or experience. *Skill* is psychomotor learning and refers to one's ability to perform or engage in an activity. *Attitude* is affective learning and refers to the feelings that influence one's leisure behavior and preferences. Certain basic principles will help facilitate learning, whether working with individual clients or groups (Flatten, Wilhite, and Reyes-Watson, 1987; Kraus, Carpenter, and Bates, 1981; Russell, 1986).

First, therapeutic recreation specialists must value and support *individual variation*. Effective leaders consider each person individually, recognizing diverse values, interests, and abilities. Personal attentiveness to variations will help specialists select the most appropriate approaches and techniques. To accomodate individual variation, therapeutic recreation specialists should not expect all clients to learn the same things, at the same rate or in the same manner.

Individual variation also implies that clients travel at their own pace and that their readiness for involvement will vary. Some clients will be ready to participate in leisure experiences while others will only go through the motions or will not participate at all. For instance, a client who has been inactive for a long time will require much encouragement and may participate during one activity and not during the next. Therapeutic recreation specialists, in attempting to structure the learning process so that clients will be motivated to seek involvement and self-direction, must meet clients at their current level of readiness and gradually help them move in desired directions. Regardless of specialists' efforts, however, some days will not be successful and efforts to learn will not be fulfilled. In this situation, it may be best to allow clients to be observers, or perhaps, to end the activity early and reschedule for another time.

Second, therapeutic recreation specialists must recognize that clients develop skills through involvement or "*doing.*" Therefore, clients should be involved in learning as early in the therapeutic recreation process as possible. To accomplish this, specialists should limit verbal explanations and use approaches that are multisensory, combining seeing, hearing, touching, smelling, tasting, and moving.

Since practice facilitates learning and the acquisition of skills, repeating activities and practicing skills are important aspects of "doing." Through repetition and practice, specialists guide efforts and make corrections when necessary.

Therapeutic recreation specialists should remember, however, that they are functioning in an enabler role, and carefully determine when and when not to assist. In the therapeutic recreation process, the ultimate leadership goal is to help clients recognize their own capacities and encourage them to assume greater responsibility for and control over their lives in general and their leisure in particular.

A related principle pertains to meaningfulness. A client's involvement is stimulated as he becomes aware of the personal relevance of the experience. His learning will be enhanced when he realizes the personal benefits to be gained through involvement and when he is encouraged to seek those activities and experiences most likely to provide the benefits he desires. Here planning "with" and not "for" clients is all-important. Experiences are meaningful when clients help determine, to the extent possible, the content of the experience and the processes used to engage in the experience.

The third area is *constructive feedback and positive reinforcement.* Feedback reinforces learning. Clients need support and encouragement when they are performing as desired, as well as when they are not. Therapeutic recreation specialists must recognize the importance of attempts to learn and acknowledge them with comments that enable clients to make necessary corrections while still appreciating their progress. For some clients, it is important for specialists to recognize partial success and reinforce all behavior that can be interpreted as an approximation of the desired activity (Crawford and Mendell, 1987). Specialists should use their best judgement when providing positive reinforcement, however. Overpraising or praising something that obviously did not turn out well is belittling and provides inaccurate feedback from which to determine progress. Clients' efforts should be acknowledged realistically.

A crucial component of providing feedback and reinforcement is the determination of realistic expectations. A person with a disability, because she may have experienced failure more often than her nondisabled peer, may have learned to expect to fail in new situations or experiences and needs opportunities to experience success relative to the new leisure interests and skills she is developing. Yet, she also needs to realize that regardless of best efforts, "success" in an experience or activity may not be achieved quickly.

Selected Teaching Strategies

As functional behaviors improve, clients move beyond the treatment component of therapeutic recreation service into leisure education, the services of which are intended to develop social interaction, recreation activity skills, knowledge of and ability to use leisure resources, and attitudes necessary for interdependent leisure participation (Dixon, 1988; Peterson and Gunn, 1984). Therapeutic recreation specialists must determine teaching strategies that are most effective in the development and acquisition of these new skills and knowledge areas. Examples of teaching strategies are discussed in the following paragraphs.

Task Analysis

Teaching or presenting an activity is aided by a technique known as task analysis: the breaking down of a recreation activity into all the necessary parts or steps and sequencing the steps for appropriate interactions within the activity. Task analysis gives a precise description, in observable and measurable terms, of each response or skill that is required to participate in an activity.

Task analysis is associated with a procedure known as *chaining*, which links the individual parts or steps. *Forward chaining* occurs when the steps are arranged and taught from the first to the last step. In *backward chaining*, the last step is listed and taught first and the steps are arranged from last to first (Crawford and Mendell, 1987; Dixon, 1988; Wehman and Schleien, 1981; Walls, Haught, and Dowler, 1982; Wuerch and Voeltz, 1982).

If a particular step in a sequence is not being performed well, therapeutic recreation specialists may break that step into a further sequence of steps, a procedure referred to as *branching*. The new sequence of steps or branch can be performed within the total sequence or can be practiced in isolation. If the branch is practiced in isolation, the step is then integrated with the total sequence after it has been mastered by the client (Gaylord-Ross and Holvoet, 1985).

Task analysis provides therapeutic recreation specialists with detailed knowledge of what clients must learn to do, step by step, in order to accomplish the activity objective. It also allows specialists to individualize their presentation by developing a skill sequence appropriate for each client.

Leader Assistance

Teaching or leading involves a combination of physical (tactile guidance), visual (e.g., modeling, gestures, diagrams), and verbal (auditory) prompts. In other words, therapeutic recreation specialists can "tell" individuals what to do, "show" them what to do, "physically help" them perform the activity, or use a combination of these prompts (Walls, Ellis, Zane, and VanderPoel, 1979). Clients and situations vary, calling for the use of various prompts, such as physical or verbal cues, gestures, directions, examples, demonstrations, and guidance. Therapeutic recreation specialists should experiment with these prompting methods to discover the ones which will facilitate successful client participation. Decisions regarding when and how much to prompt a client depend on both the individual and situation. In general, however, a client should be allowed to perform as much of the task as possible and should be provided with a minimum amount of assistance. Gradually, more restrictive prompts can be replaced with less restrictive ones.

Assistance may also be provided by peers or family members. Peer interactive approaches may include peer tutors, peer buddies, and/or special friends (Brimer, 1990). *Peer tutors* assist therapeutic recreation specialists by teaching specific skills, recording clients' progress, or attempting to modify certain behaviors. *Peer buddies* interact socially with clients, but still assume primary responsibility for directing the activities in which both are taking part. In contrast, *special friends* emphasize friendship, leisure integration, and social interaction on an equal basis.

Leadership Issues

Therapeutic recreation specialists encourage clients to develop self-awareness and to assume responsibility for meeting their leisure needs and desires. But certain transactions among specialists, clients, families, and the environment may negatively affect clients' self-awareness and self-responsibility. Some leadership issues that therapeutic recreation specialists should consider are dependency, learned helplessness, and self-fulfilling prophecy.

Dependency

All individuals in a therapeutic helping relationship may naturally feel a certain amount of dependency on the therapeutic recreation specialist (Cormier, et al., 1984; Egan, 1985), and people with serious illnesses or severe disabilities may experience feelings of dependency to an even greater extent. Kutner (1971) suggests a certain amount of dependency is important to successful intervention since positive change will more readily occur when clients allow themselves to be influenced by those involved in the intervention. If, however, clients become too dependent, they may avoid accepting personal responsibility for meeting their needs and thus delay progress toward optimal interdependent leisure functioning. Unfortunately, therapeutic recreation specialists, through efforts to support and nurture clients and their families and friends, may unintentionally foster overdependence. Clients may be psychologically attracted to this dependency state because of the attention they receive and the release from self-responsibility they experience. Moreover, therapeutic recreation specialists may be psychologically attracted to this type of relationship because it satisfies needs for acceptance, power, control, usefulness, and importance. If dependency is allowed to continue, clients learn to be helpless, relying on others rather than on themselves (Austin, 1991). Therapeutic recreation specialists must be aware of clients' dependency issues so that they help clients meet their needs in ways which positively affect personal growth and development.

Learned Helplessness

It is not uncommon for individuals receiving therapeutic recreation services initially to feel helpless. The nature of specific disabilities, the suddenness of their onset or the unpredictability of their manifestations, clients' personalities, and society's reaction to the disability may all contribute to a feeling that there is nothing clients can do about the situation. It is important for therapeutic recreation specialists to realize that this feeling of helplessness is learned through certain transactions between clients and their environments (Iso-Ahola, 1980; Seligman, 1975). Clients may perceive unsuccessful transactions as resulting from a lack of ability and come to believe that efforts cannot engender success. Therapeutic recreation specialists' responsibility is to maximize clients' abilities and the supportive properties of various environments so that they can develop feelings of competence rather than feelings of inadequacy. Therapeutic recreation content and process should allow for maximum client input, decision making, and choice so that clients can increase personal control and cease to feel helpless.

Therapeutic recreation specialists must also help clients recognize and accept the limiting realities of their particular illnesses or disabilities, primarily by making them realize that in everyone's life there are events and situations which can be controlled and those which cannot. The development of realistic goals of intervention will help clients identify abilities as well as limitations.

Self-Fulfilling Prophecy

Earlier in this chapter we stated that therapeutic recreation specialists should not question whether they *will* influence change, but rather *how*. This idea is clearly demonstrated in the self-fulfilling prophecy, a concept based on the belief that clients will, within reason, exhibit the behaviors expected of them. Much of clients' identity and thus their behaviors are based on how they are treated by others. If therapeutic recreation specialists expect them to fail, they may find it extremely difficult to succeed. On the other hand, if specialists recognize and encourage clients' ability for personal growth, they are more likely to achieve desired behavioral changes.

Summary

Therapeutic recreation specialists, because they are almost always involved in working directly with the recipients of their services, must establish and maintain cooperative relationships with clients, families, caregivers, volunteers, and community representatives. Understanding the importance of leadership and learning about effective helping strategies will enable specialists to have a positive effect on outcomes. The process of assessing, planning, and implementing individualized therapeutic recreation services is only as valuable as it is successful. Evaluation is needed to determine whether the services were implemented as planned and whether they accomplished what they intended to accomplish. Evaluation is discussed in Chapter Five, *Evaluation in Therapeutic Recreation.*

Bibliography

Anthony, P. (1985). The recreation practitioner as change agent and advocate for disabled persons. *Leisurability, 12*, 19-23.

Austin, D. R. (1991). *Therapeutic recreation: Processes and techniques.* (2nd ed.). Champaign, IL: Sagamore.

Brimer, R. W. (1990). *Students with severe disabilities: Current perspectives and practices.* Mountain View, CA: Mayfield.

Carkhuff, R. R. (1986). *The art of helping* (5th ed.). Amherst, MA: Human Resource Development.

Collingwood, T. R. (1972). The recreation leader as a therapeutic agent. *Therapeutic Recreation Journal, 6*(4) , 147-52.

Cormier, L. S., Cormier, W. H., and Weisser, R. J. (1984). *Interviewing and helping skills for health professionals.* Monterey, CA: Wadsworth Health Sciences.

Crawford, M. E. and Mendell, R. (1987). *Therapeutic recreation and adapted physical activities for mentally retarded individuals.* Englewood Cliffs, NJ: Prentice-Hall.

D'Augelli, A. R., D'Augelli, J. F., and Danish, S. J. (1981). *Helping others.* Monterey, CA: Brooks/Cole.

Dixon, J. T. (1988). The development of an effective therapeutic recreation program. In A. H. Fine and N. M. Fine, *Therapeutic recreation for exceptional children: Let me in, I want to play* (pp. 98-141). Springfield, IL: Charles C. Thomas.

Edginton, C. R. and Ford, P. M. (1985). *Leadership in recreation and leisure service organizations.* New York, NY: John Wiley.

Egan, G. (1985). *The skilled helper: A model for systematic helping and interpersonal relating.* Belmont, CA: Wadsworth.

Flatten, K., Wilhite, B., and Reyes-Watson. (1987). *Recreation activities for the elderly.* New York, NY: Springer.

Gaylord-Ross, R. J. and Holvoet, J. F. (1985). *Strategies for educating students with severe handicaps.* Boston, MA: Little, Brown, and Company.

Howe-Murphy, R. and Charboneau, B. G. (1987). *Therapeutic recreation intervention: An ecological perspective.* Englewood Cliffs, NJ: Prentice-Hall.

Iso-Ahola, S. E. (1980). *The social psychology of leisure and recreation.* Dubuque, IA: Wm. C. Brown.

Keller, M. J. (1984). Activity personnel as professional helpers. *Activities, Adaptations, and Aging, 4*(4), 51-60.

Kraus, R. G., Carpenter, G., and Bates, B. J. (1981). *Recreation leadership and supervision* (2nd ed.). Philadelphia, PA: Saunders.

Kutner, B. (1971). The social psychology of disability. In W. S. Neff (Ed.), *Rehabilitation Psychology* (pp. 143-167). Washington, DC: American Psychological Association.

McGregor, D. (1960). *The human side of enterprise.* New York: McGraw-Hill.

O'Morrow, G. S. (1980). *Therapeutic recreation: A helping profession* (2nd ed.). Englewood Cliffs, NJ: Prentice-Hall.

Peterson, C. A. and Gunn, S. L. (1984). *Therapeutic recreation program design: Principles and practices* (2nd ed.). Englewood Cliffs, NJ: Prentice-Hall.

Russell, R. V. (1986). *Planning programs in recreation.* St. Louis, MO: C. V. Mosby.

Russell, R. V. (1982). *Leadership in recreation.* St. Louis, MO: Times Mirror/Mosby.

Schmuck, R. A. and Schmuck, P. A. (1975). *Group processes in the classroom* (2nd ed.). Dubuque, IA: Wm. C. Brown.

Seligman, M. E. P. (1975). *Helplessness: On depression, development, and death.* San Francisco, CA: Freeman.

Tannenbaum, R. and Massarik, F. (1957). Leadership: A frame of reference. *Management Science, 4*(1), 1-19.

Tannenbaum, R. and Schmidt, W. H. (1958). How to choose a leadership pattern. *Harvard Business Review, 36*(2), 95-101.

Walls, R. T., Ellis, W. D., Zane, T. and VanderPoel, S. J. (1979). Tactile, auditory, and visual prompting in teaching complex assembly tasks. *Education and Training of the Mentally Retarded, 14*, 120-130.

Walls, R. T., Haught, P. A., and Dowler, D. L. (1982). *How to train new skills: Planning, teaching, evaluating.* Dunbar, WV: West Virginia Rehabilitation Research and Training Center.

Wehman, P. and Schleien, S. (1981). *Leisure programs for handicapped persons: Adaptations, techniques, and curriculum.* Austin, TX: PRO-ED.

Wuerch, B. B. and Voeltz, L. M. (1982). *Longitudinal leisure skills for severely handicapped learners: The Ho'onanea curriculum component.* Baltimore, MD: Paul H. Brookes.

Suggested Readings

Amato, P. R. (1985).   An investigation of planned helping behavior. *Journal of Research in Personality, 19,* 232-252.

Ambrose, J. A. (1989). Joining in: Therapeutic groups for chronic patients. *Journal of Psychosocial Nursing, 27*(11), 28-32.

Austin, D. R. and Crawford, M. E. (Eds.). (1991). *Therapeutic recreation: An introduction.* Englewood Cliffs, NJ: Prentice-Hall.

Beck-Ford, V., Brown, R. I., Gillberry, M., and Rolf, C. (1984). *Leisure training and rehabilitation.* Springfield, IL: Charles C. Thomas.

Bender, M., Brannan, S. A., and Verhoven, P. J. (1984). *Leisure education for the handicapped: Curriculum goals, activities, and resources.* San Diego, CA: College-Hill.

Burnside, I. M. (1984).   *Working with the elderly: Group process and techniques.* Monterey, CA: Wadsworth Health Sciences.

Farran, C. J. and Keane-Hagerty (1989). Communicating effectively with dementia patients. *Journal of Psychosocial Nursing, 27,* 13-16.

Fine, A. H. (1988). The goal of leisure within the schools. In A. H. Fine and N. M. Fine, *Therapeutic recreation for exceptional children: Let me in, I want to play* (pp. 255-281). Springfield, IL: Charles C. Thomas.

Lowenthal, B. (1986). The power of suggestion. *Academic Therapy, 21*(5), 537-541.

O'Leary, A. (1985). Self-efficacy and health. *Behaviour Research and Therapy, 23*(4), 437-451.

Purcell, B. and Keller, M. J. (1989). Characteristics of leisure activities which may lead to leisure satisfaction among older adults. *Activities, Adaptations and Aging, 13*(4), 17-29.

Romer, D. and Heller, T. (1984). Importance of peer relations in community settings for mentally retarded adults. In J. M. Berg (Ed.), *Perspectives and programs in mental retardation* (pp. 99-107). Austin, TX: PRO-ED.

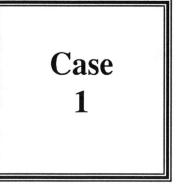

Case 1

AMANDA

In Chapter Three, *Implementing Individual Therapeutic Recreation Program Plans*, you were concerned with Amanda's physical and psychological needs (p. 95). As a ten year old sixth grader with epilepsy, she is attending a residential camp for the first time. Although she has not had a seizure in six months, she is anxious about the thought of recurring seizures.

DISCUSSION QUESTIONS

1. What is the significance of family, friends, and society accepting physical illnesses or disabilities more readily than the condition of epilepsy?

IN-CLASS EXERCISES

1. Ask an authority on epilepsy and several persons with epilepsy to host a panel discussion on how to effectively lead recreation activities with people who have epilepsy.

ROLE-PLAYING

1. Role-play Amanda's interaction with her roommate during the biweekly group discussion. As the therapeutic recreation specialist serving as the facilitator for the group session, what specific helping techniques would you employ?

Selected References for Case Study

Cowart, V. S. (1986). Should epileptics exercise? *Physician and Sports-medicine*, *14*(9), 183-184, 187, 190-191.

Manelis, J., Bloch, D., and Fell, Z. (1986). The epileptic adolescent. *International Journal of Adolescent Medicine and Health*, 2(3), 163-168.

Murphy, P. (1987). Children with medical conditions can go to summer camp. *Physician and Sportsmedicine*, *15*(7), 177-179, 183.

Case 2

BENJAMIN

You were introduced to Benjamin, age nine, in Chapter Two, *Individual Therapeutic Recreation Program Planning* (p. 59). He was having difficulty controlling his temper, refused to complete homework, would not accept parental disciplinary actions, and refused to eat at mealtimes. He was referred to the Center for Comprehensive Psycho-Educational Services in order to determine the nature of his behavioral difficulties. As the Center's therapeutic recreation specialist, you participated in the development of a program plan for Benjamin.

DISCUSSION QUESTIONS

1. Review the list of Benjamin's strengths and areas of need that you developed in Chapter Two. Did you regard Benjamin's level of self-confidence and perception of helplessness to be a strength or an area of need? Why? In either case, what

leadership techniques would you use to build his self-confidence/self-esteem and help him avoid feelings of help-lessness?

2. How would an increase in Benjamin's perceived personal control enhance his overall well-being? As a leader, how would you structure Benjamin's recreation participation so that his perception of personal control and freedom is fostered?

3. What unresolved issues or conflicts exist between Benjamin's parents and himself? Could family participation in recreation activities contribute to the resolution of these issues? If so, what leadership approaches/techniques would you employ to help Mr. and Mrs. Johnson prepare for this type of family involvement?

Selected References for Case Study

Duncan, K., Beck, D. L., and Granum, R. A. (1988). Project Explore: An activity-based counseling group. *School Counselor, 35*(3), 215-219.

Monroe, J. E. (1987). Family leisure programming. *Therapeutic Recreation Journal, 21*(3), 44-51.

Orthner, D. K. and Herron, R. W. (1984). Leisure counseling for families. In E. T. Dowd (Ed.), *Leisure counseling: Concepts and applications* (pp. 178-197). Springfield, IL: Charles C. Thomas.

Rios, D. W. (1978). Leisure education and counseling with severely emotionally disturbed children. *Therapeutic Recreation Journal, 12*(2), 30-34.

Volger, E. W., Fenstermacher, G., and Bishop, P. (1982). Group-oriented behavior management systems to control disruptive behavior in therapeutic recreation settings. *Therapeutic Recreation Journal, 16*(1), 20-24.

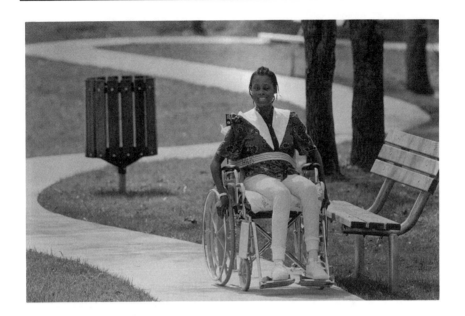

Case 3

CORA

In Chapter Two, *Individual Therapeutic Recreation Program Planning*, you developed an individual therapeutic recreation program plan for Cora (p. 68). Cora has since completed her inpatient substance abuse treatment program and has returned home. She is now receiving outpatient treatment.

ROLE-PLAYING

1. Role-play Cora and her friends as they attend a party. Cora enjoys dancing, but her friends pressure her to have a beer. ("After all, just one beer can't possibly hurt you.")

DISCUSSION QUESTIONS

1. As an outpatient, Cora attends group leisure education sessions led by a therapeutic recreation specialist and during one session, Cora discusses the above scenario. What are the possible positive and negative outcomes of the scenario? How would the therapeutic recreation specialist and other group members help Cora identify possible courses of action? What techniques would you use to help Cora identify an appropriate response? What resources should Cora use to help her handle similar scenarios?

Suggested References for Case Study

Faulkner, R. W. (1991). *Therapeutic recreation protocol for treatment of substance addictions.* State College, PA: Venture Publishing, Inc.

Francis, T. (1991). Revising therapeutic recreation for substance misuse: Incorporating flow technology in alternatives treatment. *Therapeutic Recreation Journal, 25* (2), pp. 41-48.

O'Dea-Evans, P. (1990). *Leisure education for addicted persons.* Algonquin, IL: Peapod.

Case 4

JANICE

Janice, a 15 year old white female hospitalized for the first time with a diagnosis of dysthymic disorder, has been referred by her physician to participate in an adventure group. Activities undertaken by this group include initiative problems as well as low and high ropes course elements, activities that Janice's physician believes are important for adolescents struggling with group acceptance and self-esteem, major problem areas for Janice. While the therapeutic recreation specialist recognizes the need for developing an enhanced sense of interrelatedness and group acceptance, Janice's obesity and lack of strength limit her involvement in the adventure group, and the therapeutic recreation specialist thinks the adventure activities will exacerbate Janice's perception of herself as "different" from other participants. Thus, the therapeutic recreation specialist does not assign Janice to the adventure group.

Both the physician and the therapeutic recreation specialist share their convictions with the treatment team.

DISCUSSION QUESTIONS

1. In a generic sense, what types of activities/experiences are valuable for adolescents in psychiatric treatment to (1) develop social/interactive skills and (2) enhance self-esteem/confidence?
2. Develop pro and con rationales for recommending the following activities for Janice:
    a. aerobics,
    b. swimming,
    c. expressive writing,
    d. weight training,
    e. assertiveness training, and
    f. team sports.
3. Keeping in mind your responses to questions one and two, discuss the notion that "activities that are powerful enough to help are also powerful enough to hurt!"

ROLE-PLAYING

1. Role-play the treatment team meeting during which the physician and the therapeutic recreation specialist express their opinions on Janice's involvement with the adventure group. A social worker, nurse, and counselor are also present and are involved in the discussion. What might the outcomes of this meeting be?

FIELD EXPERIENCES

1. Find out who sponsors or facilitates adventure programs in your community and make arrangements to participate.
2. Invite an adventure program facilitator to class to discuss these activities and provide feedback regarding Janice's case.

Selected References for Case Study

Davis, J. (1976). Valuing: A requisite for education for leisure. *Leisure Today/Journal of Physical Education and Recreation*, (March), 6-7.

Kottman, T. T., Strother, J., and Deniger, M. M. (1987). Activity therapy: An alternative therapy for adolescents. *Journal of Humanistic Education and Development*, 25(4), 180-186.

McKenzie, T. L. (1986). A behaviorally-oriented residential camping program for obese children and adolescents. *Education and Treatment of Children*, 9(1), 67-78.

Case 5

JIM

Jim Lowe, a 16 year old white male, was recently admitted to a private day treatment psychiatric center with a diagnosis of adjustment disorder with an anxious mood. A major factor in Jim's diagnosis was the physical and verbal abuse he received from his father for the last ten years.

The therapeutic recreation specialist and a counselor co-lead a communication skill group for adolescents. During a session concerned with self-disclosure and trust, a group of nine patients is involved in a trust circle activity in which each individual, in turn, assumes a position in the center of the other participants, closes his eyes, falls backward and trusts the group to catch him and gently pass him around the circle for a brief period. The activity goes well for the first four participants, but when Jim is asked to take the center position he states, "I'd rather not." The counselor responds, "Jim, you must do it or have your privileges restricted." Jim again refuses and the counselor escorts him away from the group. As they leave, several group members turn to the therapeutic recreation specialist and complain that the restriction is quite unfair. One participant comments, "He's been abused all his life so why should he let people touch him?" Another participant says, "I'm not going to participate in anything until Jim gets a fair deal." A third states, "I think we should just forget about this group for today." The therapeutic recreation specialist says, "Let's talk about this."

DISCUSSION QUESTIONS

1. Was this the most effective way of handling the situation with Jim? What are possible consequences of the counselor's actions? What are alternate approaches to handling the situation with Jim?
2. Discuss group process as it relates to this specific situation, and more specifically, how it influences leadership styles and approaches.
3. Discuss the efficacy of "lowest common denominator programming." This term refers to the technique of considering individual limitations/fears/weaknesses and trying to accomodate each individual when selecting activity content and process. Does this approach tend to "water things down" too much for other group members?

IN-CLASS EXERCISES

1. Write a progress note which describes Jim's behavior in the above scenario. Pay attention to both content and technical accuracy.

ROLE-PLAYING

1. Role-play and then discuss the following situations:
   a. The therapeutic recreation specialist's talk with the remaining participants;

   b. The therapeutic recreation specialist's discussion with
       the counselor which occurs at the request of the thera-
       peutic recreation specialist;
   c. The therapeutic recreation specialist's talk with Jim
       later that day; and
   d. The therapeutic recreation specialist's report of the
       incident to her immediate supervisor.

Selected References for Case Study

Hargie, O., Saunders, C., and Dickson, D. (1987). *Social skills in interpersonal communication* (2nd ed.). Cambridge, MA: Brookline Books.

Kaplan, H. I. and Sadock, B. J. (1988). *Clinical psychiatry*. Baltimore,
MD: Williams and Wilkins.

Posthuma, B. W. (1989). *Small groups in therapy settings: Process and
leadership*. Boston, MA: College-Hill.

Case 6

JOE

Joe Sizeman, a 38 year old white male, has been admitted to a private acute psychiatric hospital with a diagnosis of alcohol abuse. During his first few days of treatment, an additional diagnosis of major depression was added.

Joe was referred to the therapeutic recreation specialist for assessment and assignment to recreation programs. He was cooperative during the interview process, completed fully the therapeutic recreation questionnaire, and discussed openly his difficulties with communication, stress, and time management. The therapeutic recreation specialist recommended relaxation training, assertiveness training, and stress management groups. She also encouraged him to take part in the walking program and open gym. Since Joe's hospitalization will probably be limited to 21 days, the therapeutic recreation specialist recommended that Joe begin participating in these activities immediately.

After hearing the recommendation that he begin participating immediately, Joe became uncooperative. He stated, "I've already got something to do everyday. Alcohol is the reason I'm here so I just want to work on that." When the therapeutic recreation specialist further explained the value of the activities, Joe retorted, "You're not a doctor so why should I listen to you?" and left the room. The therapeutic recreation specialist reported the encounter to staff members on Joe's unit.

Later, Joe began participating in the relaxation group. During Joe's second scheduled relaxation session, the group facilitator introduced imagery as a modality and five minutes into the exercise Joe stood up and announced that this is a "stupid activity" and the therapeutic recreation specialist didn't explain this part to him. He then stormed out of the room.

DISCUSSION QUESTIONS

1. What leadership approaches/strategies might spark Joe's interest and motivate him to participate in therapeutic recreation activities?
2. What steps might the therapeutic recreation specialist take if Joe continues to resist program involvement?
3. Could the incident which occurred during the relaxation session have been prevented with better team planning and communication? Explain your answer.
4. How could the therapeutic recreation specialist have better prepared Joe for this experience?

IN-CLASS EXERCISES

1. Write a progress note or report which documents Joe's behavior during the relaxation sesssion.

ROLE-PLAYING

1. Role-play the incident which occurred during the relaxation session. Demonstrate how the facilitator might explain Joe's outburst to the rest of the group and then resume the activity.

2. What specific leadership approach(es) might be taken in the
    meeting between Joe and the therapeutic recreation specialist
    that occurs after the incident described in the relaxation ses-
    sion. Role-play this meeting with a classmate and discuss the
    appropriateness of the leadership approaches selected.

FIELD EXPERIENCES

1. Attend an Alcoholics Anonymous (AA) meeting in your com-
    munity.

Selected References for Case Study

Harris, G. A. and Watkins, D. (1987). *Counseling the involuntary and
resistant client.* College Park, MD: American Correctional Association.

Hazelden Educational Materials. (1985). *Now what do I do for fun?* Center
City, MN: Author.

Kaplan, H. I. and Sadock, B. J. (1988). *Clinical psychiatry.* Baltimore,
MD: Williams and Wilkins.

Kunstler, R. (1991). Substance abuse. In D. R. Austin and M. E. Crawford
(Eds.), *Therapeutic recreation: An introduction* (pp. 119-137). Englewood Cliffs, NJ: Prentice-Hall.

Case 7

JOHN

Cushing Hall, a locked 24 bed unit of
Rockingham County Hospital, is primar-
ily a long term rehabilitation unit that focuses on behavioral management.
The average length of stay is eighteen months, with a range of stay from

twelve to twenty-four months. The rehabilitation program is provided through individual and group treatment in cognitive remediation, therapeutic recreation, occupational and physical therapy, and rehabilitation counseling. John, a white male of medium build, was a high school sophomore with no significant medical problems when he was involved in a motor vehicle accident. He sustained a mild head injury with a thirty minute loss of consciousness and a temporal parietal laceration. He was hospitalized overnight and subsequently returned to school where he performed above average academically and successfully played on the high school basketball team. Several months following the motor vehicle accident, however, he became increasingly withdrawn, and two years later, his academic performance deteriorated to the point that he barely graduated from high school.

In the fall following his graduation, because of behavioral deterioration and social withdrawal, he was admitted to a psychiatric hospital. During this first admission a CT scan produced normal results. He underwent three other brief hospitalizations during the two years following graduation from high school. On his third admission to a psychiatric hospital he was diagnosed as suffering from undifferentiated schizophrenia and was treated with antipsychotic medications. Unwilling to accept the diagnosis of schizophrenia, John's mother sought out other medical opinions. During this time several specialists examined John and he was hospitalized for brief periods. On one occasion, John's behavioral deterioration was said to result from brain damage caused by the motor vehicle accident, and his antipsychotic medication was discontinued at that time. But John's condition worsened and shortly after, the medication was resumed.

In the following years, John was placed in several institutions, including both rehabilitation and psychiatric facilities. It appeared that at least part of the cause for multiple and varied hospitalizations was his mother's inability to accept John's deficiencies and her apparent frustration with the inability of the medical community to cure him. At times during these years, John lived at home with his mother and there were several episodes of his wandering and throwing objects at passing cars and people. When his mother tried to manage this behavior by locking him in the house, John responded by throwing objects and engaging in behavior that damaged personal property. His mother also reported that he occupied his time by smoking continuously and engaging in ritualistic behaviors such as toilet flushing, hand washing, and showering. Ten years following the motor vehicle accident, after assaulting a stranger who was passing by in front of his home, John was admitted to Cushing Hall with a dual diagnosis of schizophrenia and status post traumatic head injury. John's medications include Trilafon, Benedryl, and Tegretol.

John is an ambulatory man of medium height and 25 pounds over-weight. He is socially withdrawn and demonstrates lack of purposeful behavior (occupies time lying on bed or pacing hallways). His affect is blunted. Though he is occasionally able to respond to close ended questions, he generally does not speak in phrases of more than four or five consecutive words. At times, he can be directed and can engage in brief one-to-two-step tasks. His attention span is less than ten minutes and typically, after ten minutes, he will wander from the area and will not respond to verbal cues to return. Occasionally he throws objects and there are unprovoked assaults on staff.

Primarily, treatment at Cushing Hall occurs within the context of a group, and clients participate in five to six structured group sessions per day. Given John's social withdrawal and inability to attend, he is unsuccessful in participating in most of the group sessions. When he does attend a group, active participation is minimal, and after three to ten minutes he wanders from the room. Because of a low staff-to-client ratio, there is little time available for one-to-one treatment on a consistent basis. Therefore, much of John's time is unstructured.

John's mother, his most present natural support, lives nearby, visits frequently, and attends a weekly meeting with the clinical social worker. She continues to have difficulty accepting the diagnosis of schizophrenia and has extreme difficulty accepting her son's current level of functioning. She blames staff and manipulates caregivers. Although the social worker has discussed with John's mother the importance of her supporting John's treatment program, she has repeatedly acted in ways which sabotage the plan. This inability to create a cohesive environment for John is demonstrated in the way she uses her visits with John off the unit. John likes food and is unable to judge how much to consume. Although his mother is aware of his weight problem, caused by his inability to regulate his food consumption, and of his lack of an exercise program, he frequently overeats during these visits with his mother and subsequently emesis occurs.

After one month at Cushing Hall, and upon the completion of the therapeutic recreation assessment, various observations were noted regarding John's leisure behavior, interests, and abilities. John is most successful when he engages in the following recreation activities: walking, basketball, Frisbee™, football, using a rowing machine and stationary bicycle, gardening, and soccer. With cues and assistence from staff, he will also engage in painting, working with wood, and looking at magazines. He is most successful remaining in groups that are motoric in nature (e.g., exercise, painting) and has great difficulty attending language-based groups on a consistent basis. He is able to tolerate attendance in a group for the duration of the activity if the group is held outside, but the photosensitivity of his medications requires monitoring. John's present individual therapeutic recreation program plan focuses on attendance and participation in exercise and motoric groups in which he will be most successful. Treatment also focuses on increasing his attention to task. He is involved in a one-to-one weightlifting program to further develop his recreation skills and to determine his ability to learn through repetition and modeling. The therapeutic recreation specialist is also involved in leisure education sessions with John's mother to identify activities and strategies for successful participation in activities other than dining out with John.

It is expected that John will remain at Cushing Hall for 12 to 18 months to stabilize his behavior and increase his ability to engage in purposeful behavior, after which time he will probably be discharged to a less restrictive setting.

DISCUSSION QUESTIONS

1. Identify John's strengths as well as areas of need and discuss how they influence leadership decisions.

2. Recognizing that the structure for providing therapeutic recreation services at Cushing Hall is primarily that of a group format, discuss the leadership dilemma that occurs when a client's treatment needs do not conform to a group format. What can be done in this situation?

3. What issues of dependency, learned helplessness, self-fulfilling prophecy, and control are involved with John's situation? How do these issues apply to leading therapeutic recreation services with John?

4. Given the therapeutic recreation staff resources of Rockingham County Hospital, it is impossible to provide the comprehensive individual one-to-one treatment that John requires. What dilemmas does this raise for the therapeutic recreation staff? Discuss possible resolutions to these dilemmas.

5. What leadership issues are raised by John's medication (e.g., side effects, precautions) when participating in recreation activities? How would you deal with these concerns?

6. The leisure education sessions with John's mother are critical to shaping the social environment in which John is most actively involved. Identify and develop strategies for off-unit trips with John and his mother?

ROLE-PLAYING

1. Now that you have some strategies for how to engage the mother in more productive leisure experiences with her son, role-play a leisure education session with John's mother. Discuss with her the issue of involvement in alternative activities. Remember she is resistant to suggestions by clinical staff. She also has great difficulty in recognizing and accepting her son's deficiencies and blames you for some of them.

IN-CLASS EXERCISES

1. Invite therapeutic recreation specialists from county or state mental health facilities to respond with the class to the discussion questions related to John's case.

Selected References for Case Study

Bean, P. (1983). *Mental illness: Changes and trends*. New York, NY: John Wiley.

McLean, A., Temkin, N. R., Dikmens, S., and Wyler, A. R. (1983). The behavioral sequelae of head injury. *Journal of Clinical Neuropsychology*, *5*, (4), 361-376.

Snyder, S. H. (1980). *Biological aspects of mental disorder*. New York, NY: Oxford University Press.

Talbott, J. (Ed.). (1981). *The chronic mentally ill: Treatment, program systems*. Port Washington, NY: Human Science Press.

Torrey, F. E. (1983). *Surviving schizophrenia: A family manual*. New York, NY: Harper and Row.

Case 8

LAURIE

Laurie, five years old, has been admitted to the hospital for a heart valve repair. You were introduced to her case in Chapter Two, *Individual Therapeutic Recreation Program Planning* (p. 70).

DISCUSSION QUESTIONS

1. Laurie's mother is concerned because Laurie's older sister, Sarah, is jealous of the attention Laurie is receiving while hospitalized. She shares this concern with you, the therapeutic recreation specialist. How would you respond to the mother's concern and what type of support might you offer to her? To Laurie? To Sarah?
2. What type of leadership approach might you use that would foster Laurie's expression of her fears and anxieties? What types of leadership approaches could be used to help Laurie reduce her fears and anxious feelings?

ROLE-PLAYING

1. Role-play a preoperative play session including the therapeutic recreation specialist, Laurie, Sarah, and their parents. Ask a therapeutic recreation or child life specialist to critique the experience with the class.

IN-CLASS EXERCISES

1. Write a progress note based on the events of the above role-play. The progress note should include subjective and objective information, assessment, planning, and evaluation statements.

Selected References for Case Study

Froelich, M. A. (1984). A comparison of the effect of music therapy and medical play therapy on the verbalization behavior of pediatric patients. *Journal of Music Therapy, 21*(1), 2-15.

Lobato, D. J. (1990). *Brothers, sisters, and special needs: Information and activities for helping young siblings of children with chronic illnesses and developmental disabilities.* Baltimore, MD: Paul H. Brookes.

Melamed, B. G. and Ridley-Johnson, R. (1988). Psychological preparation of families for hospitalization. *Journal of Developmental and Behavioral Pediatrics, 9*(2), 96-102.

Zastowny, T. R., Kirschenbaum, D. S., and Meng, A. L. (1986). Coping skills training for children: Effects on distress before, during, and after socialization for surgery. *Health Psychology, 37*(9), 941-942.

Case 9

EDITH

Edith Miller has Alzheimer's disease and has been in an intermediate care facility for three years. You were introduced to her case in Chapter One, *Assessment in Therapeutic Recreation* (p. 31); you developed goals and objectives for her in Chapter Two, *Individual Therapeutic Recreation Program Planning* (p. 72); and you dealt with concerns that arose during implementation in Chapter Three, *Implementing Individual Therapeutic Recreation Program Plans* (p. 109). Now, as the therapeutic recreation specialist, you are observing Mrs. Miller as she watches a musical on the video. She becomes upset and grabs the arm of the resident seated next to her.

ROLE-PLAYING

1. Simulate the experience described above:
    a. How should this situation be managed?
    b. Should Mrs. Miller be removed from the room? Why or why not?
    c. How might the other residents react to Mrs. Miller's behavior?

DISCUSSION QUESTION

1. How might you interpret Mrs. Miller's behavior?

Selected References for Case Study

Mace, N. L. (1989). *Dementia care.* Baltimore, MD: The Johns Hopkins University Press.

Film

"Seven Days a Week." Terra Nova Films, 9848 S. Winchester Avenue, Chicago, IL 60643, (312) 881-8491.

"Wesley Hall: A Special Life." Terra Nova Films, 9848 S. Winchester Avenue, Chicago, IL 60643, (312) 881-8491.

Case 10

ROBERT

You were introduced to Robert Wilson in Chapter Two, *Individual Therapeutic Recreation Program Planning* (p. 74). He is a young adult male with mental retardation currently residing in a transitional living center. In Chapter

Three, *Implementing Individual Therapeutic Recreation Program Plans*, you developed a transitional plan for him to follow as he prepared for community integration (p. 118). You must now consider the following leadership concerns.

ROLE-PLAYING

1. Robert has just paid for a movie and put all of his change from the vendor into his pocket without counting or organizing it. What should the therapeutic recreation specialist say and do?
2. When the therapeutic recreation specialist asks Robert, "What would you like to do?" his usual response is, "Whatever you want to do is OK." What should the specialist say and do so that Robert will make decisions and express choices about specific leisure experiences?
3. Robert is playing cards with other residents and the therapeutic recreation specialist when his speech becomes unclear. What could the therapeutic recreation specialist say and do to facilitate Robert's enunciation without breaking up the card playing game?
4. Would it be appropriate for the therapeutic recreation specialist to involve the other residents in efforts to improve Robert's enunciation? If so, how could this be accomplished? If not, why?

Case 11

TODD

Todd Smith's case was introduced in Chapter One, *Assessment in Therapeutic Recreation* (p. 35). He is 26 years old, has Down's syndrome, and performs in the severe range of mental retardation. He was admitted to the state institution for a comprehensive evaluation. Specific behavioral concerns included interpersonal aggression, sustained yelling, and self-injurious behavior. In Chapter Two, *Individual Therapeutic Recreation Program Planning*, you began developing a program plan for Todd that included the development of a leisure skill repertoire (p. 80).

DISCUSSION QUESTIONS

1. What teaching strategies might you use and how would they be used to help Todd learn to indicate his activity preferences?
2. Describe how you might use various teaching strategies to shape Todd's attending behaviors during leisure participation? How would you reinforce appropriate attending behaviors?
3. How would responses to questions one and two change if Todd was blind? Deaf?

IN-CLASS EXERCISES

1. Let's assume Todd is blind. He has indicated an interest in listening to music. Develop one short-term instructional (behavioral) objective relative to using a cassette tape recorder. Develop a task analysis for teaching this skill. Indicate specific cues (verbal and/or physical) required for teaching the skill, materials needed for instruction, and general teaching procedures. Also consider what modifications and adaptations could be used to achieve Todd's goal of using a cassette tape recorder. How could Todd's parents support his independent participation in this activity in the home environment?

ROLE-PLAYING

1. Role-play an interaction with Mr. and Mrs. Smith in which you provide them with ideas about how to determine and support Todd's leisure preferences.
2. Role-play a team meeting in which you explain to the other members how you determined Todd's leisure preferences. Be prepared to explain how involvement in these activities contributes to the accomplishment of Todd's goals and objectives.

Selected References for Case Study

Dattilo, J. (1988). Assessing music preferences of persons with severe disabilities. *Therapeutic Recreation Journal*, 22(2), 12-23.

Ellis, R. and Whittington, D. (1981). *A guide to social skills training.* Cambridge, MA: Brookline Books.

Turnbull, H. R., Turnbull, A. P., Bronicki, G. J., Summers. J. A., and Roeder-Gorder, C. (1989). *Disability and the family: A guide to decisions for adulthood.* Baltimore, MD: Brookes.

Wehman, P. (Ed.). (1979). *Recreation programming for developmentally disabled persons.* Baltimore, MD: University Park Press.

Wehman, P. and Schleien, S. (1981). *Leisure programs for handicapped persons: Adaptations, techniques, and curriculum.* Austin, TX: PRO-ED.

Wuerch, B. B. and Voeltz, L. M. (1982). *Longitudinal leisure skills for severely handicapped learners: The Ho'onanea curriculum component.* Baltimore, MD: Paul H. Brookes.

Chapter Five

Evaluation in Therapeutic Recreation

In this text, evaluation will refer primarily to "a measurement of client progress in reaching the predetermined goals of the treatment plan within the therapeutic recreation program" (Beddall and Kennedy, 1985, p. 63). Thus specific client objectives, formulated in advance, provide the standard for determining the extent to which desired behavioral changes are obtained, with both anticipated and unanticipated outcomes being considered.

There is a close link between the evaluation of clients' progress and the intervention strategies or therapeutic recreation programs established to address clients' goals. Since such programs are considered successful when participants develop skills and behaviors needed to obtain the long-term goal of maximum interdependence, inevitably an evaluation of one involves an evaluation of the other. It follows that ascertaining clients' progress toward optimal leisure functioning enables therapeutic recreation specialists to determine indirectly the effectiveness of therapeutic recreation intervention strategies. Intervention strategies are evaluated to determine if they were implemented as planned and if the selected processes and content were appropriate relative to accomplishing stated goals. Lewis and Lewis (1983) have suggested that even subtle differences between planned and implemented services can have an effect on outcomes.

Environmental characteristics should be considered when determining the contribution that selected processes and content has made to the achievement of clients' transition goals and objectives. For example, an evaluation of possible environmental barriers, such as inaccessible facilities, lack of adapted or special equipment, or absence of natural helpers and companions could be one aspect of measuring clients' progress toward transition to natural environments such as home or community.

In order to evaluate clients' progress, therapeutic recreation specialists must establish specific goals and objectives and develop a plan that will identify the type of information needed and specify how this information will be systematically collected, analyzed, reported, and used to improve the individual therapeutic recreation program plan.

Understanding Evaluation in the Therapeutic Recreation Process

Evaluation is the last step in the individualized therapeutic recreation process. Since evaluation implies measurement against predetermined criteria, it actually begins during individual therapeutic recreation program planning, when the goals and objectives are formulated from input information, and continues until both short- and long-term goals are achieved (O'Morrow and Reynolds, 1989). Basic systems theory provides a theoretical framework for understanding the individualized therapeutic recreation process as it has been presented thus far and for appreciating the role of evaluation in this process. The input, process, output model is illustrated in Figure 5.1.

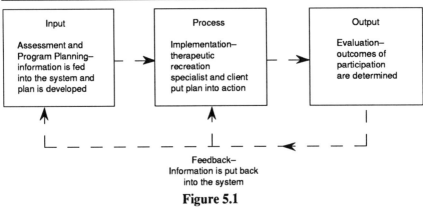

Figure 5.1
The therapeutic recreation systems model.

The assessment and individual program planning phases of the therapeutic recreation process are in fact "input" phases during which information is fed into the system. This information documents clients' baseline abilities (attitudes, skills, and knowledge existing at the beginning of treatment) against which clients' progress will be measured. During the "process" phase, therapeutic recreation specialists and clients implement the individual program plan as they engage in activities designed to bring about desired outcomes. In the "output" phase, the consequences of participation are discovered. Thus, evaluation continues when therapeutic recreation specialists and clients compare the actual participation results with the original goals and objectives. Analysis of participation produces information that is put back into the system and may lead to a modification somewhere within the system. This phase is known as the "feedback loop."

Outcomes may verify that the system is meeting its objectives, i.e., the therapeutic recreation program plan is able to facilitate the achievement of individual intervention goals. In this case, modification involves updating an individual program and/or selecting new objectives. If, on the other hand, goals are not being accomplished, modification may be needed to adjust objectives, cues, reinforcement, specific content, processes, activities, and/or leadership techniques.

Evaluation information collected and analyzed during therapeutic recreation program planning and implementation enables therapeutic recreation specialists to make necessary changes in an individual program plan while it is being designed and delivered. This approach, referred to as process or *formative* evaluation, involves more than an ongoing comparison between objectives and results, however. It also seeks to determine if the level of effort or cost of the program is appropriate in light of the results. Such analysis involves reviewing the type and extent of interventions employed by specialists as well as the total cost of resource utilization. Carruthers, Sneegas, and Ashton-Shaeffer (1986) suggest that "areas which might be evaluated include administrative concerns, costs, program benefits, appropriateness of program leadership, and the determination of whether minimal regulatory and professional standards have been met" (p. 38). Such evaluation may lead to a consideration of alternate, more effective and efficient approaches.

Evaluation information collected at the end of an individual program plan, or at preselected intervals, enables therapeutic recreation specialists to determine whether clients have achieved intended benefits and to assess the appropriateness of therapeutic recreation programs and services. This approach, referred to as outcome or *summative* evaluation, asks the basic question, "To what degree has the client or his environment changed as a result of the program's interventions?" During this phase of evaluation, therapeutic recreation specialists make decisions regarding individual program continuation, modification, and/or termination.

When clients' goals have been achieved or when agencies' services are no longer appropriate for clients, a discharge or transition plan is developed (Carter, Van Andel, and Robb, 1990). This phase of evaluation should lead to necessary referral and follow-up services.

Evaluation information can be either quantitative or qualitative. Quantitative information provides statistical answers to evaluation questions. For example, such items as the number of times a client participated in outpatient activities, the length of time a client is post-injury and/or -discharge, or the amount of time a client spent in a specified activity, constitute quantitative data. In addition, quantitative information is more significant when placed in the context of other factors such as location of the activity, staff/client ratios, and qualifications of the staff. Qualitative information is more inclusive and provides a detailed description of people and/or situations. Qualitative data could include the nature and extent of a client's disability, a client's opinions, a client's attitudes toward and/or interest in specific activities, and a client's acquisition of specific skills. Both types of evaluation information are important and should be used.

Purposes of Evaluation

As earlier stated, measuring and documenting the extent of clients' progress in the therapeutic recreation program requires that the content and process of a program plan must be evaluated. It is important to ensure that clients are receiving effective services delivered in an efficient manner. Accordingly, therapeutic recreation specialists seek evaluation information to judge the merit of the planned intervention relative to achieving client goals and objectives and identifying ways of improving it. For example, evaluation might be used to assess the appropriateness of goals and objectives, to determine program content or process strengths and weaknesses, to measure the effectiveness of program resources such as equipment, materials, supplies, and facilities, to ascertain client satisfaction, or to measure staff effectiveness.

Evaluation is also necessary to demonstrate accountability in therapeutic recreation service delivery. It confirms the efficacy of therapeutic recreation intervention, justifies program content and process relative to desired outcomes, and in general demonstrates that desired outcomes are being achieved in the most effective and efficient manner. Evaluation may also be used to justify budget expenditures as they relate to individual therapeutic recreation program plans, or to verify the need for additional staff, supplies, and equipment, as well as expanded facilities or increased access to existing facilities.

Finally, because it monitors and records the quality of therapeutic recreation services as perceived by both service providers and recipients, evaluation serves the important purpose of providing general documentation of therapeutic recreation programs. Criteria and standards for quality of care in therapeutic recreation service delivery have been developed by therapeutic recreation professional organizations, such as the National Therapeutic Recreation Society (NTRS) and the American Therapeutic Recreation Association (ATRA), and by various external accrediting groups such as the Joint Commission on Accreditation of Healthcare Organizations (JCAHO) and the Commission for the Accreditation of Rehabilitation Facilities (CARF). Therapeutic recreation specialists and clients must add to these standards by identifying other important aspects of service delivery based on their experiences and expertise. In other words, how is quality therapeutic recreation intervention best achieved for their specific situation? Therefore, evaluation serves to document the quality of therapeutic recreation programs and provides information for continuing, refining, or extinguishing existing techniques and service delivery methods.

Evaluation Models and Techniques

Using the systems analysis of input, process, and output phases of the therapeutic recreation process, the *Discrepancy Evaluation Model* (Provus, 1966; Yavorsky, 1976) provides a useful approach to individual evaluation. Discrepancy Evaluation Model (DEM) relies on the assumption that measurable objectives or outcomes serve as standards for clients' success. In this approach, actual outcomes are compared with desired outcomes, and any discrepancy between clients' performance and predetermined standards is examined. Feedback from this investigation leads to suggestions for revising the individual therapeutic recreation program plan in order to resolve discrepancies.

DEM can be employed at any stage of the system, but it is often used primarily as a summative evaluation technique. In contrast, *Utilization-Focused Evaluation* (UFE) approaches emphasize formative evaluation concerns, useful evaluation findings, and flexible methods. Connolly (1984) points out that it is inadequate merely to measure whether objectives were met. It is necessary to examine the context of the individual therapeutic recreation program along with demonstrated behaviors. Input and process characteristics that might have influenced program outcomes, either negatively or positively, must be identified. UFE emphasizes the usefulness of evaluation information as it relates to individual therapeutic recreation program revision and improvement. Thus, a desired approach to evaluation is one which compares actual outcomes with desired outcomes, during and after program implementation, and uses this information as a basis for improving intervention.

Triangulated evaluation is a systematic, multifaceted approach that uses a variety of techniques and procedures (e.g., interviews, questionnaires, tests, observation, chart analysis) from other evaluation models to gather both qualitative and quantitative information. It encourages therapeutic recreation specialists to use the full range of evaluative methods and resources to produce an in-depth portrayal of a client and program and provides both an evaluative description and a judgement of worth or merit (Howe, 1982). Howe (1982) suggests that triangulation has much practical utility because the model's evaluation design is simple and does not require a high degree of "numerical" measurement. "Human concern and the potential relevance of unanticipated outcomes are of great importance" (Howe, 1982, p. 91). Howe and Keller (1988) further explain that triangulation evaluation emphasizes clients' perspectives and makes possible a greater understanding of their needs. In addition, the use of multiple methods is desirable because it helps to confirm findings, thus permitting a more accurate interpretation and application of the results.

Gunn and Peterson (1978, pp. 265-267) describe a six-step approach that is applicable to the process of client evaluation regardless of the specific model used: (1) state the evaluation questions; (2) determine the variables; (3) determine sources of data; (4) identify the method of collecting data; (5) plan when data are collected; and (6) indicate how data will be treated.

Step 1. State the Evaluation Question. The purpose of this step is to focus the evaluation. Therapeutic recreation specialists should consider for whom the evaluation is being conducted and for what reason(s), i.e., what do specialists want to know? Audiences of the evaluation could include clients, parents or guardians, therapeutic recreation staff, treatment team members, administrators, accrediting bodies, and program funders. Examples of basic evaluation questions include: (1) What were the outcomes of the program, both anticipated and unanticipated? (2) Was the program implemented as designed? (3) Were activities and interactions appropriate in light of objectives? (4) Were objectives valid, realistic, and appropriate?

Step 2. Determine the Variables. Gunn and Peterson (1978) break each evaluation question into subquestions called variables. These are specific questions which must be asked in order to answer the broader questions raised in Step 1. For example, variables for the evaluation question concerning implementation might include the number and qualifications of staff involved, the number and characteristics of participants, the availability and characteristics of supplies, equipment, and facilities, and the number, length, and content of activity sessions. Austin (1982) points out that any subquestion is appropriate if it addresses the primary concern expressed in the broad evaluation question.

Programs can be judged by a variety of indicators; however, some will be more valid than others. For instance, therapeutic recreation specialists may use attendance figures as an indicator of a program's worth.

Attendance figures indicate how many clients were served. Yet, they cannot describe what actually happened to the clients participating in the program (Rossman, 1989).

Step 3. Sources of Data. In this step, therapeutic recreation specialists first determine what information will be needed to answer the evaluation subquestions, and then determine how to best obtain this information. The questions under investigation will influence the identification of appropriate information sources. For example, the number of program participants might be obtained through program registration or attendance records, and the characteristics of participants through individual records, files, charts, test data, staff reports, and previous evaluation reports. Therapeutic recreation specialists must also determine the validity and reliability of potential sources of information. Ideally, evaluation data should present a balanced and comprehensive view of the program or service and its impact (Rossman, 1989).

Step 4. Method of Collecting Data. Once sources of data are determined, specialists must select the actual techniques they will use to obtain evaluation information. This selection involves determining what types of resources, human and physical, are needed to conduct the evaluation, as well as the availability of these resources to therapeutic recreation specialists. As discussed earlier, the use of multiple methods of collecting data is recommended.

Very practical concerns influence methods of collecting data. For example, designing and conducting individual evaluations may require much staff time, thereby affecting the amount of interaction among program participants. External evaluators may sometimes be used, but in most cases therapeutic recreation specialists are responsible for evaluating the progress of clients and the efficacy of individualized activities and aproaches. The evaluation methods used must therefore be assessed relative to the amount of time and cost required. In addition, certain evaluation techniques require specialized training, skills, and experience.

A particular evaluation technique may be deemed inappropriate because of the characteristics of the clients being evaluated. For instance, an interview would not be the best evaluative method to use with a client with severe mental retardation who is both easily distracted and nonverbal. On the other hand, this method would be very appropriate for obtaining evaluative information from this client's parent, guardian, teacher, and caseworker. Certain methods may also produce undesirable or unnecessary intrusions into a client's affairs or activities. Keeping these factors in mind, therapeutic recreation specialists have a variety of techniques from which to choose. These include questionnaires and surveys, standardized tests and measures, attitude and interests scales and inventories, interviews and conversations, structured and unstructured observations, rating scales and checklists, case studies, and anecdotal journalistic logs or narrative writings. These various forms of data collection require a variety of physical resources including audio tape recorders, standardized test instruments, video tape recorders, computers, and biofeedback machines.

The collection of data requires recording and storing information as it is gathered. This process usually involves a filing and storage system for the various evaluation forms and narratives being completed and possibly the entering of data into a computerized classification and retrieval system.

Step 5. When Data Are Collected. Different evaluation variables or subquestions require different times and/or frequency of collection. For example, attendance records require continuous collection; characteristics of program participants probably need to be collected only once, at the beginning of the planned intervention; and data relating to program outcomes are collected at the end of the intervention and possibly at previously determined interim points.

Step 6. Treatment of the Data. In this step, therapeutic recreation specialists must determine how the information pertaining to each variable will be used to answer the evaluation questions and how results will be reported to the various evaluation audiences. Quantitative evaluation results may be analyzed and reported in terms of frequency, percentage, measures of central tendency, and measures of dispersion. More sophisticated statistical analysis, such as correlation, difference, and variance also may be used. Qualitative analysis, on the other hand, usually necessitates organizing, analyzing, and synthesizing data and then answering the evaluation questions. Basic descriptions, critical reviews or narratives, and content analysis may be aspects of qualitative analyses.

Methods of delivering evaluation reports vary and may include case studies, graphs, tables, charts, slide shows, videotapes, questions and answers, executive summaries, progress notes, and discharge plans. The reports can be both written and oral. The method of reporting is determined by the purpose of evaluation and its intended audience. Austin (1982) suggests that two evaluation approaches may be used to report data. In the first, therapeutic recreation specialists prepare a general report for all evaluation audiences. In the second, specialists prepare specific reports for different evaluation audiences. These reports are individually tailored and focus on the audience's perception of priority concerns.

Obviously, evaluation information is going to be helpful only to the extent that it is used to interpret the strengths and weaknesses of an individual therapeutic recreation program plan, determine the overall effectiveness and efficiency of interventions, and make revision decisions. The six-step approach will provide the framework for implementing a system of evaluation that will substantiate the accomplishment of goals and objectives and permit results to be applied toward revision and improvement of clients' therapeutic recreation program plans.

Summary

Individual evaluation, a vital component of program planning and implementation, is a continuous, ongoing process used to determine clients' progress towards the development of interdependent leisure lifestyles. During individual program planning, therapeutic recreation specialists specify what information needs to be collected, and how, in order to substantiate clients' progress toward goals and objectives. During and after program implementation, evaluation serves to indicate areas for possible revision and improvement of services.

In the Introduction, it was pointed out that the profession of therapeutic recreation is rapidly growing and changing. In the last chapter of this text, *Selected Issues in Therapeutic Recreation*, a variety of topics are discussed relative to their implications for the future development of the profession.

Bibliography

Austin, D. R. (1982). *Therapeutic recreation: Processes and techniques.* New York, NY: John Wiley.

Beddall, T. and Kennedy, D. W. (1985). Attitudes of therapeutic recreators toward evaluation and client assessment. *Therapeutic Recreation Journal, 19*,(1), 62-70.

Carruthers, C., Sneegas, J. J., and Ashton-Shaeffer, C. A. (1986). *Therapeutic recreation: Guidelines for activity services in long term care.* Urbana-Champaign, IL: University of Illinois.

Carter, M. J., Van Andel, G. E., and Robb, G. M. (1990). *Therapeutic recreation: A practical approach.* Prospect Heights, IL: Waveland Press.

Connolly, P. (1984). Program evaluation. In C. A. Peterson and S. L. Gunn, *Therapeutic recreation program design: Principles and procedures* (2nd ed.) (pp. 136-179). Englewood Cliffs, NJ: Prentice-Hall.

Gunn, S. L. and Peterson, C. A. (1978). *Therapeutic recreation program design: Principles and procedures.* Englewood Cliffs, NJ: Prentice-Hall.

Howe, C. Z. (1982). Some uses of the multi-modal of curriculum evaluation in therapeutic recreation. In L. L. Neal and C. R. Edginton (Eds.), *Exetra perspectives: Concepts in therapeutic recreation* (pp. 87-98). Eugene, OR: Center of Leisure Studies, University of Oregon.

Howe, C. Z. and Keller, M. J. (1988). The use of triangulation as an evaluation technique: Illustrations from regional symposia in therapeutic recreation. *Therapeutic Recreation Journal, 22*(1), 36-45.

Lewis, J. A. and Lewis, M. D. (1983). *Management of human service programs.* Monterey, CA: Brooks/Cole.

O'Morrow, G. S. and Reynolds, R. P. (1989). *Therapeutic recreation: A helping profession* (3rd ed.). Englewood Cliffs, NJ: Prentice-Hall.

Provus, M. (1971). *Discrepancy evaluation.* Berkeley, CA: McCutchan.

Rossman, B. (1989). *Recreation programming: Designing leisure experiences.* Champaign, IL: Sagamore.

Yavorsky, D. K. (1976). *Discrepancy evaluation: A practitioner's guide.* Charlottesville, VA: University of Virginia.

Suggested Readings

Austin, D. R. (1991). *Therapeutic recreation: Processes and techniques* (2nd ed.). Champaign, IL: Sagamore.

Berk, R. A. and Ross, P. H. (1990). *Thinking about program evaluation.* Newbury Park, CA: Sage Publications, Inc.

Bullock, C. C. and Coffey, F. (1980). Triangulation as applied to the evaluative process. Leisure Today. *Journal of Physical Education and Recreation, 50*(8), 50-52.

Chen, H. (1990). *Theory-driven evaluations*. Newbury Park, CA: Sage Publications, Inc.

Connolly, P. (1984). Analyzing program cause as well as effect: A model for program analysis. *Therapeutic Recreation Journal, 18*(1), 31-39.

Hunter, I. R., Reynolds, R. P., and Williams, M. L. (1984). The elaboration model in adapted activity research: Increasing the programmatic value of program evaluations. *Adapted Physical Activity Quarterly, 1*(1), 12-18.

Jewell, D. L. (1980). Documentation: Shibboleth for professionalism. *Therapeutic Recreation Journal, 14*(1), 23-29.

Kennedy, D. W. and Lundegren, H. M. (1981). Application of the discrepancy evaluation model in therapeutic recreation. *Therapeutic Recreation Journal, 15*(1), 24-34.

Levy, J. (1982). Behavioral observation techniques in assessing change in therapeutic recreation/play settings. *Therapeutic Recreation Journal, 16*(1), 25-32.

Love, A. J. (1991). *Internal evaluations*. Newbury Park, CA: Sage Publications, Inc.

Riley, B. (Ed.). (1987). *Evaluation of therapeutic recreation through quality assurance.* State College, PA: Venture Publishing, Inc.

Shadish, W. R., Cook, T. D., and Leviton, L. C. (1991). *Foundations of program evaluation.* Newbury Park, CA: Sage Publications, Inc.

Touchstone, W. A. (1975). The status of client evaluation within psychiatric settings. *Therapeutic Recreation Journal, 9*(14), 166-172.

Wyatt, W. J. and Hunt, S. K. (1976). Using parents as evaluators of a therapeutic recreation camping program for the retarded. *Therapeutic Recreation Journal, 10*(4), 143-148.

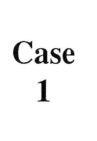

Case 1

CARRIE

Carrie Collins, a 78 year old white female, was admitted to a 550-bed general medical and surgical hospital with a diagnosis of right cerebrovascular accident (CVA). Ms. Collins also shows transient slurred speech and dysphagia.

Ms. Collins has a medical history of significant hypertension, presumed hypertension cardiovascular disease with congestive failure, type II diabetes mellitus, and hyperthyroidism. Her hyperthyroidism has been treated surgically. Ms. Collins was also treated for a hip fracture approximately one year prior to her current admission.

Ms. Collins is felt to have fairly good potential as a rehabilitation candidate. The rehabilitation care team suggested a treatment program with the following goals: enhance abilities to dress and bathe self, enhance transfer and ambulatory skills, and enhance awareness of and participation in recreation activities.

DISCUSSION QUESTIONS

1. It has been determined by the rehabilitation care team that Ms. Collins should be discharged to her home with appropriate home care follow-up. According to the National Therapeutic Recreation Society's *Standards of Practice for Therapeutic Recreation Service*, and/or the American Therapeutic Recreation Association's *Standards of Practice for Therapeutic Recreation*, what should Ms. Collins' discharge/transition plan include?

2. During inpatient treatment, the therapeutic recreation specialist was able to discuss problems connected with Ms. Collins' past leisure participation and attitudes and explored former recreation activities. However, since the period of rehabilitation time was limited, she was not able to adequately discuss

new recreation activities, appropriate use of present leisure time, and where to find community leisure resources. Discuss recommendations for post-discharge/transition planning relative to what should be done following Ms. Collins' discharge.

3. Since Ms. Collins is being discharged home, what would the therapeutic recreation specialist want to know about her home and community prior to developing a discharge/transition plan?

4. What type of communication and discharge planning could the therapeutic recreation specialist at the hospital initiate with the therapeutic recreation specialist working in the community?

5. What approach(es) would you use to determine the effectiveness of the discharge/transition plan?

Selected References for Case Study

American Therapeutic Recreation Association. (1991). *Standards of Practice for Therapeutic Recreation*. Hattiesburg, MS: Author.

Caplan, B. (Ed.) (1987). *Rehabilitation psychology desk reference*. Rockville, MD: Aspen.

Coyle, C. P. and Kinney, W. B. (1990). Leisure characteristics of adults with physical disabilities. *Therapeutic Recreation Journal, 28*(4), 64-73.

Hough, S. and Brady, D. (1988). Avocational skill development for neurobehaviorally impaired inpatients. *Therapeutic Recreation Journal, 22*(4), 39-48.

Lindemann, J. E. (1981). *Psychological and behavioral aspects of physical disability: A manual for health practitioners*. New York, NY: Plenum Press.

Logigian, M. K. (Ed.). (1982). *Adult rehabilitation: A team approach for therapists*. Boston, MA: Little, Brown, and Company.

National Therapeutic Recreation Society. (1990). *Standards of practice for therapeutic recreation service* (revised). Alexandria, VA: National Recreation and Park Association.

O'Morrow, G. S. and Reynolds, R. P. (1989). *Therapeutic recreation: A helping profession* (3rd ed.). Englewood Cliffs, NJ: Prentice-Hall.

Stolov, W. C. and Clowers, M. R. (Eds.). (1981). *Handbook of severe disability: A textbook for rehabilitation counselors, other vocational practitioners, and allied health professionals.* Washington, DC: U.S. Department of Education, Rehabilitation Services Administration, U.S. Government Printing Office.

Case 2

MAGNOLIA HILLS

In Chapter One, *Assessment in Therapeutic Recreation*, you were introduced to Magnolia Hills, a congregate residence for older adults (p. 26). As the residents age, their needs change, possibly producing an increase in the incidence of chronic conditions such as memory impairment, sensory impairment, heart and respiratory diseases, and depression. Staff realized that a systematic and comprehensive assessment of the residents' ongoing needs was necessary if they were to continue to plan and implement an effective therapeutic recreation program. You were hired as a therapeutic recreation consultant to develop, implement, and evaluate the assessment system. Program revisions and additions were made based on comprehensive assessment data. Staff have now asked you to develop a plan for systematically evaluating the results of new programming efforts.

DISCUSSION QUESTIONS

1. In this scenario, what is the relationship between assessment and evaluation?

2. Many of the recreation activities provided at Magnolia Hills are group activities. Discuss specific evaluation questions the activities coordinator should consider. Suggest possible sources of evaluation information. Suggest a variety of methods that could be used to evaluate group activities.

3. Professionals often evaluate group activities by the degree to which *program* objectives were met. How do program objectives (or outcomes) differ from individual (behavioral) objectives or outcomes?

4. Periodic evaluation of individual progress must also take place at Magnolia Hills. Suggest a variety of methods (e.g., use of behavioral objectives) for measuring changes in: (1) residents' functional abilities; (2) residents' leisure skills; and (3) residents' leisure interests and attitudes. Functional abilities could include orientation, sensory response, mobility, and activity tolerance.

5. How would the techniques and strategies used for individual evaluation differ from those used for program evaluation?

6. How are you going to use your evaluation data? How will your interpretation of the meaning of your results relate to decisions regarding resources, policies, procedures, and/or individuals?

Case 3

PREPARING A PROGRAM EVALUATION PLAN

You are the director of a therapeutic recreation department in an acute physical rehabilitation center. Administrators at the center have noted that an increasing number of adults, sixty-five and older, are being admitted with head injuries resulting primarily from falls or motor vehicle accidents. These administrators have decided to open six new beds in the rehabilitation center and designate them specifically for older adults with head injuries.

The present therapeutic recreation program in the head injury service section is structured for children and young and middle-aged adults, and the program serves patients at Levels II to IV on the Rancho Scale (Hagen, Malkmus, and Durham, 1972). Therapeutic recreation services currently include sensory stimulation, orientation, social skills retraining, animal assisted therapy, adaptive aquatics, community functional skills training, memory exercises, and leisure education.

DISCUSSION QUESTIONS

1. Discuss Rancho Los Amigos Medical Center's Levels of Cognitive Function. What behaviors might you expect at each level?

IN-CLASS EXERCISES

1. Develop a plan to evaluate the impact that the addition of six beds for older adults with head injuries will have on the therapeutic recreation program in these two areas:
   a. Management concerns, such as the cost of supplies, time, space, and staff to work with these older adults.
   b. Functional skills that will be targeted as the primary treatment focus, such as socialization, cognition, and orientation.

The evaluation plan should include evaluation questions and subquestions, sources for evaluation data, data-collecting procedures and instruments, schedule for collecting evaluative information (formative and summative), data analysis, data summary, and process for making revisions based on evaluative feedback. The evaluation is being conducted for the center's administrators. You are concerned about providing quality services, meeting requirements for Medicare and Medicaid reimbursement, and addressing the needs of older patients.

FIELD EXPERIENCES

1. Invite a therapeutic recreation specialist and administrator from a rehabilitation facility that serves older clients to participate in the in-class exercise described above.

Selected References for Case Study

Gunn, S. L. and Peterson, C. A. (1978). *Therapeutic recreation program design: Principles and procedures.* Englewood Cliffs, NJ: Prentice-Hall.

Hagen, C., Malkmus, D., and Durham, P. (1972). *Levels of cognitive functioning.* Downey, CA: Rancho Los Amigos Hospital, Division of Neurological Sciences.

Case 4

EVALUATION PRIORITIES SIMULATION

When evaluating therapeutic recreation programs, therapeutic recreation specialists must not only analyze program content and process characteristics, but must also determine participant characteristics and the effects that the intervention strategy has produced. Thus, determining the worth of a program involves evaluating the effectiveness of the program relative to achieving individual objectives and goals. Deciding what evaluation questions and subquestions should be asked is crucial. Since most often it is not practical or feasible to include all suggested evaluation questions, choices must be made. The following scenario is designed to force you to decide which questions to include in an evaluation and to experience the consequences of your decisions.

As the therapeutic recreation supervisor for a city recreation department serving a community with a population of 50,000, the recreation director has assigned you the task of evaluating the summer therapeutic recreation programs. During the summer you operated an eight-week day camp for various populations with disabilities, a learn-to-swim program for people with physical disabilities, and a weekly "Dance Under the Stars" program for adults with mental retardation. In addition, people with disabilities were encouraged to participate in regular departmental offerings—especially special events.

The day camp program had 55 campers with 12 staff and an operating budget of $25,000. It operated from 8:00 a.m. to 4:00 p.m. Monday through Friday for 12 weeks. Fifteen individuals participated in the learn-to-swim program, which operated one hour a day, three days per week for 12 weeks. Since the swimming instruction ratio was one-to-one, volunteer leaders were used, and you employed only one staff member to supervise the program and train and supervise the volunteers. Your budget for the swim program was $1,500. The dance program operated on Saturday nights from 9:00 p.m. to 12:00 midnight, for 12 weeks, and you had a budget of $500 per night for hall rental, band, decorations, and refreshments. Attendance at the dances averaged 40 individuals an evening. The policy of including people with disabilities in recreation programs offered to the general public did not increase the cost of these programs, but you were expected to consult with other programs as needed to enable their leaders to accommodate individual needs. You received 10 such requests over the summer.

ROLE-PLAYING

There are several evaluation audiences interested in determining the worth of the therapeutic recreation program. Select five of the following evaluation audiences. It is recommended that three of the audiences include the city council, the therapeutic recreation supervisor, and the participants. Each class member should be assigned to one of the five evaluation audiences:

City Council (interested in how many were served and the cost per participant),

Therapeutic Recreation Advisory Board (interested in how many were served, the populations served, and the outcome of individual participation),

Director of Recreation (interested in how many were served, how well the program was managed, and how the program contributed to the department's mission),

Therapeutic Recreation Supervisor (interested in how well the program was managed; whether or not supplies, equipment, timing, location, were satisfactory; how well the leaders and volunteers performed; whether or not individual expectations and behavioral changes were realized; and whether or not participants intend to participate again),

Therapeutic Recreation Leaders (interested in how important this program was to the participants, whether or not the participants had fun, what benefits the participants received, how well the participants performed, and which activities the participants liked best), *Participants* (interested in how well the program was managed, what happened to them as a result of their participation, which activities they liked best, and overall level of satisfaction with services), and
Lions Club, which provided 10 percent financial support for the summer program (interested in how many participated, what benefits the participants received, and whether or not the participants intend to participate again).

You will role-play the interests of the group you are assigned for the remainder of the simulation. Each group will select a spokesperson.

On page 177 there are ten evaluation questions (do not turn to page 177 yet) which may be included in the evaluation. Not all questions can be included so some must be eliminated. The simulation leader will propose each question, one at a time, to the interest groups. Each group, from its role perspective, must make one of the following decisions on each question:

    a.   We insist that this question *be included* in the evaluation.
    b.   We insist that this question *be excluded* from the evaluation.
    c.   We are *ambivalent* and don't care one way or the other about this question.

But it isn't that easy! Each group must elect to include at least two questions, to exclude at least two questions, and to be ambivalent and abstain on at least one question. In addition, no group can insist on including more than five questions, excluding more than five questions, or remaining ambivalent about more than three questions. A group will have only two minutes to determine its vote on each question, and may not communicate with other groups. Those who are unable to vote at the end of two minutes are recorded as abstentions.

Points are awarded based on the decision of each group compared to the other groups' decisions. The meaning of the points do not become apparent until all points are awarded. Scores for teams will range from negative through positive numbers, and various team scores will cluster, indicating the teams shared similar views.

ISSUE	GROUP VOTES					POINTS				
	1	2	3	4	5	1	2	3	4	5
1	I	A	E	A	E	-2	0	+2	0	+2
2										
3										
4										
5										
6										
7										
8										
9										
10										
Sum										

I = Include   A = Ambivalent   E = Exclude

Figure 5.2

Scoring is done on the matrix included as Figure 5.2. The simulation leader reveals each evaluation question to the groups, one at a time, and gives each group two minutes to decide how to vote on the question. Rotate the order of voting so all groups must eventually vote first. The leader then records each group's vote. Once the votes are recorded, they are scored (votes and scores for one round are already recorded on the matrix included as Figure 5.2). Points are awarded as follows:

a. If all teams vote either to exclude or include an issue, all teams receive four points.

b. If a majority of teams vote to exclude or include an issue (ambivalent votes are counted as abstentions and do not figure in computing the majority view), each of the teams in the majority receives as many points as there are teams in the majority and the minority team loses the same number of points. Ambivalent votes are recorded as zero.

c. In the event of a tie vote, all teams voting either to include or exclude the issue lose two points; those abstaining receive four points.

d. If all teams vote that they don't care one way or the other, all teams lose four points.

Once all the issues have been revealed, voted on, and scored, simply sum the score for each group and rank order the scores. Group debriefing can be facilitated by discussing the following questions:

(1) How did teams decide which issues to emphasize?

(2) Why were these issues considered important by these audiences?

(3) Why do different evaluation audiences have different evaluation interests and how does this affect the design of the evaluation?

(4) Why not include all evaluation issues?

(5) How does the selection of evaluation issues impact the eventual conclusion of the evaluation?

Because this is a simulation, not a game, there is no winner and the objective is not to acquire as many points as possible but to *role-play faithfully the interests of your group* in deciding on which evaluation questions to include.

TEN EVALUATION QUESTIONS

1. How well did program leaders perform?

2. How important was participating in this program to participants? How does it compare to their other recreation activities?

3. How well was the program managed?

4. What was the impact of the program, i.e., who was served and how many were served?

5. Were the equipment and supplies for the program satisfactory?

6. What happened to the participants in the program? What outcomes did they experience?

7. Do participants intend to participate again?

8. What agency mission did this program accomplish?

9. What were the cost data for this program, i.e., what was the cost per participant, the percent of user support provided, the percent of third party support?

10. Was the program scheduling (day, time, location) effective for participants?

Selected References for Case Study

House, E. R. (1977). *The logic of evaluative argument.* Los Angeles, CA: Center for the Study of Evaluations, University of California.

Patton, M. Q. (1981). *Creative evaluation.* Beverly Hills, CA: Sage Publications, Inc.

Patton, M. Q. (1978). *Utilization focused evaluation.* Beverly Hills, CA: Sage Publications, Inc.

Rossman, J. R. (1989). *Recreation programming: Designing leisure experiences.* Champaign, IL: Sagamore.

Weiss, C. H. (1972). *Evaluation research.* Englewood Cliffs, NJ: Prentice-Hall.

Case 5

ANOTHER BANQUET AT SIERRA MADRE

Through the years, the Sierra Madre Adult Day Care Center has enjoyed the commitment and continuity of an excellent volunteer staff. These volunteers have enabled the Center to offer a diversity of therapeutic recreation services and have provided input and assistance in developing and implementing individual program plans. Several years ago, the Center received a national award for its volunteer program.

The Center's first program director, a capable volunteer recruiter, initiated a yearly awards banquet to honor volunteers who give their time and talents to the Center. This year the banquet is to honor twenty-six volunteers of all ages, including nine members of a Girl Scout Troop and the Mayor of Sierra Madre. As in years past, the banquet will be held in the all-purpose room at the Center. This year's budget is $500 and must cover food, decorations, programs, and all other supplies and materials.

The awards banquet, however, seems to have grown stale, and in the past two years attendance at the banquet by Center participants has been declining, even though the volunteer honorees still seem to appreciate the gesture. This year the Center's Advisory Board has had difficulty convincing Center volunteers and participants to serve on the awards banquet planning committee, and already this committee is having difficulty selecting a date for the banquet as everyone seems to be busy on every date suggested. Even the Center's program director has lost his enthusiasm for the event. He does not know if his lack of enthusiasm is the result of boredom with the year-after-year sameness of the banquet or because of frustration in trying to cajole and inspire the lethargic planning committee. Yet he recognizes the valuable resources these volunteers provide and freely admits that the progress of individual Day Care Center participants would suffer if these resources were lost.

DISCUSSION QUESTIONS

1. In this scenario, what is the relationship between using Center volunteers and increasing the effectiveness of therapeutic recreation intervention strategies?

2. What are possible reasons for the decline in enthusiasm of Center participants for the awards banquet?

3. What evaluation questions should the program director formulate to help determine whether to revitalize or terminate the awards banquet? What sources of evaluation information are available to the program director and how will he collect this information?

4. If the program director decides to encourage the planning committee to develop an alternative program format in order to revitalize the awards program, what changes in frequency, promotion, leadership, program location, and financial support would you recommend? By what other means could the Center honor its volunteers?

5. One of the themes that emerges from this scenario is the concept of program life cycles. Recreation programs go through periods of introduction, growth, maturity, saturation, and decline, and though this cycle can be modified by careful program management, the decline of a program's appeal is inevitable. Does the concept of program life cycles have implications for the volunteer banquet?

6. How could the program life cycle concept apply to determining and/or modifying the process and content of individual therapeutic recreation program plans?

IN-CLASS EXERCISES

1. Select a program with which you have had personal experience as a participant or program leader over an extended time period. Discuss the life cycle of this program and predict its future accordingly.
2. Form a panel of two to three students and have the panel present this scenario and its possible solutions to the class. Use the above questions as a guide for preparing the presentation.
3. Select five to eight students to serve as the Sierra Madre banquet planning committee. These students are seated in a circle in the middle of the classroom and discuss question four listed above. Others in the class are seated in a circle behind the committee and afterwards offer feedback and discussion on the committee's solutions and processes in reaching the solutions.
4. In small groups of four to five students, brainstorm at least 10 ideas for honoring volunteers. Follow up with each group reporting their results to the whole class for discussion.
5. Engage in a timed writing exercise where for 10 minutes each student independently writes his or her reactions to the Sierra Madre case. Use these writings to initiate full class discussion of various issues.

FIELD EXPERIENCES

1. Invite to class a guest who has implemented a very successful and long lasting therapeutic recreation program and ask him to describe the evaluation and revitalization strategies he has used. Ask the guest to describe the extent to which program participants were involved in the evaluation and revitalization process and how program changes affected their individual therapeutic recreation program plans.
2. Visit an adult day care center in your community and interview three to five randomly chosen participants concerning their participation in the center's activities. Then do the same with various staff members. Formulate some general truisms about program life cycles from your interview data.

ROLE-PLAYING

1. The panel of students involved in the second in-class exercise described above may choose to role-play the situation as a way of initially presenting the problem to class.
2. Role-play a planning meeting of the Sierra Madre banquet planning committee after they have selected a date and have gathered data related to the evaluation questions formulated in discussion question three.

Selected References for Case Study

Crompton, J. (1979). Recreation programs have life cycles, too. *Parks and Recreation, 14*(10), 52-57.

Kraus, R. (1985). *Recreation program planning today.* Glenview, IL: Scott, Foresman, and Company.

Rossman, R. (1989). *Recreation programming: Designing leisure experiences.* Champaign, IL: Sagamore.

Russell, R. V. (1982). *Planning programs in recreation.* St. Louis, MO: C. V. Mosby.

Case 6

WILDERNESS GROUP

Wilderness Group (WG) is a nonprofit organization which contracts with state agencies to provide treatment for adjudicated youth. The average adjudicated youth serves either nine months in a traditional juvenile correctional institution or 30 days in WG and eight months at home on parole. For obvious reasons, the young people have volunteered readily to participate in the program and selection has been based on a subjective evaluation by

the WG program director, who interviews all of the youth who volunteer for the program and selects those whom she thinks will "succeed." Past program participants have included males and females ranging in age from 15 to 17 years. Their personal histories vary and their violations range from status offenses to multiple felonies.

A WG program usually consists of 10 participants and two instructors, lasts 30 days, and involves an extended lake/flat-river canoe trip, rock climbing, rappelling, trust exercises, and ropes course activities. A run followed by a dip-in-the-river and group incentives are daily features. Reality Therapy is used to guide instructor/participant interactions. The program is not co-educational and costs about $3,000 per participant. A new WG program begins approximately every two weeks with the number of programs split evenly between males and females.

Six instructors have been affiliated with WG at any one time. These instructors, who are only on the payroll while they are leading a program, earn about $3,000 for each 30 day program. The instructor turnover rate has averaged 25 percent per year. In addition, there have generally been six non-instructor staff positions, including program director, chief instructor, operations manager (facilities, equipment, food, transportation), assistant to the operations manager, and two secretaries/clerks. Recent data collected on the WG program have enabled cumulative recidivism rates to be calculated. Participant recidivism one year following WG is 19 percent; after two years, 40 percent; after three and four years, 42 percent and 47 percent, respectively.

DISCUSSION QUESTIONS

1. What are some common treatment needs of delinquents? Relate these needs to the benefits expected from participation in outdoor rehabilitation programs.
2. What client characteristics have been linked to success in outdoor rehabilitation programs?
3. What short- and long-term outcomes or behavioral indicators could be utilized to measure client success in an outdoor rehabilitation program?
4. What evaluation model or techniques would be most appropriate for measuring client success in an outdoor rehabilitation program?
5. How would results of client evaluation influence program modification? Discuss specific examples based on the Wilderness Group scenario.

IN-CLASS EXERCISES

1. Formulate three behavioral objectives for a participant in the WG program and develop a plan to evaluate the participant's success. The evaluation plan should address both the formative and summative phase of evaluation and should include both quantitative and qualitative evaluation information.* (See page 184.) For each behavioral objective:
   a. List several evaluation questions;
   b. Determine evaluation subquestions or variables;
   c. Determine sources of evaluation information;
   d. Designate methods of collecting evaluation information;
   e. Specify when data will be collected; and
   f. Determine how evaluation information will be used.
2. There are a number of programs like Wilderness Group throughout the country. Try to locate one in your area and request that personnel come to class and participate with you as you complete exercise one.
3. You are the program director for WG. The state agency which contracts with WG for services is requesting an evaluation report to determine whether or not to renew this contract.

Create a table of contents of what you would include in your evaluation report. Determine the resources (human, physical, and financial) needed to design, conduct, and prepare this evaluation.

*There are a host of problems when one uses standardized evaluation instruments with delinquents. Examples include attention span, literacy, tendency-to-lie, and subculture-based norms and definitions.

Selected References for Case Study

Baer, D. J., Jacobs, P. J., and Carr, F. E. (1975). Instructors' ratings of delinquents after outward bound survival training and their subsequent recidivism. *Psychological Reports*, *36*(4), 547-553.

Glasser, W. (1975). *Reality therapy*. New York, NY: Harper-Row.

Heaps, R. A. and Thorstenson, C. T. (1974). Self-concept change immediately and one year after survival training. *Therapeutic Recreation Journal*, *8*(1), 60-63.

Hunter, I. R. (1987). The impact of an outdoor rehabilitation program for adjudicated juveniles. *Therapeutic Recreation Journal*, *11*(3), 30-43.

Hunter, I. R. (1984). The impact of voluntary selection procedures on the reported success of outdoor rehabilitation programs. *Therapeutic Recreation Journal*, *18*(3), 38-44.

Hunter, I. R. and Purcell, K. D. (1984). Program characteristics and success in a resocialization program for adjudicated delinquents. *Corrective and Social Psychiatry*, *10*(2), 25-34.

Willman, H. and Chun, R. Y. F. (1973). Homeward bound: An alternative to institutionalization of adjudicated juvenile offenders. *Federal Probation*, *37*(3), 52-58.

Witman, J. P. (1987). The efficacy of adventure programming in the development of cooperation and trust with adolescents in treatment. *Therapeutic Recreation Journal*, *11*(3), 22-29.

Wright, A. N. (1983). Therapeutic potential of the outward bound process: An evaluation of a treatment program for juvenile delinquents. *Therapeutic Recreation Journal, 17*(2), 33-42.

Case 7

ANNIE

Annie, a white 53 year old adult with moderate mental retardation, had lived with her mother and father in a rural area on the family farm until five months ago, when her father died and her mother was no longer able to manage the farm. Her mother sold the farm and went to live with her sister in an older adult congregate living center in a nearby city. Her mother, 83, sought an appropriate placement for Annie as she realized she would be unable to care for her always and Annie was placed in a group home in the same city where her mother is now residing.

Annie had no formal education, had lived her entire life on the farm with her mother and father, and enjoyed feeding the animals, helping out around the house, going to the small rural church, watching television in her room, and helping her mother cook. Each day on the farm had its regular routine and Annie liked that. She is about 20 pounds overweight, in good general health, has good social skills, is unable to read or write, enjoys communicating with people, is outgoing and friendly, and is generally well-groomed. Her dress is usually neat and clean but almost always she wears overalls, as she wore these on the farm every day except Sunday. She did not want to move and she cannot understand why her mother made her live in the group home. While she says she is mad with her mother, she longs for the weekend visits with her. Annie tends to stay in her room most of the time and becomes very upset when the other women touch her personal possessions or enter her room without permission. She often cries when upset and totally withdraws from the group. She does not like to share the attention of the house parents when the group does recreation activities; however, as long as she is the center of attention, she seems to enjoy the group activities. She enjoys watching television in her room and loves to feed the group home dog, Lucky.

Annie was placed in a group home with five other women, who range in ages from 35 to 63 years with mild to moderate mental retardation. All the women, except Annie, have lived in group homes for most of their adult lives. The group home is operated by the Association for Retarded Citizens (ARC) and you are employed as the therapeutic recreation specialist to design, conduct, and evaluate recreation services for several group homes. You work closely with the house parents, who help you implement therapeutic recreation services.

You met with Annie, her mother, house parents, and social worker to assess her needs, interests, and abilities and then created an individual therapeutic recreation program plan for Annie. The quarterly goals on Annie's individual program are:

(1) To be able to identify when she has free time during the week and on weekends.

(2) To be able to identify three recreation activities she can do independently in the group home.

(3) To be able to identify two recreation activities she can do with others in the group home.

(4) To participate in the exercise program at least two times per week during the quarter.

(5) To attend two out of the four special recreation events offered during the quarter.

(6) To reduce the number of crying outbursts when she is not the center of attention in group recreation activities.

(7) To help her adjust to the routine and women in the group home through participation in recreation activities.

(8) To wear appropriate clothing to the recreation activities, outings, and special events.

(9) To visit her mother, in her mother's home, one weekend a month and to have her mother visit her at the group home one day each week.

(10) To lose six pounds.

The following individual therapeutic recreation program plan was created for Annie:

(1) To participate in the group's weekly leisure education program.

(2) To participate in the exercise program and to lose six pounds.

(3) To participate in the special recreation events and outings.

(4) To have monthly weekend and weekly visits with her mother.

(5) To work with house parents on a behavior modification plan to reduce crying as a means of getting attention and her way.

(6) To participate in a one-to-one 30 minute session with the therapeutic recreation specialist once every two weeks to address needs identified on the individual therapeutic recreation program plan.

The therapeutic recreation specialist with consultation from the house parents completed the following progress note on Annie three months after she entered the group home: "Annie is slow in adjusting to the group home recreation program and the other women. She spends most of her time in the yard playing with Lucky, the dog, or in her room watching TV. She regularly attends the weekly 30-minute leisure education class and seems to enjoy it. She has developed a positive relationship with the therapeutic recreation specialist. She is unable to discriminate between work and free time. She is able to identify three recreation activities she can do independently in the group home: (1) watch TV; (2) play with the dog; and (3) take care of her plants. She cannot identify any recreation activities she enjoys doing with the other women. She refuses to attend the exercise program and has gained five pounds. She refused to attend the special recreation events, except when food was the focus. For example, she attended only the ice cream social and cook out. She is reducing the crying outbursts when she is not the center of attention through a structured behavior modification program using positive social reinforcers. She enjoys the one-to-one interactions with the therapeutic recreation specialist and asks frequently when they will take place. Annie begs the specialist to stay longer and do special activities with her such as going to the zoo or washing the dog as they have done during visits. She has begun to wear more appropriate clothing, again through a behavior modification program that uses going to her mother's home as the reward. The visits with her mother are the highlight of her life. She looks forward to seeing her mother and cries when they must be separated."

DISCUSSION QUESTIONS

1. The goal for Annie, to be able to identify two recreation activities that could be done with other women in the group home, was not met. Why not? How would you structure Annie's program to meet this goal during the next quarter?

2. Annie has never engaged in a formal, structured exercise program and she did not participate in the one at the group home. Discuss why this type of exercise may not have been appropriate to help Annie lose weight. After this discussion, suggest or design another recreation activity that may help Annie achieve this goal. The activity needs to be better tailored to meet Annie's needs, interests, past experiences, and abilities.

3. How would you measure the goal to wear appropriate clothing on recreation outings and to special events?

4. Review the progress note and identify subjective and objective data.

5. You need to write a discharge plan regarding recreation and leisure participation to go into Annie's files. What would you include and why?

FIELD EXPERIENCES

1. Invite community-based therapeutic recreation specialists who work with group homes to visit class and discuss the questions listed above with the students.

2. Invite a representative from the State Developmental Disabilities Council or a local Association for Retarded Citizens to discuss the issue of the growing number of older adults from rural areas, with mental retardation and their needs as they relate to designing and evaluating recreation services.

Selected References for Case Study

Edgerton, R. B. and Gaston, M. A. (1991). *"I've seen it all!" Lives of older persons with mental retardation in the community.* Baltimore, MD: Paul H. Brookes.

Keller, M. J. (Ed). (1991). *Activities with developmentally disabled elderly and older adults.* New York, NY: The Haworth Press.

Chapter Six

Selected Issues in Therapeutic Recreation

Because therapeutic recreation is, as we have seen, a profession in rapid transition, various points and issues are being discussed and, in some cases, disputed by therapeutic recreation specialists. In this chapter, selected issues that influence the delivery of quality therapeutic recreation services will be discussed. These issues have implications for therapeutic recreation assessment, program planning, implementation, leadership, and evaluation. Some of these issues have emerged through cases previously presented while others will be introduced for the first time. For organizational purposes, selected issues have been categorized as professional, individual, or environmental.

Professional Issues

The following two issues have philosophical orientations with professional practice implications. The first issue concerns the efficacy of therapeutic recreation service. The desire to satisfy both lower and higher order basic human needs (Maslow, 1970) through recreation is as old as mankind. Broadly speaking, people within and outside the profession define recreation as pleasurable, voluntary, individualized, and meaningful. In addition, most agree on the potential benefits of recreation participation, such as happiness, self-development, renewal, socialization, education, and physical fitness. Questions remain, however, regarding recreation's significance as a medium through which positive individual change, the perspective that has been presented throughout this text, occurs. Frye and Peters (1972) state that positive benefits or values above and beyond pleasure are secondary to the recreation experience; yet, often these accompanying benefits or values, be they physical, intellectual, emotional, spiritual, or social, become the focus of therapeutic recreation intervention. As Frye and Peters (1972) point out, values of recreation may not be achieved for an individual "unless purposefully sought and emphasized according to the individual's specific needs as related both to his capacities and to the effects of various illnesses and disabling conditions" (p. 44). When changes occur, however, to what extent has the interplay of intervention skills, recreation content, and interaction processes used by therapeutic recreation specialists actually helped to achieve clients' goals and objectives? Increasingly, answers to questions regarding the scope and efficacy of therapeutic recreation are being sought in practice and academic settings. Research activities in therapeutic recreation, heavily used to substantiate a profession's claim to competence and reason for existing, are increasing in quantity and quality (Witt, 1988). A specific example is the opportunity provided to the Department of Recreation and Leisure Studies at Temple University, in 1990-91, by the National Institute on Disability and Rehabilitation Research, U. S. Department of Education, to study the efficacy of therapeutic recreation as a treatment modality. In addition, standards, in academic education preparation, credentialling, and service delivery, have made it easier to account for the purposes and benefits of therapeutic recreation. Unfortunately, in a volatile and changing society, health care industry, and social service system, the support for therapeutic recreation may begin to wane unless rigorous evidence of its value is demonstrated and articulated among therapeutic recreation practitioners, educators, and researchers, and between other health and allied health care professionals and consumers.

Another issue related to therapeutic recreation's efficacy is the distinction between recreation experience as an end in itself, and as a tool for treatment and rehabilitation. The first distinction is based on the belief that because recreation promotes the general well-being of individuals, it is important. The second distinction emanates from a belief that recreation has more value than simply "wholesome activity"; that is, it can be used for purposeful intervention and treatment to address physical, intellectual, emotional, or social behaviors. The Therapeutic Recreation Service Model (Peterson and Gunn, 1984) which was described in Chapter Two, provides therapeutic recreation with a philosophical basis which seems to incorporate both the "recreation as treatment" and "recreation for its own sake" perspectives. As depicted in this model, adopted as the philosophical basis for therapeutic recreation practices by the National Therapeutic Recreation Society in 1981, a client may move between treatment and recreation participation focuses. Such movement implies that one progresses from participation in activities of a recreational nature for specific habilitative or rehabilitative benefits to participation in these activities for their inherent values. Both ends of the continuum imply a needs based, person centered approach to therapeutic recreation. The acceptance of this model, however, as the philosophical basis for the design and delivery of therapeutic recreation services has been repeatedly questioned (e.g., Halberg and Howe-Murphy, 1985; Howe-Murphy and Halberg, 1987; Hemingway, 1986; Lee, 1987; Mobily, 1987; Mobily, 1985; Shank, 1987; Sylvester, 1987).

In 1984, the American Therapeutic Recreation Association proposed a statement of purpose which reflects a philosophical orientation in the direction of therapy: "to promote independent functioning and to enhance optimal health and well-being of individuals with illnesses and/or disabling conditions" (p. 2). Interestingly, it appears that at a time when health and social services are moving away from institutionalized, medically dominated practices to outpatient, transitional, and community-based services, a portion of the therapeutic recreation profession remains focused primarily on treatment.

Individual Issues

Therapeutic recreation has been characterized as a helping profession (Austin, 1982; Carter, Van Andel, and Robb, 1985; O'Morrow, 1976) and Gunn and Peterson (1978) point out that regardless of the population with whom therapeutic recreation specialists work or the setting in which they work, they share two important aims of the helping relationship: (1) to promote positive change in people with disabilities; and (2) to facilitate enjoyment of independently chosen and personally rewarding leisure lifestyles. A therapeutic recreation specialist's approach to this helping relationship raises several important issues.

Of particular importance are one's beliefs about the value and dignity of human life and one's perceptions of persons who have disabilities. Traditionally, disability, illness, disease, impoverishment, psychological distress, and social deviancy have been perceived as abnormal (deviations from the norm) and unfortunately, those who are labeled abnormal or deviant in society are often rejected and isolated (Howe-Murphy and Charboneau, 1987). But it is usually an emphasis on the disability or deviation, because it implies that there is a need for change or improvement, that brings clients and therapeutic recreation specialists together in helping relationships. In fact, clients are often perceived primarily in terms of their disabilities, and because disabilities become the focus of attention, other individual qualities, such as their capabilities and aspirations, are often ignored. (Howe-Murphy and Charboneau, 1987). While therapeutic recreation specialists may insist that they do not view their clients primarily in terms of their disabilities, it is common to hear them refer to these individuals by such names as "paras," "quads," "MR's," and "bifas" (people with spina bifida). Ideally, therapeutic recreation specialists should enter helping relationships with great respect for the "whole" human being, indeed, great respect for the value and dignity of life in general.

Self-Responsibility and Self-Determination

A primary prerequisite to personally chosen leisure lifestyle is client self-responsibility. Therapeutic recreation specialists are not trying to remake clients' lives but to help them overcome barriers to achieving appropriate leisure lifestyles so that they may refashion their lives accordingly. In essence, therapeutic recreation specialists negotiate with clients concerning how to go about change in regard to developing, maintaining, and expressing an appropriate leisure lifestyle. The helping relationsip is participative rather than directive and should assist clients to function more interdependently and make meaningful decisions. Hence, the ultimate responsibility for decision making should remain with clients as much as possible.

The opportunity to exercise control by making choices from an array of recreation alternatives may be difficult, even bewildering. McDowell (1984) suggests that client choice is concerned with three major areas: (1) knowing/learning what is out there, how to get it, and how to use it; (2) knowing what is important to value; and (3) knowing consequences and risks of choices as well as alternatives. For various reasons at different times, however, clients may not be able to independently choose recreational pursuits or choices may be discouraged by therapeutic recreation specialists because they infringe upon the rights of others. In other situations, clients who are able to choose independently among various recreation alternatives may believe their decisions will have unfavorable repercussions, even if this is not a valid concern. For example, Sylvester (1982) found that a therapeutic recreation specialist was likely to reject "the commonly shared philosophical tenet espousing the right to freedom of choice during one's discretionary time" (p. 31) if this choice interferred with or was in conflict with treatment. Finally, some therapeutic recreation specialists may influence clients' decisions by limiting recreation alternatives to only those considered acceptable.

In some instances, clients may not know or believe that they have leisure related problems. A difficult question to answer is, "Upon whose standards do therapeutic recreation specialists determine that leisure related problems exist?" In other instances, clients simply do not care that they have leisure related problems or lack the interest and energy to participate in the process of change. In such cases, how do therapeutic recreation specialists intervene while still fostering a sense of self-responsibility and promoting personal control and choice?

Concerns about client freedom, that is, the opportunity to exercise control and choice, to express and pursue personal preferences, necessitate additional discussion of issues relating to client rights. The National Therapeutic Recreation Society's (NTRS) *Code of Ethics* (1990) as well as NTRS *Standards of Practice for Therapeutic Recreation* (1990) speak to the need to respect the basic human and legal rights of clients and their families. Certain rights are guaranteed by law to people with disabilities. Velleman (1990) lists the "Big Ten Civil Rights of People With Disabilities" as the right to: (1) a barrier-free environment; (2) appropriate housing and independent living; (3) transportation and travel; (4) financial assistance; (5) health care; (6) insurance; (7) certain social services; (8) work; (9) education; and (10) consumer involvement. In a setting where purposeful intervention occurs, such as in therapeutic recreation, people with disabilities and their parents or guardians, where appropriate, maintain these basic legal rights and more. For example, people receiving treatment or intervention services have the right to receive proper assessment and evaluation as well as the right to due process. Due process includes the right to be involved in the development of individual program plans, to be adequately informed regarding the goals and objectives of these plans (informed consent), to obtain information regarding the process by which these plans may be challenged in an impartial hearing, and to privacy. In addition to these legal rights, clients have the human right to be treated with respect and full recognition of their dignity and individuality.

Clients also have the right, to the maximum extent possible, to self-determination, to be in control of their futures, and to choose freely from meaningful and appropriate options. Self-determination implies that clients also have the right to refuse or challenge participation or treatment, and in various court cases, the constitutional right to refuse treatment has been upheld. Refusal of participation or treatment may be denied, however, in situations where clients' welfare is clearly and immediately threatened and when they are unable to make rational decisions on their own because of incapacity (Sylvester, 1985). Self-determination also implies that clients have the right to dignity of risk—the right to experience both success and failure during participation or treatment interactions.

Confidentiality

Privacy in treatment dictates that information pertaining to clients must be handled confidentially. In the helping relationship, therapeutic recreation specialists are exposed daily to confidential information, partially because many therapeutic recreation specialists work in clinical or institutional settings where the communication of confidential information is necessary.

In addition, however, the very nature of therapeutic recreation activity often creates an atmosphere in which clients feel free to communicate confidential information to specialists.

Confidential information is any written or verbal communication to, or observations by therapeutic recreation specialists which are not clearly intended to be shared with another person. Exceptions occur when the law "absolutely and explicitly demands it or it can be unequivocally demonstrated that the client's well-being or the fundamental welfare of others is clearly and immediately at stake" (Levy, 1976, p. 142). Examples of confidential information include: (1) the fact that a person is or has been a client; (2) information given in confidence by a client in the course of receiving treatment; (3) information given in confidence by family, friends, and colleagues; (4) any opinion, summary, or instruction concerning the client given by the treatment team or other agency personnel in the course of treatment; and (5) personal information which, if told to others, could possibly be detrimental to the best interests of the client.

To illustrate the above categories of confidentiality, the following scenario is presented: Anne Black is a client at a mental health facility (Anne's status as a client). She was voluntarily admitted, disclosing that she was very depressed and had considered suicide (information given in confidence by Anne). During a community outing to which Anne's husband was invited, he asks you, the therapeutic recreation specialist, for information about what's been bothering his wife so that he can be more helpful (opinions, summaries, or instructions concerning Anne). He goes on to share with you that Anne seemed to start "going downhill" after he admitted having a one-time affair (information given in confidence by a member of Anne's family). He adds, "Of course, it didn't help that she found out about my affair at about the same time she was fired. She had missed quite a few days at work and her boss thought she was acting strange" (personal information which, if disclosed to others, could be detrimental to Anne).

A study conducted by Sylvester (1982) provides insight regarding how some therapeutic recreation specialists interpret the limits of confidentiality. Sylvester reports that when a client's well-being was in jeopardy, the responding therapeutic recreation specialists did not perceive confidentiality as unconditional. The general feeling expressed was that the safety of others was more important than the need for absolute confidentiality. Matters of confidentiality also appeared to be situation specific, and in some situations, specialists felt it was ethical to breach confidentiality. For example, if the responding therapeutic recreation specialists felt certain clients' behaviors, such as dishonest or illegal acts, were serious, they were less protective of confidentiality than if they considered the behaviors to be less critical. But in other cases, such as situations involving sexual matters, the specialists were in disagreement. Sylvester concluded that in essence, confidentiality is a matter of individual choice influenced heavily by the values of each therapeutic recreation specialist. Debates regarding the limits of confidentiality are ongoing and this important topic will continue to be of great concern to the therapeutic recreation profession and individual therapeutic recreation specialists.

Self-Advocacy

In the past several decades, governmental, professional, and public awareness and concern for persons with disabilities have been heightened. People with disabilities are becoming more assertive and insistent in their demands for access to education, employment, recreation, and independent living. They have participated in a broad range of group and individual efforts to improve conditions, campaign for their rights, preserve service benefits, and educate the public regarding their abilities. Yet dependency, rather than self-advocacy, has historically been the expected role of people with disabilities. Therefore, these individuals may lack advocacy skills and knowledge of how to influence decision makers.

Advocacy may be best approached as a partnership between therapeutic recreation specialists and other helping professionals and their clients. When these professionals support their clients by teaching advocacy procedures and by adhering to program concepts such as self-determination, dignity of risk, freedom of choice, and personal responsibility, these clients are empowered and challenged to become advocates for themselves. As stated by Kathy Hoffman: "'I' became 'we.' I experienced others' pain in being different. We realized that collectively we could bring about changes in our own lives and for others. To me, the disability movement means the right to have and express a positive identity. Each of us must choose that identity" (Hoffman cited in Roth, 1981, p. 34).

Environmental Issues

The types of issues designated as environmental relate to the characteristics of clients' environments that enable their inclusion and full participation in activities of choice. The specific issues to be discussed include normalization and integration, legal factors, and outreach.

Normalization and Integration

Perhaps no other single concept has influenced the design and delivery of
therapeutic recreation services more than normalization. First described by
Nirje (1969), normalization was intended to make "available to the mentally
retarded patterns and conditions of everyday life which are as close as
possible to norms and patterns of the mainstream of society" (p. 181).
Wolfensberger (1972) later helped to bring this Scandinavian philosophy
into the service delivery systems in the United States and Canada. He
defines normalization as the "utilization of means which are as culturally
normative as possible in order to establish and/or maintain personal behaviors and characteristics which are as culturally normative as possible"
(1972, p. 26). Normalization and its related principles emphasize abilities
and stress similarities between people rather than differences. Normalization is grounded in the basic human and legal rights which allow all people
the opportunity to choose the ways in which they will participate in their
community.

The desire to deliver services in environments and under circumstances
that are as culturally normal as possible has influenced the development and
implementation of related principles and practices such as deinstitutionalization, mainstreaming, and integration. *Deinstitutionalization* emphasizes
moving people with disabilities out of institutions and into home-like communities which are more normal than large impersonal institutions. *Mainstreaming* is primarily a movement in public education in which students
with disabilities, who used to be placed in special schools segregated from
the mainstream, are educated in the same buildings and ideally in the same
classrooms as students of their chronological age. The implementation of
PL 94-142, the Education for All Handicapped Children Act, provided the
impetus for mainstreaming and brought concepts such as "least restrictive
setting" to the forefront. The least restrictive setting is that one which is the
least "different," closest to the mainstream of society. It is believed that
within this environment clients have the best opportunities to maximize
their individual abilities. A more recent term, integration, often used as a
synonym for mainstreaming, includes the delineation of a continuum of
services leading to normalized participation.

A continuum of recreation integration, described in Chapter Two, is
progressive and sequential and could include segregated services, "special"
or physically integrated services, and socially or fully integrated services.
As in the Therapeutic Recreation Service Model (Peterson and Gunn,
1984), it is possible for a client to participate in different levels of recreation

integration simultaneously, based on individual need and readiness. Therapeutic recreation specialists strive to develop a range of opportunities offered in situations and settings with as few restrictions as possible, preferably in settings also used by persons without disabilities. These recreation opportunities are those that are valued and supported by clients, their family members, friends with or without disabilities, and other significant individuals. While it is not necessary or desirable for families and friends to share *each* recreation interest of clients, it is desirable that they share some common interests. This integration continuum will enable individuals to have as satisfying and as interdependent leisure lifestyles as possible.

Legal Factors

The United States once supported a system of "separate but equal" in regard to public education for blacks and whites. This notion was struck down by the U. S. Supreme Court as being in violation of the spirit and the letter of the Constitution. In the field of recreation, professionals have long touted a "recreation for all" concept. Yet, in regard to people with disabilties, the most prevalent service delivery pattern of the past has been a continuation of the separate but equal concept.

> "America told itself that such [segregated] opportunities were best for people with disabilities because they had 'special' capabilities, 'special' needs, 'special' goals, 'special' means, 'special' bodies, 'special' minds. Special but equal took the place of separate but equal, but the segregation was just as real" (Project LIFE, 1988, p. 1).

Legislation passed in the 1960s and 1970s coincided with the emphasis on integration. Several legislative acts challenged the "separate but equal" concept as it related to community participation. For example, The Architectural Barriers Act of 1968 (PL 90-480), The Rehabilitation Act of 1973 (PL 93-112), as amended in 1974 (PL 93-516), and The Education for All Handicapped Children Act (PL 94-142), as amended in 1986 (PL 99-457), guaranteed access for individuals with disabilities to facilities and activities that are available to the general public. All of these acts ensure access to services in the least restrictive and most appropriate environment.

In 1989, The Americans with Disabilities Act (ADA) was introduced in the U. S. Senate and House of Representatives and signed into law by President George Bush on July 26, 1990. This piece of legislation is an omnibus civil rights statute that prohibits discrimination against people with disabilities in private sector employment, all public services, public accommodations, transportation, and telecommunications. It is broader in scope and impact than the aforementioned laws and its provisions extend to the private sector as well.

In signing the ADA into law, the federal government sent a strong message that inaccessibility, whether physical, programmatic, or administrative, intentional or unintentional, is discrimination. The ADA provides comprehensive guidelines on banning discrimination against people on the basis of disability.

Outreach

In the early years of organized recreation in the United States, concern was directed toward those members of society who found themselves temporarily displaced or out of the mainstream. These individuals were primarily disadvantaged youth and adults, many of whom were immigrants, in transition from rural agricultural settings to urban industrial ones. Recreation was considered socially purposeful and necessary to improve the quality of life for these individuals perceived as having unique needs. There seemed to be a feeling of moral responsibility for individuals who were having difficulty fitting society's norms. Programs, such as those offered on the playgrounds and in the settlement houses, were easily accessible to the people they were intended to serve.

As the profession of recreation has grown, however, it seems to have lost some of its earlier concern for the "common good" (Lahey, 1991), and its focus on "outreach." Indeed, to take advantage of recreation opportunities as they are currently conceived and delivered requires individual initiative and the ability to be mobile for participation (Pomeroy, 1977). Recreation professionals seem to assume all citizens are equally prepared to enter the public arena and seek desired recreation services. Yet, in reality, participation may be limited, because of chronic or temporary disability, lack of transportation, unawareness or nonacceptance of opportunity, and/or economic circumstances. Many professionals in community recreation programs consider themselves underfunded, hence they may have avoided specific attempts to bring "hard-to-reach" citizens into mainstream community recreation services. Perhaps of greatest concern is the possibility that because therapeutic recreation has claimed to be the primary professional discipline concerned with the recreation needs of people with disabilities, community recreation professionals have felt little responsibility to provide recreation to all persons within communities, specifically, those with disabilities (Carter and Kelley, 1981). Yet, as Kennedy, Smith, and Austin (1991) point out, "most persons in our society are not served by therapeutic recreation specialists but by community recreation personnel" (p. 9).

Clinical therapeutic recreation specialists and general and therapeutic recreation professionals working in the community share a responsibility in regard to clients' transition from clinical to community settings. This responsibility implies that all recreation professionals assume an active role in facilitating the community recreation involvement of populations such as individuals with disabilities living in urban or rural areas who may be isolated, and individuals, who because of chronic illness, disability, or frailness caused by advanced age, spend a disproportionate amount of time in their homes. Individuals with disabilities who are in an ethnic or cultural minority and thus face even greater obstacles relative to community acceptance and involvement may also be members of this population. The expertise of therapeutic recreation specialists can be used to provide consultation, technical assistance, and training to community recreation personnel regarding specific access issues such as attitudes, adaptations, human resources, architectural barriers, communication, and transportation. In addition, therapeutic recreation specialists can function as consumer advocates and help to ensure that the rights and needs of people with disabilities remain in the forefront of community recreation service delivery.

Summary

In this chapter, issues that influence the delivery of therapeutic recreation services were discussed. Each professional, individual, and environmental issue that was presented has implications for individual therapeutic recreation assessment, program planning, implementation, leadership, and evaluation. As the therapeutic recreation profession continues to emerge, therapeutic recreation specialists must grapple with these issues to ensure that individual program planning practices facilitate the development, expression, and maintenance of appropriate and meaningful leisure lifestyles of clients.

Bibliography

American Therapeutic Recreation Association. (1984). *Newsletter of ATRA* (available from ATRA, P.O. Box 15215, Hattiesburg, MS).

Austin, D. R. (1982). *Therapeutic recreation: Processes and techniques.* New York, NY: John Wiley.

Carter, M. J. and Kelley, J. D. (1981). Recreation programming for visually impaired children. In J. D. Kelley (Ed.), *Recreation programming for visually impaired children and youth* (pp. 63-79). New York, NY: American Foundation for the Blind.

Carter, M. J., Van Andel, G. E., and Robb, G. M. (1985). *Therapeutic recreation: A practical approach.* St. Louis, MO: Times Mirror/Mosby.

Frye, V. and Peters, M. (1972). *Therapeutic recreation: Its theory, philosophy, and practice.* Harrisburg, PA: Stackpole.

Gunn, S. L. and Peterson, C. A. (1978). *Therapeutic recreation program design: Principles and procedures.* Englewood Cliffs, NJ: Prentice-Hall.

Halberg, K. and Howe-Murphy, R. (1985). The dilemma of an unresolved philosophy in therapeutic recreation. *Therapeutic Recreation Journal, 19*(3), 7-16.

Hemingway, J. L. (1986). The therapeutic in recreation: An alternative perspective. *Therapeutic Recreation Journal, 20*(2), 59-68.

Hoffman, K. (1981). In W. Roth, *The handicapped speak* (p. 34). Jefferson, NC: McFarland.

Howe-Murphy, R. and Charboneau, B. G. (1987). *Therapeutic recreation intervention: An ecological perspective.* Englewood Cliffs, NJ: Prentice-Hall.

Howe-Murphy, R. and Halberg, K. (1987). Evolution of a philosophy in therapeutic recreation: An essential and continual quest. *Therapeutic Recreation Journal, 21*(2), 79-80.

Kennedy, D. W., Smith, R. W., and Austin, D. R. (1991). *Special recreation: Opportunities for persons with disabilities.* (2nd ed.). Dubuque, IA: William C. Brown.

Lahey, M. P. (1991). Serving the new poor: Therapeutic recreation values in hard times. *Therapeutic Recreation Journal, 25* (2), 9-18.

Lee, L. (1987). A panic attack in therapeutic recreation over being considered therapeutic. *Therapeutic Recreation Journal, 21*(2), 71-78.

Levy, C. S. (1976). *Social work ethics.* New York, NY: Human Sciences.

Maslow, A. H. (1970). *Motivation and personality.* New York, NY: Harper and Row.

McDowell, C. F. (1984). Leisure: Consciousness, well-being, and counseling. In E. T. Dowd (Ed.), *Leisure counseling: Concepts and applications* (pp. 5-51). Springfield, IL: Charles C. Thomas.

Mobily, K. (1987). A quiescent reply to Lee. *Therapeutic Recreation Journal, 21*(2), 81-83.

Mobily, K. (1985). A philosophical analysis of therapeutic recreation: What does it mean to say "We can be therapeutic?" Part I. *Therapeutic Recreation Journal, 19*(1), 14-26.

National Therapeutic Recreation Society. (1990). *Code of ethics* (revised). Alexandria, VA: National Recreation and Park Association.

National Therapeutic Recreation Society. (1990). *Standards of practice for therapeutic recreation service* (revised). Alexandria, VA: National Recreation and Park Association.

Nirje, B. (1969). The normalization principle and its human management implications. In R. Kugel and W. Wolfensberger (Eds.), *Changing patterns in residential services for the mentally retarded* (pp. 227-254) Washington, DC: President's Committee on Mental Retardation.

O'Morrow, G. S. (1976). *Therapeutic recreation: A helping profession.* Englewood Cliffs, NJ: Prentice-Hall.

Peterson, C. A. and Gunn, S. L. (1984). *Therapeutic recreation program design: Principles and practices* (2nd ed.). Englewood Cliffs, NJ: Prentice-Hall.

Pomeroy, J. (1977). Outreach: An approach to serving the leisure needs of the isolated elderly. *Journal of Physical Education and Recreation, 48*(8), 45-47.

Shank, P. A. (1987). Therapeutic recreation philosophy: A state of cacophony. In C. Sylvester, J. L. Hemingway, R. Howe-Murphy, K. Mobily, and P. A. Shank (Eds.), *Philosophy of Therapeutic Recreation: Ideas and Issues* (pp. 27-40). Alexandria, VA: National Recreation and Park Association.

Sylvester, C. (1987). Underground notes on Laura Lee's theme. *Therapeutic Recreation Journal, 20*(3), 6-10.

Sylvester, C. (1985). An analysis of selected ethical issues in therapeutic recreation. *Therapeutic Recreation Journal, 19*(4), 8-21.

Sylvester, C. (1982). Exploring confidentiality in therapeutic recreation practice: An ethical responsibility in need of response. *Therapeutic Recreation Journal, 16*(3), 25-33.

Velleman, R. A. (1990). *Meeting the needs of people with disabilities: A guide for librarians, educators, and other service professionals.* Phoenix, AZ: Oryx Press.

Witt, P. A. (1988). Leisure programs and services for special populations. In L. A. Barnett (Ed.), *Research About Leisure: Past, Present, and Future.* Champaign, IL: Sagamore.

Wolfensberger, W. (1972). *The principle of normalization in human services.* Toronto, Canada: National Institute on Mental Retardation.

Suggested Readings

Bedini, L. A. (1990). Separate but equal? Segregated programming for people with disabilities. *Journal of Physical Education, Recreation, and Dance, 61*(8), 40-44.

Buchanan, T. and Buchanan, J. P. (1987). Rural change and social institution: Implications for providers of leisure services. In S. H. Smith and D. D. McLean (Eds.), *Leisure Today: Selected Readings IV* (pp. 90-92). Reston, VA: American Alliance for Health, Physical Education, Recreation, and Dance.

Carter, M. J. (1988). Defining therapeutic recreation. *Parks and Recreation, 22*(12), 28-31.

Compton, D. M. (Ed). (1989). *Issues in therapeutic recreation: A profession in transition.* Champaign, IL: Sagamore.

Edginton, C. R. and Compton, D. M. (1975). Consumerism and advocacy: A conceptual framework for the therapeutic recreator: *Therapeutic Recreation Journal*, *9*(1), 26-32.

Fain, G. S. (1984). Toward a philosophy of moral judgement and ethical practices. In E. Dowd (Ed.), *Leisure counseling: Concepts and applications* (pp. 277-300). Springfield, IL: Charles C. Thomas.

Goldman, C. D. (1987). *Disability rights guide: Practical solutions to problems affecting people with disabilities.* Lincoln, NE: Media Publishing.

James, A. (1980). Historical perspective: The therapy debate. *Therapeutic Recreation Journal*, *14*(1), 13-16.

Kunstler, R. (1991). There but for fortune: A therapeutic recreation perspective on the homeless in America. *Therapeutic Recreation Journal*, *25* (2), 31-40.

Lahey, M. P. (1987). The ethics of intervention in therapeutic recreation. In C. Sylvester, J. L. Hemingway, R. Howe-Murphy, K. Mobily, and P. A. Shank (Eds.), *Philosophy of Therapeutic Recreation: Ideas and Issues* (pp. 17-26). Alexandria, VA: National Recreation and Park Association.

Nichols, S. (1988). Trends in the United States: Life, liberty, and the pursuit of happiness? *Journal of Leisurability*, *15*(2), 8-11.

O'Morrow, G. S. and Reynolds, R. P. (1985). *Problems, issues and concepts in therapeutic recreation.* Englewood Cliffs, NJ: Prentice-Hall.

Schleien, S. J., Heyne, L. A., Rynders, J. E., and McAvoy, L. H. (1990). Equity and excellence: Serving all children in community recreation. *Journal of Physical Education, Recreation, and Dance*, *61*(8), 45-48.

Taylor, S. J. (1988). Caught in the continuum: A critical analysis of the principle of the least restrictive environment. *Journal of the Association for Persons with Severe Handicaps*, *13*(1), 41-53.

Throne, J. M. (1975). Normalization through the normalization principle: Right ends, wrong means. *Mental Retardation*, *13*(5), 23-25.

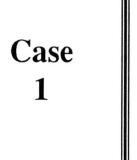

RECREATION AND SOCIAL DEVIANCY

In Chapter Two, *Individual Therapeutic Recreation Program Planning*, you reviewed the case entitled "Recreation in Corrections" (p. 56). In Chapter 6, *Evaluation in Therapeutic Recreation*, the case entitled "Wilderness Group" was presented (p. 181). Both cases dealt with recreation programs in settings serving people who exhibit socially deviant behavior—the former a more traditional program with incarcerated adults and the latter a less traditional approach with adjudicated youth.

DISCUSSION QUESTIONS

1. Some state legislators and citizens think of recreation in correctional settings as "paid vacations," and in the last few years there has been a move away from the philosophy of treatment to one of punishment. In addition, the benefit/cost ratio of less traditional treatment alternatives, such as illustrated in "Wilderness Group," has been questioned. Discuss the value of therapeutic recreation in settings serving people who have exhibited socially deviant behavior. What do you consider to be the major role of therapeutic recreation in these settings?

2. Compare and contrast the value of treatment and diversional recreation in correctional programs. Is there a place for both treatment and diversional programs? Explain your answer.

3. What strategies could you formulate to help your legislators, the general public, and, perhaps, department of youth services and correctional program administrators, understand and appreciate the role and value of therapeutic recreation in these settings?

IN-CLASS EXERCISES

1. Conduct a class debate on the issue that recreation opportunities are a privilege that inmates do not deserve. Establish criteria for the debate and have the audience participate in discussion after the debate.

ROLE-PLAYING

1. The state legislature is considering cutting the Wilderness Group program described in Chapter Five. Role-play an open meeting between two legislators, two department of youth services officials, and two citizens each opposed to the program and the program director, chief instructor, operations manager, and two former Wilderness Group program participants and their parents each in favor of the program. This may be Wilderness Group's last opportunity to justify the value and cost effectiveness of its program.

FIELD EXPERIENCES

1. Visit a state or federal correctional facility and discuss its recreation programs and services with officials.

Selected References for Case Study

Aguilar, T. E. (1986). Recreation—An untapped resource. *Corrections Today, 48*(2), 173-175, 178.

Aguilar, T. E. (1991). Social deviancy. In D. R. Austin and M. E. Crawford (Eds.), *Therapeutic recreation: An introduction* (pp. 100-118). Englewood Cliffs, NJ: Prentice-Hall.

Anderson, S. C. (1991). Corrections. In D. R. Austin and M. E. Crawford (Eds.), *Therapeutic recreation: An introduction* (pp. 352-372). Englewood Cliffs, NJ: Prentice-Hall.

Card, A. P., Poole, C. A., and Romero, V. A. (1985). Turning recreation into education. *Corrections Today, 47*(5), 88-90.

Gibson, P. M. (1979). Therapeutic aspects of wilderness programs: A comprehensive literature review. *Therapeutic Recreation Journal, 13*(2), 21-31.

Krug, J. L. (1979). Correctional recreation: A stalemate on progress. *Parks and Recreation, 14*(11), 36-38.

Case 2	JERRY

Jerry, a 38 year old male with C5/6 quadraplegia, is a patient at a spinal cord rehabilitation center. He wants to learn how to fish again. The patient's treatment team questions the therapeutic recreation specialist's plans to pursue this goal since Jerry's discharge plan includes placement in a nursing home because he has no family or social support system. Jerry is used to staying busy and is worried about his future.

Jerry self-initiated involvement with the therapeutic recreation specialist soon after admission because he was interested in "getting busy." Through the assessment process, the specialist finds that Jerry's former leisure interests included fishing, camping, and enjoying the outdoors in general with his wife. But he has had no leisure lifestyle in the six years since his divorce because he has worked two jobs. Jerry admits that he did not need the money: "It was just something to do." He tells the specialist that in the past year or so, he has been thinking about getting back into his outdoor interests, but has not gotten around to it. He indicates that fishing is his main interest.

The therapeutic recreation specialist reports that the resumption of fishing is one of Jerry's discharge goals. Team members oppose this goal because they believe that: (1) fishing adaptations for someone at Jerry's level of injury are expensive; (2) the nursing home setting will probably not offer many opportunities for Jerry to go fishing; and (3) Jerry will require moderate assistance with all aspects of fishing with the exception of set-up, during which he will require maximum assistance. Since he has no friends or family, this last point is a major barrier to the likelihood of his participation in fishing after discharge.

At the end of a lengthy discussion, the therapeutic recreation specialist still wants to pursue the goal and the other members of the treatment team are opposed to it.

DISCUSSION QUESTIONS

1. As a member of the treatment team, what are the various roles the therapeutic recreation specialist could assume in this situation (e.g., patient advocate, team member, turf protector)? What are the positive and negative aspects of each role?
2. What, if any, ethical questions are raised in this situation? For example, what about the role of patient rights, dignity of risk, opportunity, or choice?
3. When does allegiance to the treatment team begin and end and concern for the patient's preferences begin and end?
4. What should the therapeutic recreation specialist's next step be?

ROLE-PLAYING

1. Assume the therapeutic recreation specialist decides to actively pursue approval from the team to maintain fishing as a discharge goal. Simulate a discussion about this issue, identifying the points that the specialist would want to address and the issues the treatment team would want to address.

Selected References for Case Study

Carley, L. (1982). *An examination of the effectiveness of a leisure counseling programme on rehabilitation patients with spinal cord injuries.* Unpublished master's thesis, University of Waterloo, Ontario, Canada.

Batavia, A. (1988). Needed: Active therapeutic recreation for high level quadriplegics. *Therapeutic Recreation Journal, 22*(2), 8-11.

Trieschmann, R. B. (1988). *Spinal cord injury: Psychological, social and vocational rehabilitation* (2nd ed.). New York, NY: Demos.

Case 3

MAX

Max, a 32 year old with T5/6 paraplegia, was admitted to the spinal cord rehabilitation unit following a suspicious gun accident. Although unable to confirm it, his family, the police, and the rehabilitation center psychologist strongly suspect that it was a suicide attempt. Max denies this.

The psychologist assigned to Max elects to tell the treatment team of the suspected nature of Max's accident but does not put him on suicide precautions at this time. The therapeutic recreation specialist assigned to Max in turn notifies members of the therapeutic recreation department who may come in contact with Max.

Three weeks after his admission, Max stops a therapeutic recreation department staff member, who is not his therapist, in the hallway, shows him the model airplane he has been working on, and asks for a razor blade to complete the next step. The staff member says that he will check on it and tells Max's assigned therapeutic recreation specialist of Max's request. The assigned specialist refers the request immediately to Max's psychologist.

DISCUSSION QUESTIONS

1. Review and critique the actions taken by Max's assigned therapeutic recreation specialist. Are there any confidentiality issues? If you were the therapeutic recreation specialist, would you handle this situation the same way? Why or why not?

ROLE-PLAYING

1. Role-play the interchange between Max and his assigned therapeutic recreation specialist if the specialist had not gone to the psychologist but decided to talk directly with Max about his need for the razor blade to complete his model airplane.

Selected References for Case Study

DeLoach, C. and Greer, B. G. (1981). *Adjustment to severe physical disability: A metamorphosis*. New York, NY: McGraw-Hill.

Thurer, S. and Rogers, E. S. (1984). The mental health needs of physically disabled persons: Their perspective. *Rehabilitation Psychology*, *29*(4), 239-249.

Case 4

THE TOWN MEETING

Pat Farlap, a city council member in the town of Sherwood, a small midwestern city of 5,320 people, is approached by Mr. and Mrs. Brown about their daughter Marie, who has spina bifida and uses a motorized wheelchair. The Browns are very upset because they haven't been able to find out whether or not Marie can participate in the summer playground program with her friends. Believing that Marie has a right to participate in the program, they sent in the registration form and were told that their request is pending. They then talked to C. J. Rogers, director of the city park and recreation department, but couldn't get a final response to their request. Since the program is tax-supported, they have threatened to bring the issue before the city council if Marie is left out.

Because it is an election year Pat doesn't want to create a scene at a city council meeting. To avoid trouble and to get all the right people talking to each other, she has called a friendly neighborhood meeting of all parties involved. She anticipates that things can be worked out through good communication and has decided to serve as moderator of the meeting to keep things running smoothly and to bring the group to some conclusions. She has invited to the meeting the people listed and described below.

ROLE-PLAYING

Simulate the town meeting by playing the characters described below. Prior to the simulation, you may want to interview people in positions represented by the characters included in this role-play. In addition, you may want to review readings related to the issues your character will raise:

Pat Farlap—city council member, moderator of the meeting. (see description above).

Marie Brown—eight year old girl born with spina bifida. She is bright, cheerful, friendly and has many friends at school and in town. She uses a motorized wheelchair for mobility and most activities. Her overall play performance, compared to that of her peers, is somewhat delayed. (Marie will not be attending the meeting.)

Ernest Brown—Marie's father. Ernest believes that as a taxpayer, he is entitled to have his daughter in the summer playground program. He wants more than just talk, he wants action! He is going to make sure something good comes out of this meeting. He wants a clear "yes" that Marie is in! Also, he is pleased that the school superintendent will be at this meeting because he can discuss some school issues as well. Ernest is tired of seeing how hard it is for Marie to get around, even when she is at play, and wants the school to install some special playground surfaces and equipment so Marie can play like everyone else during recess. The school playground has a sandy surface in places, and Marie's wheelchair often gets stuck.

Jane Brown—Marie's mother. Because Jane wants Marie to have all the opportunities that other children have to play, learn, and grow normally, she expects the city and school to provide Marie with access to all programs and services. She believes Marie is smart and doing well in spite of missing quite a bit of school because of surgeries and hospitalizations. She has also been reading about the Americans with Disabilities Act of 1990, the Education of All Handicapped Children Act of 1975, and section 504 of the Rehabilitation Act of 1973.

C. J. Rogers—director of the local park and recreation department. C. J. would prefer not to be involved in this meeting. Although C. J. knows the Browns and likes Marie, he can't see how to include her in summer T-ball, swimming, and trips to the amusement park without special staff and transportation. He isn't sure how to handle her or her wheelchair and is afraid of liability issues. He never had any educational training in working with people with disabilities. The whole situation is scary to him and a "pain in the neck." Moreover, Sherwood is a small town, the recreation budget is VERY limited, and there is barely enough money to support the two parks and a few children's programs during the summer. There is no money for extra qualified staff for Marie! The Browns should hire an attendant for Marie if that's what she needs.

Toni Reed—superintendent of Sherwood school. Toni knows Marie is a bright child, but her mobility problem complicates things at school enough, to say nothing about the playground. Toni has already insisted that the school board make everything in the district accessible to people with disabilities. Now Marie's parents want special playground equipment for her, too. That's going too far! Toni does think the city should make its parks accessible to everyone, but the school has only so much money to spend! If there are some special requests for Marie's summer playground activity, the money should come from the park and recreation budget, not from the school.

Billie Block—playground director for the city's summer program. Like C. J. Rogers, Billie is uneasy about getting Marie into the summer play-ground program. Billie has no formal training or education regarding people with disabilities, and now the Browns want Billie to get Marie into T-ball, swimming, and all the other activities! Billie thinks the city should hire an attendant to help Marie if she comes to the playground. There will be plenty to do just handling all the other kids. How could one person possibly manage Marie and the other kids, too?

Mrs. Temple—president of the local Parent-Teacher Association. (Mrs. Temple has taken the liberty of inviting a few guests to the meeting.) The Browns have asked Mrs. Temple for help at this meeting, seeing her as a strong ally. Mrs. Temple believes Marie should be allowed to participate in play programs both at school and in town—like everyone else! Mrs. Temple is willing to fight for what is right, yet she realizes she could easily get in trouble with some people in town who think Marie is getting too much attention and too much money for "extras" their children don't get.

Fran Nelson—therapeutic recreation specialist at a long-term care facility in Sherwood. Mrs. Temple has asked Fran to attend this meeting because of Fran's education and experience. Fran believes that if people understood Marie and her particular needs (as well as spina bifida), they would be less fearful of the situation. She is willing to volunteer her time to train C. J. and Billie in disability awareness and helping techniques so that Marie can function as independently as possible. Knowledge of current legislation regarding the rights of people with disabilities is a strong point for Fran.

Leslie Allen—therapeutic recreation specialist in a group home in Glendale, a nearby town. Mrs. Temple has also invited Leslie to this meeting, thinking her therapeutic recreation education and experience will be helpful. Leslie believes that it will be easier than most people think to include Marie in the summer playground program. Not having time to volunteer (as Fran has), Leslie would be happy to train and work with the summer staff on normalization principles and integration techniques, provided the city can pay a consulting fee. Leslie wants to emphasize that the summer playground program will not meet all of Marie's needs. Leslie successfully used integration strategies in Glendale, working with local clubs and volunteers, to include people with disabilities in a wide variety of recreation activities. Besides getting Marie onto the school playground and into the town's summer programs, Leslie thinks the Browns should contact organizations such as the Girl Scouts to expand Marie's community recreation opportunities.

Glenn Bower—president of the regional Association for Retarded Citizens (ARC). Mrs. Temple wants Glenn to be present for this meeting because he has had experience integrating persons of varying abilities into community life. Glenn believes the process must develop gradually, with effective communication. Everyone must be prepared so that they can work together for success. Since he expects that one meeting of this group will not be enough to resolve all the issues, he wants the group to meet on a regular basis to work out what is best for Marie. Also, Glenn believes Marie should attend these meetings too!

DISCUSSION QUESTIONS

After role-playing the characters in the town meeting, engage in a discussion of the following questions to help analyze what transpired during the meeting:

1. What was resolved or accomplished through the meeting? Were specific outcomes achieved?
2. Was your character satisfied with the outcome(s) of the meeting?
3. How did you feel playing your character?
4. Did you feel that the other characters understood your position(s)?
5. What interrelated issues are involved in this situation? How can they be resolved?
6. Respond to Glenn's idea that Marie should attend meetings concerning this issue.

Selected References for Case Study

Bedini, L. A. (1990). Separate but equal? Segregated programming for people with disabilities. *Journal of Physical Education, Recreation, and Dance*, *61*(8), 40-44.

Edwards, D. and Smith, D. (1989). Social interaction in an integrated day camp setting. *Therapeutic Recreation Journal*, *24*(3), 71-78.

Goldman, C. D. (1987). *Disability rights guide: Practical solutions to problems affecting people with disabilities*. Lincoln, NE: Media Publications.

Halberg, K. J. (1989). Issues in community-based therapeutic recreation services. In D. M. Compton (Ed.), *Issues in therapeutic recreation: A profession in transition* (pp. 305-324). Champaign, IL: Sagamore.

Halberg, K. J., Earle, P., and Turpel, L. T. (1985). Implementing recreation integration: Specific issues and practical solutions. *Journal of Physical Education, Recreation and Dance*, *56*(5), 29-31.

Park, D. (1980). *Legislation affecting park services and recreation for handicapped individuals*. Washington, DC: Hawkins.

Schleien, S. J. and Ray, M. T. (1988). *Community recreation and persons with disabilities: Strategies for integration*. Baltimore, MD: Paul H. Brookes.

U. S. Department of Justice. (1990). *The Americans with disabilities act*. Government Printing Office: 273-170.

Zoerink, D. A. (1988). Effects of a short-term leisure education program upon the leisure functioning of young people with spina bifida. *Therapeutic Recreation Journal*, *22*(3), 44-52.

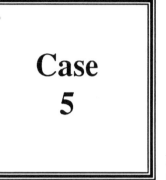

Case 5

THE PASSING OF A FRIEND

Immediately after they met, Jeanette Cox, a new resident at the Water Gardens Life Care Center, and Al Roberts, also a resident, became fast friends. Because of her generous and outgoing personality Jeanette made friends easily, and since she had never married and had few living relatives, she treasured these friendships.

Mr. Roberts' health was failing, but he still maintained his dry sense of humor and quick wit. He was a wonderful storyteller and Ms. Cox looked forward to their visits. One morning his door was closed and he did not answer when she knocked. That afternoon she peeked in on Mr. Roberts only to find a new resident in his bed. Confused, scared, and angry, she made her way to the nurses' station to find out what was going on regarding Mr. Roberts.

DISCUSSION QUESTIONS

When a resident dies at the Water Gardens Life Care Center, the typical practice is to close the door of the resident's room, vacate the corridors, and quietly remove the deceased from the Center. The room is then assigned to a new resident and life at the Center goes on.

1. Should the death of a fellow resident be formally recognized in a long-term health care setting? Why or why not?

2. How should residents be informed of the death of other residents? Should all residents be informed? Why or why not?

3. What benefits could be achieved through a scheduled memorial service in a long-term health care setting to recognize the death of residents?

4. Would you involve clergy in a memorial service? Should the service be nondenominational in nature? Who would be invited to attend—family, residents, staff, others? Why? If so, by what method or means would you contact the family?

5. Discuss the role of religious programs within the overall therapeutic recreation activities program.
6. Should other disciplines be involved in the organization of the service? If so, how?

ROLE-PLAYING

1. Ms. Cox approaches you, the Director of Activities and Volunteers, regarding a memorial service for her friend Al. Although your initial reaction to her idea is positive, you fear the administrative staff will not support such a service, so you decide to play "the devil's advocate" with Ms. Cox and challenge her to explore her reasons for requesting the service. You say, "If we can come up with a good rationale for a memorial service and a good plan, I will present the idea to the administration." "Let's get to work, then," replies Ms. Cox. "All of us need to know we will be remembered and missed." Ask a director of a long-term health care facility to play the administrator role of Water Gardens Life Care Center for this exercise. Present the plan for a memorial service to the administrator of the Life Care Center. As you discuss your ideas for Mr. Roberts' service, present your rationale for instituting memorial services as a regular part of the activities program.

FIELD EXPERIENCES

1. In consultation with appropriate professionals, interview older adults, both those in the community and those in long-term health care facilities, regarding their opinions about how to handle the death of a fellow resident.

Selected References for Case Study

Conway, P. (1988). Losses and grief in old age. *Social Casework*, *69*(9), 541-549.

Hoffman, J. (1990). The memorial service. *Great Ideas for Long Term Care*, *4*(10), 5-6.

Siegel, J. M. and Kuykendall, D. H. (1990). Loss, widowhood, and psychological distress among the elderly. *Journal of Consulting and Clinical Psychology*, *58*(5), 519-524.

Case 6

ROBERT

You were introduced to Robert in Chapter Two, *Individual Therapeutic Recreation Program Planning* (p. 74), and worked with his case again in Chapter Three, *Implementing Individual Therapeutic Recreation Program Plans* (p. 118), and Chapter Four, *Leadership in Therapeutic Recreation* (p. 152). Robert, a 30 year old male with Down's syndrome, resides in a transitional living center with five to eight other individuals. The mission of the center is to prepare these residents for community living in supervised apartments. Individual program plans are developed with each resident and include responsibilities in the center as well as skill development in various areas supportive of his integration into the community. One such skill is the ability to plan each day's events, including use of free time.

In order to live independently in a supervised apartment in the community, Robert needed to improve: (1) money management and budgeting skills; (2) food preparation and weight control; (3) decision-making skills; (4) verbal expression; and (5) ability to initiate, stay on, and complete tasks.

DISCUSSION QUESTIONS

1. Many of the residents at the center or already living in the community display needs similar to Robert's. In addition, residents have large amounts of free time during the day, in the evenings, on weekends, and during holidays. The center does not currently employ a therapeutic recreation specialist. Develop a rationale for this agency's employing a qualified therapeutic

recreation specialist and include in it the purpose and goals of a therapeutic recreation program in this setting. Describe the philosophical orientation from which you would design a therapeutic recreation program that coincides with the overall mission of the center.

2. You are a therapeutic recreation specialist with the local community recreation department and have recently been contacted by the director of the center where Robert lives about providing recreation and leisure experiences for him and seven other residents. Resources are very limited at this time and the recreation director has indicated no new programs will be approved. You have discussed this issue with your advisory board and a nearby university therapeutic recreation faculty member suggested integrating the center's residents into existing programs. Discuss the pros and cons of doing this. Discuss issues of readying the residents as well as community participants.

3. Invite a community based therapeutic recreation specialist to class to discuss the benefits and obstacles to segregated and integrated recreation programs and services.

Selected References for Case Study

Bullock, C. C. and Howe, C. Z. (1991). A model therapeutic recreation program for the reintegration of persons with disabilities into the community. *Therapeutic Recreation Journal*, 25(1), 7-17.

Carter, M. J. (forthcoming). *Designing therapeutic recreation programs in the community*. Reston, VA: American Alliance for Health, Physical Education, Recreation, and Dance.

Richardson, D., Wilson, B., Wetherald, L., and Peters, J. (1987). Mainstreaming initiative: An innovative approach to recreation and leisure services in a community setting. *Therapeutic Recreation Journal*, 21(2), 9-19.

Wilhite, B., Keller, M. J., and Nicholson, L. (1990). Integrating older persons with developmental disabilities into community recreation: Theory to practice. *Activities, Adaptation, and Aging*, 15(1/2), 111-129.

| Case 7 | ROGER |

Roger McAndless, a 45 year old white male, has been in a coma for fourteen weeks as a result of skull and brain injuries received in an automobile accident. Following surgery to relieve pressure on his brain, Roger spent the next twelve weeks in the Intensive Care Unit. After his vital signs improved, he was placed in a private room. Roger's neurosurgeon informed Roger's family that his recovery depends upon his coming out of the comatose state. "At this point there is nothing more we can do but wait," he told them. At the request of his family, Roger was moved to a nursing home where he could receive constant supervision and be closer to his family. The sixty bed facility provides services for patients requiring either intermediate or skilled care.

Pamela, a therapeutic recreation specialist and the facility's activities consultant, assists the activities director, Susan, who has a high school education. Pamela provides consultation on a monthly basis. Today Susan greets Pamela with a look of concern; she has a new admit who is her first comatose resident—Roger. "I just don't know what to do," Susan states hopelessly. "What in the world can be done for anyone in a coma?"

"Let's first have a look at his chart," Pamela says.

After discussing various aspects of Roger's medical chart with Susan, Pamela asks to be escorted to Roger's room. As she and Susan arrive, Pamela knocks on Roger's door and announces their arrival. Roger's private room is devoid of any stimulation other than a small silent radio left by his family. Pamela asks Susan to open the curtain and as she does, rays of sunshine fall on Roger's bed, landing on his hands and neck as far as the shadow will allow. Pamela looks at Roger and says, "Good morning, Mr. McAndless. My name is Pamela. I'm a consultant helping Susan, the activities director. You're at Ocean View Rest Home and we are going to take good care of you." Susan looks at Pamela as though she is not playing with a full deck. Pamela continues, "Mr. McAndless, I am going to open your hand," and lifts his hand, which is slightly constricted. She begins to massage his hands and fingers very gently, slowly progressing in range of motion to the fingers and wrist. While she works, she talks to Roger, describing his room to him, mentioning current events at the nursing home, etc. She looks around the room and activity ideas came to mind. She asks Susan, "What type of recreation has Mr. McAndless been receiving?" Susan replies, "Well, his family brought this radio," and she gestures to the small radio sitting on the night stand.

DISCUSSION QUESTIONS

1. Back at her office, Susan turns to Pamela and says, "You talked to Mr. McAndless as if he could hear everything you said." As Pamela, how would you respond?

2. Susan, concerned about the very important issue of program plans, says, "The surveyors say we must write our goals in behavioral terms. How can I write a goal with Mr. McAndless performing the action?" As Pamela, how do you respond?

3. How should you involve Roger's family in the development and implementation of his care plan? What rights, roles, and responsibilities do guardians have for persons who are comatose?

4. Ocean View is a relatively new nursing home and Roger is the facility's first comatose resident. Pamela asks Susan for her permission to provide an in-service to all disciplines. What topics should Pamela cover during the in-service? Why would Pamela ask for Susan's permission to present an in-service to other disciplines?

5. An in-service for all staff is scheduled for the following week. Pamela begins the in-service by telling staff members that they are not nursing home employees. This raises some eyebrows. She says, "You are caregivers," and goes on to talk about Roger. "The first thing we need to remember is that Mr. McAndless is not a comatose man. Rather, he is a man who happens to be in a coma." What principles is Pamela emphasizing with her opening remarks? Is this an effective way to begin the in-service? Why or why not?

6. Therapeutic recreation is generally thought of as a process of helping a person function as independently as possible during leisure. Is this concept appropriate to use with Roger? If so, how? If not, why?

7. Susan says, "I have 59 other residents who seem to really benefit from my efforts. I find it hard to make time to work with Roger since I never get a response. Could you help me with this?" As Pamela, give Susan some ideas to consider that may help her.

IN-CLASS EXERCISES

1. Discuss the importance of sensory stimulation with an individual who is comatose. List a variety of activities that would provide stimulation for Roger in the following senses:
    a. hearing,
    b. smelling,
    c. touching, and
    d. tasting.
2. Explain how individual issues, such as age appropriateness, Roger's preferences, and family preferences influenced your activity decisions. What interaction approach(es) would you use with Roger?

Selected References for Case Study

Balicki, M. (1984). An interdisciplinary team approach to the assessment of initial stages of cognitive recovery. *Cognitive Rehabilitation*, 2(3), 12-17.

Johnson, D. A. and Roethig-Johnston, K. (1988). Coma stimulation: A challenge to occupational therapy. *British Journal of Occupational Therapy*, 51(3), 88-90.

Johnson, G. M. (1987). Hypnotic imagery and suggestion as an adjunctive treatment in a case of coma. *American Journal of Clinical Hypnosis*, 29(4), 255-259.

Uomoto, J. M. and McLean, A. (1989). Care continuum in traumatic brain injury rehabilitation. *Rehabilitation Psychology*, 34(2), 71-79,

Whyte, J. and Glenn, M. B. (1986). The care and rehabilitation of the patient in a persistent vegetative state. *Journal of Head Trauma Rehabilitation*, 1(1), 39-53.

Case 8

JUST SAY NO?

This major rehabilitation hospital contains a substance abuse, inpatient treatment unit. There are two separate components: a twenty-eight patient detoxification service and a fourteen patient rehabilitation service. Clients are racially mixed, poor to lower middle class males and females, ranging in age from eighteen up. Average length of stay for detoxification patients ranges from five days to three weeks, depending upon the type of drug addiction and client motivation. Rehabilitation clients typically remain inpatients for six to nine months, although they can remain for longer periods of time.

The therapeutic recreation program consists of leisure education (group sessions), leisure counseling (individual sessions), sports programs, arts and crafts, socialization programs, community readjustment programs, and special events. All therapeutic recreation programs are suggested for rehabilitation clients.

Each year the substance abuse unit takes part in a competition called the "Sober Olympics," which includes participants from local, state, and international treatment facilities. The events include track and field, volleyball, basketball, golf, and social games (chess, checkers, dominoes, etc.). The objective of the competition is to provide sober/clean substance abusers an opportunity to engage in competitive activities in order to increase their self-esteem, awareness of leisure activities, and team camaraderie. The event is highly successful and participants typically choose to return each year as alumni from their respective facilities. Again, the primary emphasis is on being drug free.

The substance abuse unit values the special event and each year teams composed of current inpatients, staff, and prior rehabilitated patients are formed. All rehabilitation clients from the substance abuse unit are encouraged to participate and practice sessions become a major focus of the therapeutic recreation program prior to the "Olympics."

This year rumors have been circulating that some former patients planning to participate in the event are using substances, and in order to provide a "clean" program, the therapeutic recreation specialists have decided to conduct a drug test on all participants. Current inpatients engage in random weekly drug testing and anyone refusing to take the test is considered "dirty" and is discharged from the facility. Staff who are participating, including the therapeutic recreation specialists, have all agreed to engage in the drug testing, and all prior patients, with the exception of one, have agreed to be tested. These individuals believe this is the only way to ensure a drug-free team. But one former patient and one psychologist have voiced opposition to drug testing, stating that it violates constitutional rights guaranteed to individuals. This former patient has had a long history of substance abuse and demonstrated significant manipulation while an inpatient. The therapeutic recreation specialists feel justified in their action and support from the interdisciplinary team, with the exception of the psychologist, has been continuous.

The situation has escalated and the psychologist has taken the issue before the hospital ethics committee, which has ruled against the therapeutic recreation specialists and the other team members. The hospital ethics committee is supportive of voluntary drug testing for all "Sober Olympics" participants but feels mandatory drug testing, in this situation, is inappropriate.

DISCUSSION QUESTIONS

1. Do the therapeutic recreation specialists have the right to institute a voluntary drug testing procedure with participants involved in a community based program such as "Sober Olympics"? Why or why not?
2. What ethical concerns face therapeutic recreation specialists in substance abuse facilities who attempt to involve former clients in programs, such as "Sober Olympics" and others, and want to ensure that these programs are drug-free?
3. Does across-the-board drug testing violate individual confidentiality of inpatients? Of outpatients? Why or why not?
4. Should therapeutic recreation specialists involve aftercare clients in their programs, if these individuals are suspected of current substance abuse? Why or why not?

5. When substance abuse programs have an aftercare component, should the programs mix client populations, i.e., current inpatients and aftercare clients? Why or why not?
6. What is the proper relationship between individual rights and program rules and guidelines?
7. What types of hospital and therapeutic recreation policies and procedures should be in place to address drug testing?

IN-CLASS EXERCISES

1. Construct a list of planning guidelines for developing therapeutic recreation programs for people with substance abuse histories involved in aftercare.
2. Ask a hospital administrator or attorney who is up-to-date on the legal and ethical issues of drug testing of employees and patients to discuss this case with the class.
3. Review standards for accreditation (JCAHO, CARF, etc.) and your state licensure guidelines regarding drug testing and discuss how they apply to this situation.
4. Invite a therapeutic recreation specialist who conducts a "Sober Olympics" program to share the policies and procedures for this event with the class.

ROLE-PLAYING

1. In an effort to prevent the drug testing issue from going before the hospital ethics committee, representatives from the therapeutic recreation department meet informally with the psychologist and client in question. Role-play each of these individuals as they present their concerns and try to resolve the issue satisfactorily.

Selected References for Case Study

Diwan, S. (1990). Alcoholism and ideology: Approaches to treatment. *Journal of Applied Social Sciences*, *14*(2),221-248.

Gold, M. (1986). *The facts about drug and alcohol.* New York, NY: Bantam Books.

Kunstler, R. (1991). Substance abuse. In D. R. Austin and M. E. Crawford (Eds.), *Therapeutic recreation: An introduction* (pp. 119-137). Englewood Cliffs, NJ: Prentice-Hall.

Lewis, M. J. (1990). Alcohol: Mechanisms of addiction and reinforcement. *Advances in Alcohol and Substance Abuse, 9*(1-2), 47-66.

National Institute on Alcohol Abuse and Alcoholism. (1987). *Sixth special report to the U.S. Congress on alcohol and health.* Rockville, MD: U.S. Department of Health and Human Services.

Ransom, G., Waishwell, L., and Griffin, J. A. (1987). Leisure: The enigma for alcoholism recovery. *Alcoholism Treatment Quarterly, 4*(3), 103-116.

Case 9

SHAWN

Shawn, a 26 year old with T-8 paraplegia who is one week from discharge, was injured in a car accident involving alcohol. He feels much guilt and remorse about the accident and has expressed a desire to turn his life around.

Shawn was a successful high school athlete, but except for his construction job, he has not been physically active since. He says that there was nothing to do after work in his rural community but drink and play pool with co-workers. He has been very active in the therapeutic recreation program at the spinal cord rehabilitation center and has become a competent swimmer. His therapeutic recreation specialist has instructed him on pool transfers, which he can do independently, and on measures to protect his skin integrity. Shawn enjoys swimming and has been swimming at least three times per week for the last month. He is pleased with his level of fitness, which he reports is the best since he left high school.

Shawn is committed to continuing swimming. He believes that it will help him to stay away from drinking, which he now acknowledges was a problem. But during his last weekend pass, when he went to the community pool to check out the accessibility and swim some laps, the pool manager told him he could not swim there because the county, which owns the pool, cannot accept the liability. Shawn was humiliated and angry and now accuses his therapeutic recreation specialist of "setting him up!"

DISCUSSION QUESTIONS

1. How should the therapeutic recreation specialist diffuse and effectively channel Shawn's anger to help him resolve the situation?
2. What are Shawn's rights as protected by Section 504 of the Rehabilitation Act of 1973 and the Americans with Disabilities Act of 1990? Read both pieces of legislation and indicate what role the therapeutic recreation specialist should play, if any.

ROLE-PLAYING

1. Role-play the initial interchange between Shawn and the therapeutic recreation specialist which leads to developing a step-by-step plan that offers Shawn a viable short- and long-term solution to this problem through self-advocacy.
2. Based on your response to question two above, help Shawn draft a letter to the pool manager.

Selected References for Case Study

Edginton, C. R. and Compton, D. M. (1975). Consumerism and advocacy: A conceptual framework for the therapeutic recreator. *Therapeutic Recreation Journal, 9*(1), 26-31.

Oestreicher, M. (1990). Accessible recreation: 20 years behind the times. *Parks and Recreation, 25*(8), 52-55.

| Case 10 | STEVEN |

Steven, whose case first appeared in Chapter Two, *Individual Therapeutic Recreation Program Planning* (p. 77), is a 28 year old male who was involved in a car accident resulting in a severe traumatic head injury. He is currently a patient in the neurobehavioral unit of a treatment facility for individuals with head injuries who exhibit severe behavioral deficits. Prior to Steven's admission to the neurobehavioral unit, he lived at home. One of Steven's primary treatment goals was to return to and live successfully in a less restrictive setting.

DISCUSSION QUESTIONS

After reviewing the specifics of Steven's case, respond to the following questions:

1. Describe how the principle of normalization can be applied in the development of Steven's treatment program. Elaborate on specific program examples.
2. Identify and describe barriers Steven might encounter as he seeks participation in community recreation programs. Offer possible ways of overcoming these barriers.
3. What do you perceive to be the role of the therapeutic recreation specialist working in the clinical setting relative to preparing Steven's home and community environment for his return? What are specific steps the specialist could take to assist in Steven's transition to community life?
4. Should community recreation departments formally reach out to newly disabled persons and/or those persons who have not been traditionally included in community recreation and leisure services? Why or why not?

5. Some states and communities have established a network system for integration of persons from clinical based therapeutic recreation programs to community based therapeutic recreation programs. How could the state professional therapeutic recreation association be involved with establishing this network system? Discuss issues of confidentiality, legal liability, and programming as you explore the possibilities of establishing an integration network and referral system.

IN-CLASS EXERCISES

1. Develop a job description for an outreach worker with a community parks and recreation department. Include the job title, qualifications, objectives of the position, and examples of specific job responsibilities and duties.

Selected References for Case Study

Carlton, T. O. and Stephenson, M. D. (1990). Social work and the management of severe head injury. *Social Science and Medicine*, *31*(1), 5-11.

Pomeroy, J. (1974). The handicapped are out of hiding: Implications for community recreation. *Therapeutic Recreation Journal*, *8*(3), 120-128.

Reynolds, R. P. (1979). What is normalization and how can you do it? *Parks and Recreation*, *14*(8), 33-34, 51.

Prigatano, G. P. (1989). Work, love, and play after brain injury. *Bulletin of the Menninger Clinic*, *53*(5), 414-431.

Wankel, L. M. and Berger, B. G. (1990). The psychological and social benefits of sport and physical activity. *Journal of Leisure Research*, *22*(2), 167-182.

<table>
<tr><td>

Case
11

</td><td>

TODD

</td></tr>
</table>

You were first introduced to Todd Smith's case in Chapter One, *Assessment in Therapeutic Recreation* (p. 35). He is 26 years old, has severe mental retardation, and demonstrates inappropriate behavior such as interpersonal aggression, sustained yelling, and self-injurious behavior. In Chapter Two, *Individual Therapeutic Recreation Program Planning* (p. 80), you began developing a program plan for Todd and in Chapter Four, *Leadership in Therapeutic Recreation* (p. 153), you suggested strategies for developing Todd's leisure skill repertoire.

ROLE-PLAYING

1. In Chapter Four, you role-played an interaction with Todd's parents, Mr. and Mrs. Smith, in which you provided them with ideas about how to determine and support Todd's leisure preferences. During the discussion Mrs. Smith asks, "Is it realistic to expect Todd to participate in community recreation activities or should we try to find activities designed specifically for people with similar needs?" How do you respond?

FIELD EXPERIENCES

1. Invite to class a panel of parents whose children have severe mental disabilities and/or behavioral problems along with community therapeutic recreation specialists. Ask each group to discuss issues concerning the integration of children with mental and emotional disabilities into community recreation programs.

Selected References for Case Study

Rynders, J. E., Schleien, S. J., and Mustonen, T. (1990). Integrating children with severe disabilities for intensified outdoor education: Focus on feasibility. *Mental Retardation, 28*(1), 7-14.

Case 12

TOMMY

Tommy, a seven year, eleven month old boy with spina bifida, has been referred for a psychological evaluation by his family physician. Tommy's mother has recently expressed concerns about his behavioral difficulties. These concerns include the following:

(1) Tommy's increased frequency of negative behaviors. He is angry at times, expresses extreme self-criticism, demonstrates combativeness, and indulges in temper tantrums. These behaviors occur primarily at home.

(2) School-related behavioral difficulties. Tommy's teacher reports that since entering second grade, Tommy has become increasingly disruptive (e.g., inappropriate remarks, "silly" behaviors, shouting). In addition, although Tommy is capable of catheterizing himself independently, recently he has refused to perform this activity at school.

(3) Decreased frustration tolerance level.

(4) Occasional somatic complaints when it is time to go to school.

Tommy is seen regularly at the Children's Clinic for myelodysplasia and V/P shunt where he has undergone two surgical procedures for release of hip contractures. He ambulates with reciprocating braces and crutches and occasionally a wheelchair. He is independent in most self-help skills, including bowel and bladder management. He needs minimal help in dressing.

He was recently evaluated by his school psychologist and found to be functioning well within the average intelligence range. He is in a regular second grade classroom, and his teacher reports that his academic performance is adequate. She believes his current behavioral difficulties are the result of frustration. This is her second year teaching Tommy, and he reportedly had no behavioral difficulties in first grade.

Tommy participates in horseback riding, swimming, and neighborhood activities with peers. Additionally, he is enrolled in the Northside Recreation Center's programs for children with disabilities as well as music therapy at Music House. Mrs. Conner reports that Tommy participates in most of these activities enthusiastically. He is quite competitive and interested in winning. Tommy's preferred activities involve gross motor skills (e.g., climbing structures, dodge ball), and "all of the activities that regular kids do," but he sadly acknowledges his limitations in these activities relative to his peers.

Regarding his participation in music therapy, Mrs. Conner reports that Tommy has recently begun to lose interest, and his therapist reports that for the past several months he has appeared angry and withdrawn during his sessions. He resists formal instruction and his level of participation has decreased. When paired with another child—an 11 year old boy with mild mental retardation—Tommy behaved very competitively, insisting on being first, etc. The music therapist reports that despite his unwillingness to participate or to practice at home, he is quite enthusiastic about performing for his parents or for recitals. Although Tommy is unable to identify reasons for his dissatisfaction with music therapy, he does say that he doesn't know why he and not his siblings have to go.

Tommy also has recently expressed dissatisfaction with the quality of his school art work relative to that of his peers. (His drawing of a person consisted of a head only, and he explained that he "couldn't draw bodies" and therefore omitted it.)

Tommy has begun asking questions regarding his condition (e.g., "Will I ever get better?") and expresses annoyance at having to engage in required activities (e.g., bowel management).

When asked if he understands the reasons for his psychological evaluation, Tommy states that sometimes he feels bad about himself. He goes on to say that even though "kids try to make me feel better, I know I'm not doing good." He also states that "there's nothing anyone can do" to make him feel better about himself.

DISCUSSION QUESTIONS

1. To what extent might Tommy's currently observed behavioral changes be a function of the influence of his physical disability on the social and cognitive developmental processes occurring at this time? What needs might be reflected in his competitiveness, his desire to be first, to win?
2. Discuss issues of personal control and choice as they pertain to Tommy's situation. Consider, for instance, whether Tommy is able to engage in those activities which would enhance his self-concept. Are his choices of activities limited by his physical disability? Could his disruptive behavior in school and his resistance to formal music therapy represent his attempts to exert some control over his environment? Why or why not?
3. Apparently Tommy is beginning to think about the future and thus about the permanency of his condition. As a therapeutic recreation specialist, how would you respond to his questions regarding his disability and his ability to participate in certain activities?
4. Present a rationale for expanding Tommy's current participation in recreational activities. What therapeutic recreation service or combination of services—treatment, leisure education, recreation participation—would you recommend for Tommy?

IN-CLASS EXERCISES

1. Divide students into debate teams for each of the following recommendations. Present arguments, pro and con, to the class:
   a. Continue Tommy's participation in activities with able-bodied peers.
   b. Avoid those activities which may create excessive frustration or be perceived by Tommy as a failure experience.
   c. Encourage Tommy's participation in activities in which he is successful and which emphasize his strengths.
   d. Let Tommy decide whether or not he will participate in music therapy (music therapy versus music lessons).

    e.   Arrange for Tommy to interact with a role model who also has a physical disability, ideally a male, somewhat older than Tommy.

    f.   Allow Tommy the maximum level of independence in those situations which necessitate a certain amount of dependence on others.

Selected References for Case Study

Dattilo, J. and Barnett, L. A. (1985). Therapeutic recreation for individuals with severe handicaps: An analysis of the relationship between choice and pleasure. *Therapeutic Recreation Journal, 21*(3), 79-91

Dixon, J. (1978). Expanding individual control in leisure participation while enlarging the concept of normalcy. *Therapeutic Recreation Journal, 12*(3), 20-24.

Loesch, L. C. (1984). Leisure counseling with youth. In E.T. Dowd (Ed.), *Leisure Counseling: Concepts and applications* (pp. 129-156). Springfield, IL: Charles C. Thomas.

Zoernik, D. A. (1988). Effects of a short-term leisure education program upon the leisure functioning of young people with spina bifida. *Therapeutic Recreation Journal, 22*(3), 44-52.

Case 13

RICHARD

Richard Taylor, a 32 year old, white male, is in the later stages of Acquired Immunodeficiency Syndrome (AIDS). He was employed as a hotel manager up to eight months ago and lived in a large metropolitan community until three months ago, when he began to demonstrate some signs of memory loss, impaired concentration, increased aggression, social disinhibition, irritability, and incontinence, along with severe weight loss and weakness. He was placed in a small, rural nursing home which accommodated primarily geriatric patients and had never served people with AIDS. Richard's sister lives in this small, conservative, rural community with her family. Her husband is the mayor and from a very prominent local family. She visits Richard weekly and he responds well to her.

Richard is up nearly every day and sits in the day/activity room with the other residents. He is a wonderful piano player and an accomplished singer and the residents have enjoyed the several times he has played and sung. Painting, drawing, gardening, and snow skiing had been favorite activities and the therapeutic recreation specialist has encouraged Richard to participate in these activities, but he refuses. The only activity he has actively engaged in since he entered the facility is playing the piano and singing. He mainly stares out the window and watches television. He may address staff when spoken to and on occasion ask for personal care assistance.

In the patient care (team) meeting about Richard, the team expresses a strong need to provide meaningful recreation activities that will help him with his adjustment to the facility and will address his lack of socialization. Richard is sitting in the meeting and says, "I wish I could just die." His sister, who is also in attendance, indicates, "He needs services that are different from those offered the older adults. Richard is talented and using his talents brings so much pleasure to him."

DISCUSSION QUESTIONS

1. As a new therapeutic recreation specialist having never worked with persons with AIDS, you must answer several questions: Should Richard be expected to fit into the regular program of activities at the long-term care facility? Does Richard have the right to refuse therapeutic recreation services? Why or why not? Should Richard's sister decide what type of activities should be offered to him?
2. An alert resident asks you, "Why is that young man here? He looks so bad; what's wrong with him?" How would you respond to this resident's questions? What issues concerning confidentiality should be considered?

3. While having lunch in the dining room with several staff members, one comments, "That Richard Taylor is going to hell, as that is God's way of punishing him for his sins. I just can't work with him. When he is assigned to me I don't give him a bath. I do change his linens, but I'm not touching him. I have no respect for his kind." What is your responsibility in this situation? You have always felt that the dignity and worth of the individual should be respected. You also know that the nurses' aides are required in your facility to bathe the residents daily.

4. A local volunteer church group that has been a strong supporter of the nursing home's therapeutic recreation program for years, informs you that they will not be back to conduct the weekly religious program nor the monthly birthday party, even though both activities are very popular, if Richard is in the day/activity room when they come. What are you going to do?

5. You have been working with Richard now for seven months and have established nice rapport. He indicates to you that he would like to go skiing one last time. You have discussed your concern regarding his health with the nurse and his physician and both agree, he is too weak. He has continued to ask you to take him and indicated that it is his "right" to go skiing. What are you going to do?

IN-CLASS EXERCISES

1. Create an in-service training program for a long-term care facility to prepare all staff members to work effectively with people with AIDS. What topics should be included and who should present them?

FIELD EXPERIENCES

1. Invite a panel of experts (legal counsel, nurse, therapeutic recreation specialist, doctor, and a person with AIDS) to discuss the legal, health, and ethical issues of working with people with AIDS.

Selected References for Case Study

Centers for Disease Control. (1987). Recommendations for prevention of HIV transmission in health care settings. *Morbidity and Mortality Weekly Report, 36*(20), 306-308.

Dunphy, R. (1987). Helping persons with AIDS find meaning and hope. *Health Progress, 68*(4), 58-63.

Frierson, R. L. and Lippmann, S. B. (1987). Psychologic implications of AIDS. *American Family Physician, 35*(3), 109-116.

Ginzburg, H. M. and Gostin, L. (1986). Legal and ethical issues associated with HTLV-III disease. *Psychiatric Annals, 16*(3), 180-185.

Kadzielski, M. A. (1986). Legal implications for health care providers. *Health Progress, 67*(4), 48-52.

O'Donnell, L. and O'Donnell, C. R. (1987). Hospital workers and AIDS: Effect of in-service education on knowledge and perceived risks and stresses. *New York State Journal of Medicine, 87*, 278-280.

Turner, N. H. and Keller, M. J. (1988). Therapeutic recreation practitioners' involvement in the AIDS epidemic: Rationale and implications. *Therapeutic Recreation Journal, 22*(3), 12-23.

Video

AIDS, Psychosocial Interventions. Carle Medical Communications, 110 West Main, Urbana, IL 61801-2700 (25 minutes).

Index of Cases

BOOKS FROM VENTURE PUBLISHING

Acquiring Parks and Recreation Facilities through Mandatory Dedication:
  A Comprehensive Guide
    by Ronald A. Kaiser and James D. Mertes

The Activity Gourmet
    by Peggy Powers

Adventure Education
    edited by John C. Miles and Simon Priest

Amenity Resource Valuation: Integrating Economics with Other Disciplines
    edited by George L. Peterson, B. L. Driver and Robin Gregory

Behavior Modification in Therapeutic Recreation: An Introductory Learning Manual
    by John Dattilo and William D. Murphy

Benefits of Leisure
    edited by B. L. Driver, Perry J. Brown and George L. Peterson

Beyond the Bake Sale—A Fund Raising Handbook for Public Agencies
    by Bill Moskin

The Community Tourism Industry Imperative—The Necessity, The Opportunities,
  Its Potential
    by Uel Blank

Dimensions of Choice: A Qualitative Approach to Recreation, Parks, and Leisure
  Research
    by Karla A. Henderson

Doing More With Less in the Delivery of Recreation and Park Services: A Book of
  Case Studies
    by John Crompton

Evaluation of Therapeutic Recreation Through Quality Assurance
    edited by Bob Riley

The Evolution of Leisure: Historical and Philosophical Perspectives
    by Thomas Goodale and Geoffrey Godbey

The Future of Leisure Services: Thriving on Change
    by Geoffrey Godbey

Gifts to Share—A Gifts Catalogue How-To Manual for Public Agencies
    by Lori Harder and Bill Moskin

Great Special Events and Activities
    by Annie Morton, Angie Prosser and Sue Spangler

Leadership and Administration of Outdoor Pursuits
    by Phyllis Ford and James Blanchard

The Leisure Diagnostic Battery: Users Manual and Sample Forms
  by Peter A. Witt and Gary Ellis

Leisure Diagnostic Battery Computer Software
  by Gary Ellis and Peter A. Witt

Leisure Education: A Manual of Activities and Resources
  by Norma J. Stumbo and Steven R. Thompson

Leisure Education: Program Materials for Persons with Developmental Disabilities
  by Kenneth F. Joswiak

Leisure Education Program Planning: A Systematic Approach
  by John Dattilo and William D. Murphy

Leisure in Your Life: An Exploration, Third Edition
  by Geoffrey Godbey

A Leisure of One's Own: A Feminist Perspective on Women's Leisure
  by Karla Henderson, M. Deborah Bialeschki, Susan M. Shaw and
    Valeria J. Freysinger

Marketing for Parks, Recreation, and Leisure
  by Ellen L. O'Sullivan

Outdoor Recreation Management: Theory and Application, Revised and Enlarged
  by Alan Jubenville, Ben Twight and Robert H. Becker

Planning Parks for People
  by John Hultsman, Richard L. Cottrell and Wendy Zales Hultsman

Private and Commercial Recreation
  edited by Arlin Epperson

The Process of Recreation Programming Theory and Technique, Third Edition
  by Patricia Farrell and Herberta M. Lundegren

Quality Management: Applications for Therapeutic Recreation
  edited by Bob Riley

Recreation and Leisure: An Introductory Handbook
  edited by Alan Graefe and Stan Parker

Recreation and Leisure: Issues in an Era of Change, Third Edition
  edited by Thomas Goodale and Peter A. Witt

Recreation Economic Decisions: Comparing Benefits and Costs
  by Richard G. Walsh

Recreation Programming And Activities For Older Adults
  by Jerold E. Elliott and Judith A. Sorg-Elliott

Risk Management in Therapeutic Recreation: A Component of Quality Assurance
  by Judith Voelkl

Schole VI: A Journal of Leisure Studies and Recreation Education

A Social History of Leisure Since 1600
by Gary Cross

Sports and Recreation for the Disabled—A Resource Manual
by Michael J. Paciorek and Jeffery A. Jones

A Study Guide for National Certification in Therapeutic Recreation
by Gerald O'Morrow and Ron Reynolds

Therapeutic Recreation Protocol for Treatment of Substance Addictions
by Rozanne W. Faulkner

Understanding Leisure and Recreation: Mapping the Past, Charting the Future
edited by Edgar L. Jackson and Thomas L. Burton

Wilderness in America: Personal Perspectives
edited by Daniel L. Dustin

Venture Publishing, Inc
1999 Cato Avenue
State College, PA 16801
814-234-4561